COUNSELING EFFECTIVELY IN GROUPS

COUNSELING EFFECTIVELY IN GROUPS

JOHN VRIEND AND WAYNE W. DYER, EDITORS
Wayne State University and St. John's University

**educational technology publications
englewood cliffs, new jersey 07632**

Library of Congress Cataloging in Publication Data

Vriend, John, comp.
    Counseling effectively in groups.

    Consists of articles reprinted from the Jan. and Feb.
1973 and Mar. 1969 issues of Educational technology
magazine.
    1. Group counseling--Addresses, essays, lectures.
I. Dyer, Wayne W., joint comp. II. Title.
LB1027.5.V74   371.4'044   73-7937
ISBN 0-87778-062-5

Printed in the United States of America.

Library of Congress Catalog Card Number: 73-7937.

International Standard Book Number:
0-87778-062-5.

First Printing: June, 1973.

To the young ones, Diana Lee, Laurel Joan, Tamara Lynn, Bonita Ellen, and to the youngest, Tracy Lynn.

Table of Contents

COUNSELING EFFECTIVELY IN GROUPS

1.
Introduction:
Effectiveness Is the Name and
Technology the Game

John Vriend and
Wayne W. Dyer

As a highly effective educational and therapeutic practice, group counseling is like no other. When competent counselors ply their expertise in a group setting, they maximize their effectiveness because of the built-in conditions which vitalize the experience and because they can service greater numbers of clients. If this is true, ought we not to have at our disposal, we in the helping professions, all the technology about group counseling that is available? This is the idea, at least, which has been swirling in the heads of the editors for a good many years and which has sparked the beginning assemblage of group counseling technology which comprises this collection of original contributions.

The editors have attempted to bring together the salient features of a technological approach to the study and practice of group counseling, primarily in the educational setting. These include a precise identification of the techniques, concepts, practices and innovations which lead to appropriate group counseling outcomes, a labeling of efficient training practices for group counselors, a look at what kinds of technical and programmatic aids, both hardware and software, facilitate the trainer and the practitioner, and an extended, clear statement of what is meant by group counseling and how it differs from other group work of a kindred nature.

When properly conducted, group counseling is a potent instrument for making positive, healthful differences in the lives of people. The process of unequivocally identifying self-defeating behaviors, actively working at understanding the maintenance system and psychological motivation for such behaviors, and establishing workable alternatives to them in a group setting—a crucible employing the powerful peer influence resources so vital to human development—basically comprises the components of effective group counseling.

But this view, essentially remedial, is only half the story. Membership in a counseling group can benefit *anyone*. It is a supercharged learning environment where new behaviors can be acquired and practiced, where members can learn to master themselves and develop competencies and skills which are useful in more and more areas of their lives, where even creative and self-actualized geniuses can get more mileage out of their natural endowments. For each member the over-all personal goal becomes the greatest totality of personal effectiveness: How can I take charge in more parts of my world?

Given the great promise of group counseling for helping human beings in their living and growing, particularly if institutionalized in the nation's schools, the need for delineating a technology becomes crucial. The literature which elaborates effective procedures for conducting group counseling sessions is scant. What are the best methods for training would-be helpers as group counselors? How can group counseling productivity be enhanced by the employment of visual and mechanical aids, by the introduction of particular structures, programs, systematized leader behaviors, even gimmickry? These and a multitude of similar questions go more than partially unanswered in a careful search of the pertinent literature.

In commissioning each contribution which appears in this book the editors' principal criterion was: How would it add to a sorely needed collection of group counseling technology? Leading researchers, practitioners, theorists and group counselor trainers were invited to contribute their own unique efforts within the outlined parameters. Each author's expertise in the group counseling world has been established either through published texts, research studies, actual leading of counseling groups in various settings, or years of experience in training group leaders.

Most of this extensive gathering of writings on group counseling first made its appearance in two special issues of *Educational Technology* Magazine, in January and February, 1973. Now the collection comes to you in book form and is intended for use by practicing counselors in every therapeutic community where group counseling is an appropriate and significant component of the repertoire of counseling services to be delivered; but most particularly for those professionals who function in educational settings. Certainly the ideas contained herein, both theoretical and utilitarian, the reports of experimental research, of effective group counseling practice, and of procedure and technique development are all of important interest to counselor educators engaged in the very difficult business of helping to train counselors who will enter the profession with the capability of delivering group counseling skills and competencies at acceptable performance levels.

What this book is about is *effectiveness*. In their editorial role, soliciting and working with the contributors to refine ideas and focus on potent variables, as authors endeavoring to communicate their knowledge of group counseling components, as practitioners actually functioning as group counselors and as trainers of counselors, the editors have continued to stress productivity and effectiveness. It is the dominant theme of this book. Making healthful, positive and lasting differences in the lives of people through the process of group counseling is a point of view shared by all the contributors, a theoretical core around which all can rally. Simply stated, this means group counselors knowing why, when and what they are going to do—and doing it.

A reader looking to locate a stylized or formalized approach to counseling, either individually or in groups (i.e., those approaches customarily labeled behavioral, developmental, client-centered, rational-emotive, or whatever) won't find it here, even though some of the writers might have found it convenient at one time or another to allow their names to be associated with a particular "camp." Nor will the reader find much discussion of group norms, tasks, values, dynamics, member roles and such theorizing about the nature of groups as social structures taking particular forms over the accumulated time of their existence and going through predictable stages. The literature on groups is endlessly extensive in this regard and the editors saw little reason for the inclusion of such group material as would be largely repetitious. What the reader will find, if he is seeking to label this collection, is an approach which can be called *pragmatic*. The direction of most of the writings is toward what *works*, what gets results and toward the development of expertise and professionalism.

But this is not to say that all of the contributions are totally practical in nature or intent. The book contains a veritable smorgasbord of writings generated to focus on many adjunctive issues which are significantly related to and have a bearing on whether or not effective group counseling can be encountered in a given fashion or setting.

The Contents

However much some authorities would tend to separate individual and group counseling, there remains the important connection that the end goal of both is the improvement in the mental outlook and behavior of the individual client. Thus, several of the authors address themselves to the task of delineating counseling aspects and process variables which are important to effectiveness in the traditional counseling dyad and work toward an extension and transformation of counseling principles, procedures and techniques to the more complicated structured environment that comprises a counseling group (for example, see the writings of Carkhuff, Doverspike, Kagan and Ivey). The first chapter following this introduction, "Toward a Comprehensive Framework Unifying All Systems of Counseling" by H. Jon Geis, has been included specifically to provide the reader with the kind of important theoretical and practical background information about counseling in general which undergirds much of the thrust of this entire book.

In this same regard, the editors felt it was vital to an understanding of the way in which they and some of the other writers have used the term "technology" that the reader be given a full exposure to the careful thought which is behind its application to counseling, both individually and in groups. Thus, they have included John Vriend's "Counseling Technology: A Needed Conceptualization" among what is essentially a collection of writings on group counseling.

Surprisingly, the term technology is anathema to some professionals and they are reluctant to give it the credence which is its due. They associate technology with what is mechanical, not human, and in their minds never the twain shall meet. The editors are challenging this perspective and seeking to ward it off by restoring this useful word and the ideas subsumed under it to a prominent place in the hierarchy of paramount concerns professionals have when they contemplate the behavioral discipline of counseling.

Following these two orientation and foundation-laying discussions comes a treatise wherein the editors collaborate to make a case for the development of a technology of group counseling which includes an extended definition of how group counseling is differentiated from a host of other "group experiences," an important separating out process which school counselors in particular need to ingest and be able to articulate, if they are to satisfy critics and help group counseling to flourish in the educational settings where it is urgently needed.

Goal-setting in group counseling has been a neglected area, many counselors espousing an opportunistic approach, an open-ended, come-what-may point of view hardly consonant with a technology of group counseling. In her contribution, T. Antoinette Ryan has provided readers with a step-by-step schema for goal-setting in counseling groups. John D. Krumboltz and Beverly Potter follow this with a detailed model of techniques for achieving certain specific behavioral objectives.

Robert R. Carkhuff makes a case for a "human technology" in the group world and emphasizes the need for utilizing effective procedures and personnel at each stage in the training of competent and potent helpers. In his powerful essay on the application of counseling procedures in groups for the educationally distraught, Milton Schwebel has provided readers with numerous thoughtful insights and delineated important group counseling principles for counselors to consider. Doris Jefferies has taken a position against using the group counseling process to produce agents of the "system" by making membership in the counseling group contingent upon the adoption of "other-directed" value systems. Beyond this, she and her assistant, Kathy Schiaffino, present an annotated bibliography of selected sources for information about group counseling with children.

George M. Gazda and Roger W. Peters have carefully outlined the most recent research on group work, that which has been published since 1969, and have made pointed and practical comments on their findings. In an unusual synthesizing of observations, Wayne Rowe and Bob B. Winborn have critiqued 36 articles which are critical or cautionary about group experiences, and have ˙tabularized the most common fears and objections that people have. Walter M. Lifton's manuscript draws an absorbing analogy between group societal prac-tices and current societal norms, and suggests an application of group counseling procedures to the resolution of general social problems. Merle M. Ohlsen has written about the significant precondition of readiness for group counseling by offering methods of assessing readiness and implementing a viable group counseling program. The editors have collaborated on an effort which attempts to make explicit both the rationale and the specific occasions when certain leader interventions are called for, a model of the kind of detailing of leader behaviors in counseling groups which so seldom gets written.

Clarence A. Mahler has written an essay for educational decision-makers on the minimally needed conditions in the school environment for effectuating a practical group counseling program. James E. Doverspike makes clear distinctions between goal setting in developmental and problem-solving counseling groups, while making a forceful case for individualizing the goals of group members. Allen E. Ivey has adapted microcounseling methods to group counseling, and has provided readers with a model for the identification of the components of group counseling micro-training. The editors have again collaborated, to produce an argument which eliminates "playing" from what we label "role-working," and important structures, principles, techniques and precautions for role-working in counseling groups are specified. In an analogous vein, James M. Sacks delineates an array of techniques that are traditionally employed in group psychodrama, a rich therapeutic methodology too often overlooked by professionals interested in group counseling. Not unrelatedly, Barbara B. Varenhorst has described how game theory and simulations can be a pragmatic part of effective group counseling practice.

Norman Kagan has written an engrossing account of one particular approach to the harnessing of technology in influencing human interaction in groups. Writing in a corresponding tone, Randolph B. Tarrier has shown how technology can be engaged productively in the preparation and training of counselors who will work with groups. John Vriend has described in imaginative detail an ideal facility for the training of group counselors, for the studying of the group counseling process from every conceivable angle and for doing needed not-yet-dreamt-of research. The laboratory he describes is not so futuristic as it might seem at first: it is constructible with present-day technological know-how. Benjamin Cohn writes about a stimulating training innovation utilizing a bug-in-the-ear device which allows absentee-cueing by a training supervisor while a counselor is in the process of leading a group.

While encounter groups are not seen as synonymous nor even closely similar to counseling groups by the editors, they have nevertheless invited Jim Bebout to contribute his report because he is the director of a project in a California community which constitutes a massive experimental research effort in encounter group experiences for volunteering adults; his findings will be of interest to group counseling professionals. Anna L. Miller and David V. Tiedeman, writing in a future-oriented cast, tie together significant ideas about technology and the lives of us all in the groups, real and potential, that we do and can inhabit.

H. Jon Geis, as he does in his earlier manuscript in this book, winds up the offerings by making another in-depth contribution to the profession of outstanding merit. He has very carefully set about to debunk a number of common (and often obstructive to gainful practice) group work myths. His highly personalized account presents the conditions and rationale under which he works, as he details from his own therapeutic practice a comprehensive look at these myth areas and how the beguiling traps they harbor may be avoided. Although his ideas are founded on and arise out of a highly "therapeutic" matrix, as he is an active group-therapy practitioner, his systematic analysis of the nine myth areas is nevertheless applicable to any and all who seek to become knowledgeable and proficient group counselors. The misbeliefs that he thoroughly disputes are common stumbling blocks in counseling groups, and his presentation represents an imaginatively conceived and carefully thought-out approach to improving effectiveness in all psychological helping groups.

This concludes the line-up. The editors feel they have brought together a collected body of thought which is unlike any other in the currently existing literature, but they also see this book as a beginning. The storehouse of group counseling technology which they envision is a long way from being filled. But the guidelines for doing so are laid out in this volume and the directions that a full development of a technology of group counseling ought to take are established.

2.
Toward a Comprehensive Framework
Unifying All Systems of Counseling*

H. Jon Geis

The original task I set for myself in this exposition was a definition and delineation of some of the more important and result-producing critical counselor behaviors or effective counselor practices. It was my belief that such a presentation would benefit would-be counselors, those who are already practitioners and those engaged in the complex work of training counselors, all of whom are concerned about the applied aspects of counseling.

As I set to work on this task, however, it became clear that it would be impossible to isolate any few techniques or practices which could adequately represent counseling as a whole. For one thing, there are so many formal counseling systems—Harper (1959) has identified 36—that any selection of techniques invariably would overlook some major counseling interventions felt to be important by leading theorists and practitioners. Secondly, this multiplicity of counseling systems strongly suggests that counseling cannot be a unitary term; any consideration of fundamental aspects of "counseling" must consider the fundamental aspects of *all* counseling systems. Thirdly, an attempt to arrive at a group of significant techniques revealed that these techniques cannot be considered apart from the nature of the counselee, his environment and the counseling goals set forth for him (explicitly or implicitly) by the counselor.

Therefore, it developed that I would be of most help to the educator, would-be counselor, or even to theorists and counseling practitioners themselves, if I could outline a comprehensive, yet brief,

*Under the same title, with minor differences, this manuscript first appeared in the March, 1969 issue of *Educational Technology* Magazine.

frame of reference within which to consider the great variety of counseling systems, concepts and techniques potentially useful for helping particular counselees in particular circumstances to achieve particular goals when counseled in particular ways by particular counselors.

No claim is made that the material in this contribution is a fully comprehensive description of counseling-in-general. It is offered in an attempt to help counseling professionals view counseling in a way that is *more* comprehensive than any single presentation that is, to my knowledge, already available in the literature of counseling.

Three separate, but related, sections follow which describe in somewhat different ways many of the elements of counseling-in-general, each section attempting to identify and/or comment about the major aspects of counseling in a way which contributes to an over-all functional description.

The first section sets forth a necessarily detailed definition of counseling. The second section presents some considerations which amplify the definition and cut across the third section, which elaborates a model of what are, when looked at from a still different point of view, the three main interrelated parts of counseling: (1) a theory of what people-in-the-world are like, (2) a theory of what is good for people-in-the-world and (3) a theory of the stimulus conditions which may constructively influence people-in-the-world as a function of their characteristics and what the counselor holds to be good for them.

The theory of the good, or the ethically valued counseling outcomes, is viewed as the inescapable (and, for most counselors and counseling systems, unrecognized) tie that binds the counselee-in-the-world to the counselor's choice of stimulus conditions.

A Definition of Counseling

What do we mean when we speak of "counseling?" We must distinguish the kind of counseling with which we are concerned from kinds which may be considered, for example, mainly medical, legal, religious or school grade "counseling." Therefore, a useful working definition—one which would appear to encompass virtually all systems of counseling—is proposed*:

---

*The reader is invited to consider a similar, yet in many ways different, omnibus definition presented by Harper (1959).

Psychological counseling is an activity in which a person who is trained and experienced in the psychological theory and practice of understanding and changing human behavior seeks to influence, mainly but not exclusively by the technique of talking, the perceptions, thinking, feelings, emotions and actions of one or more counselees, with the intention of producing short- and/or long-range changes in the counselee and/or in his reality situation which are more self-benefiting and self-actualizing and less self-defeating and self-inhibiting, with regard to what the counselee and/or counselor define as the counselee's self-interest as it relates to his personality and/or his reality problems.

As the reader can see, there are many separate elements in this definition of counseling. Each element is considered to be integral to an over-all conceptual framework which can include the particulars of any actual counseling situation. Some of the elements are discussed briefly in the following section, the remainder not being discussed because they appear to be self-explanatory.

Some Considerations Bearing
on Counseling

A number of considerations amplify the definition of counseling as well as the three-part model offered in the last section, and should be kept in mind because they add considerably to the meaning of the unifying conceptual framework sought in this chapter.

1. The most important single feature of the kind of counseling of concern here is the fact that its primary emphasis is *psychological*—the knowledge and skills of the counselor and the main aspects of his work with the counselee deal with psychology; what English and English (1958) in their *Comprehensive Dictionary of Psychological and Psychoanalytical Terms* define as "a branch of science dealing with behavior, acts, or mental processes, and with the mind, self, or person who behaves or acts or has the mental processes."

The subject matter of greatest concern and the comparatively low level of sophistication and skill of the counselor in activities designated as, for example, medical, legal, religious or school grade counseling, do not permit them to fall within the scope of the definition offered. While all school grade advisors no doubt use at least *some* kind of psychological approach, it would generally be on a "common sense" basis, and the focus would be more exclusively on curriculum considerations for the student rather than mainly (or even also) on behavior change.

It is important to note, however, that even though many counselors do not operate primarily within a psychological framework, their particular kind of counseling may be enhanced immeasurably to the extent that they are knowledgeable and skilled in psychological aspects of counseling. The major reason for this is quite simple: it is impossible to divorce the subject matter of an interview (e.g., which course of study to choose or how and whether to lose weight) from the psychology of the counselee and psychological skills helpful in getting the material thoroughly considered by him.

2. The counseling process, the role of the counselor and the nature of the counselor himself may vary somewhat in terms of a host of factors beyond the specifics of the three-part model to be offered, including the specific nature of the counselor's work setting, the duration and frequency of the contacts with the counselee, the specific goals of the counselor, the amount and kind of training and experience of the counselor, the counselor's access to adjunctive techniques and resources, and the related underlying and developing problems of the counselee.

3. As concluded by C.H. Patterson (1966), a leading critical authority in the field, "there are no essential differences between counseling and psychotherapy in the nature of the relationship, in the process, in the methods or techniques, in goals or outcomes (broadly conceived), or even in the kinds of clients involved."

Efforts have been made along a number of lines to separate counseling from psychotherapy. For example, counseling has been said to focus on decision-making, the identification of the counselee's assets and limitations, some special kind of content such as educational or vocational material, or dealing only with normal individuals; and psychotherapy to focus on psychopathology, unconscious mental processes or basic personality change. Yet, theoretically and in actual practice, the categories tend to overlap so much that no such separatist attempt seems to hold up. Concepts and techniques comprising systems identified as "psychotherapy" should, therefore, not be overlooked in efforts to understand, learn and practice effective counseling.

4. Counseling outcomes traceable to the effect of the counseling itself (rather than, for example, to fortuitous changes in the counselee's life situation) may be characterized as *learned* behavioral changes.

It is difficult to conceive of a professional psychological counselor undertaking an intervention with a counselee for any purpose other than to help the counselee learn something or change his behavior by acquiring some kind of knowledge so that he can act differently—with the occasional exception of interventions which are designed to be supportive or maintain the individual in a current status rather than allowing him to slip back.

Principles of learning underlie all counseling systems. For example, positive and negative reinforcements (rewarding or penalizing the counselee for an act or verbalization), chaining of responses (e.g., building one positive experience upon another) and concern for readiness for behavioral change (e.g., interpreting to the counselee only insofar as he can find the interpretation meaningful and profit from it) are principles used by virtually all counselors. However, learning principles are identified explicitly and built into their formal counseling approach by only a few theorists, even though this type of approach to counseling is having an increasingly significant impact on the field at the present time (Eysenck, 1960; Wolpe, 1958; Dollard and Miller, 1950).

5. Systems of counseling and psychotherapy have been described in terms of various dichotomies, such as those emphasizing action versus insight, directiveness versus non-directiveness (or a relatively non-directing approach which Carl Rogers [Rogers, 1951] came to identify as client-centered) and a medical model (conceiving of an "underlying disease" which had to be "treated" before the "symptom" behavior would change) versus a psychological (Ullmann and Krasner, 1965) model (viewing the problem behavior as changeable by working directly upon the relationship between it and its usual stimulus environment).

Perhaps one of the most useful distinctions between systems of counseling is along the lines marked out by Harper (1959), who classifies the great majority of approaches as emphasizing "emotional reconditioning" and a minority as concerned with "intellectual reeducation."

The former group of systems emphasizes behavior change based upon conditioning during the interview, often encouraging affective arousal by the counselee with regard to personality aspects of the counselor, and stressing the importance of the counseling climate as a special therapeutic kind of experience.

The latter group emphasizes more rational discussion and a greater focus on cognitive elements.

Harper fails to make clear, however, that the intellectual reeducation theorists actually take a teaching approach, which holds that counselees can change by rational enlightenment and persuasion, and which appears to use the environmental experiences occurring during the period *between* counseling sessions (rather than only or mainly the time spent in the counselor's office) for reconditioning experiences.

6. To the degree that counseling systems seek similar outcomes, *efficiency* must be an overriding goal in counseling. Any system which seeks to relieve distress and unhappiness and promote greater happiness for members of a society who vastly outnumber the professionals trying to help them must always be attempting to accommodate greater numbers of counselees—by conserving time and effort on those currently being helped. Too, besides making room for more counselees, it is obviously of intrinsic value to the profession to help any counselee change as quickly as possible. It is not success alone, but the economy of time and effort with which a system achieves its degree of success, by which it must be evaluated.

7. The psychological counselor, like the educator, takes a short-range point of view within a long-range context. He knows that, in most cases, he must help a counselee learn and change over a period of time (perhaps days or weeks, maybe months or even years) rather than immediately. Therefore, he focuses mostly on current data and strives for small but cumulative short-range gains, while keeping in mind the longer-range goals.

8. The major focus for any psychological counselor must be on counselee *problems*, no matter how broadly defined. That is, conceiving what the counselee presents as "problems" to be solved whether with regard to the counselee's personality traits or his relations with reality—makes the counselor's work specifically *task-oriented*.

9. There are two major overlapping ways of viewing the goals of psychological counseling: in terms of minimizing or eliminating the presence of self-defeating behavior patterns and, beyond that, stimulat-

ing self-actualizing aspects of the counselee's personality.

The advent of counseling psychology as a specialty after World War II and the emphases on vocational and educational guidance, with their focus on helping the counselee make self-benefiting decisions, probably were the beginnings of more formal attempts to move the counselee beyond a status quo life situation. And every attempt at eliminating self-defeating behavior must have in it some effect, at least, of furthering the counselee's life situation. But direct efforts at intervention for the sake of stimulating *all* individuals, as potential counselees, beyond their present life status is, I believe, the promise of the future in counseling.

There is no reason why the insights and skills of the counselor cannot be used to give all persons the push toward maximum development of their potential. Such an interventionist approach is truly an educational conception, since it is designed to aid all individuals, not only those in felt distress or in anti-social difficulties.

10. Psychological counseling works not only philosophically but also in psychological strategy in terms of the counselee's *self-interest*. Counseling which either disregards proceeding in terms of the counselee's self-interest or is undertaken for some *other* party's sake (such as a parent or teacher) not only is antithetical to counseling philosophy but also is found to be relatively ineffective—and can actually worsen the counselee's situation. To change for the better, the counselee must see that, at least in the long run, the contemplated changes in his behavior and situation are either to help him get more good things for himself or, at the very least, avoid what will very likely be a worse situation than his present one.

11. All counseling systems guide the counselee, but some systems take a much more explicit and forceful role in directing counselee activity, by virtue of their choice of stimulus conditions as related to counseling goals, both within and outside of the counseling session. The greater the active and explicit guiding on the part of the counselor, the more competence and greater responsibility would seem to be required of him.

12. Insofar as the counselor conceives of his task as one which requires a greater range of knowledge and change interventions, he will have greater responsibility, in the ethical as well as the factual (causal) sense, for the counselee's welfare, in the choices of goals and in

stimulus conditions potentially available.

13. If the counselor is conceived to be a change strategist who *influences* his counselee, it may be seen from the foregoing definition that the counselor need not limit his interventions to those undertaken during an interview, but may use, potentially, the universe of possibilities to influence changes. (For example, he may plan a seemingly casual but potentially influential two-minute encounter with his counselee in the school hall, or he may manipulate the counselee's environment by having him placed in a different class.)

14. Although it is not dealt with in this chapter, psychological counseling with *groups* of individuals is covered by the definition, and is with good warrant rapidly increasing in use in the field of counseling.

A Three-Part Model for a Unified Theory of Psychological Counseling

I. A Theory of What People-in-the-World Are Like

This portion of the model is really self-explanatory. Based on all the information we can put together, most importantly from research sources, we should have as good an idea as possible of what people and their environments are like in all respects. As may be seen from Figure 1, this dimension of the model is descriptive: it considers the physical-biological and psychological characteristics of people-in-themselves, what the world-in-itself (the variety of environments) is like, and what people and the world in interaction are like. The counselor is potentially more helpful to his counselees to the extent he is informed about people and world facts.

The counselor cannot be an expert in all areas, but he may become increasingly sophisticated in areas not directly involving his counseling expertise in itself, such as medicine, economics, sexual practices, religious institutions, the range and depth of the world of work, etc. For example, it might be highly desirable that a counselor have knowledge of a particular ghetto adolescent he is counseling with regard to his energy level, intelligence, supportive or negatively influential home and neighborhood environments, expectations he may have for persons like this youngster (as well as for the particular child), the

Figure 1

*A Three-Part Model for a Unified Theory of
Psychological Counseling*

I.   *A Theory of What People-in-the-World Are Like*

      A.   What People-in-Themselves Are Like
            1.   Physical-Biological Characteristics
            2.   Psychological Characteristics

      B.   What the World-in-Itself Is Like

      C.   What People-and-the-World-in-Interaction Are Like

II.   *A Theory of What Is Good for People-in-the-World*

III. *A Theory of Stimulus Conditions Which May Constructively
      Influence People-in-the-World as a Function of Their Character-
      istics-in-the-World and What Is Good for Them*

      A.   Counselor Personal Qualities

      B.   Counselor Techniques

      C.   Counseling-Related Adjuncts

channels available for career achievement in the society at large (and
particularly with regard to this individual), how drugs of various kinds
may act upon his counselee to inhibit self-actualization, etc.

*II. A Theory of What Is Good for
People-in-the-World*
Based upon their knowledge of what people-in-the-world are like,

most particularly the present and potential counselees, the counselors have in mind a number of desired counseling outcomes or goals. In turn, their choice of goals has a great deal to do with the choice of stimulus conditions most useful for achieving these goals. From this point of view, then, counseling may be conceived as, in one important aspect, an *ethical values system* which, according to the emphasis on certain valued goals, ties what we believe factually about people-in-the-world to the stimulus conditions which are believed to influence their behavior.

Counselors most frequently upset themselves about the notion that they "know what is good" for the counselee. This difficulty would seem to disappear if they would forthrightly realize the ethical values inherent in *any* approach to helping people—since values indicate the making of a choice, which has definite action implications, about what is good in human affairs—and take a stand in that regard as to the *general* values held for the counselee. That is, counselors often believe that to take a value stand means that they are choosing or requiring for the counselee what is good for him in the *specific* situation and thereby potentially thwarting him, choosing wrongly or denying him his right to choose for himself. Rarely is this done. Rather, the counselor elaborates in detail with the counselee all the options bearing on any such situation, so that the counselee has the greatest freedom to move in his own self-interest. This is done in terms of a number of *general* values held for the counselee, including the crucial value of the counselee's right to go ahead and do what may or will be against his own self-interest. (The counselor's professional obligation in such a case is to make sure the counselee understands all the options before he decides to act against himself.)

Following is a list of some of the more important general values or desired counseling outcomes held by psychological counselors from virtually all schools of counseling. It should be noted that they are self-*freeing* values rather than, as specific values would be, self-limiting. The categories overlap to some extent.

1. *Psychological independence.* This includes the freedom to be oneself, do what one wishes, when there are no realistic restrictions, and to take responsibility for one's actions. True psychological independence means that one does not *need* to have things a certain way even though he might strongly *prefer* or wish it. It emphasizes the

ability to tolerate the opposite of that which is highly important to oneself.

2. *Self-acceptance and accepting other people*. This requires that the individual not blame or condemn himself or lower his self-value even though he might have acted below his standards or even permanently be deficient in some way. He sees himself as responsible for (as causing and even being accountable for) some act, but does not blame himself for it. His worth does not depend upon his actions, be they good or bad, wrong or right. He feels adequate as a person and self-approving despite his deficiencies and disapproval by others. The same philosophy he applies to other people, not requiring them to be "perfect."

3. *Increase in enlightened self-interest*. The individual is for himself first, but not in an overfocused way or in a way which is socially irresponsible (the latter because he realizes that to act unfairly against others now might in some way penalize him in the long run).

4. *Accepting reality*. This means seeing and tolerating reality for what it is without emotionally protesting against it ("I can't *stand* it" and "It *shouldn't be* that way!") even while trying to change it, as far as this is at all possible. Other important aspects of accepting reality include giving up perfectionistic requirements for the world and oneself, acquiring self-discipline, and learning to postpone present pleasures in the service of some longer-range value.

5. *Decrease in self-defeating emotions, feelings and habit patterns*. Anger, fear, anxiety, low frustration tolerance, depression and other emotions and feeling states can be shown to be at least potentially always self-defeating. Greater control and decrease of these emotions, if not their virtual elimination, is a desired outcome for many counselors. Similarly, habit patterns of various kinds also interfere with self-actualization, and the counselor works to eliminate them.

6. *More fully experiencing oneself and the world*. This includes greater knowledge and awareness of oneself and other people, places and things; greater openness to all aspects of living, most importantly to one's own internal experiences. It implies having the motivation and developing the skills for greater involvements, which in turn may imply taking the initiative, "risk-taking" and even at times an adventurous disposition. One has greater perspective on oneself as a part of a large world, and there is the experience—and fact—of having greater power to

participate in it in self-fulfilling ways.

7. *Increase in problem-solving and decision-making abilities.* These crucial facets of effective human functioning can be taught, and are often directly or indirectly an outcome of counseling, especially since much of counseling involves these behaviors. The counselee seems to learn principles of problem-solving and decision-making and how to generalize these to other situations in his life.

8. *Learning new concepts and principles.* Counselors want their counselees to learn new concepts, ideas and principles for more effective living.

9. *Maintaining current self-benefiting behavior.* The counselor's task is often that of helping the counselee maintain levels of functioning and actualization in the face of tendencies to slip back or when potentially disruptive stresses come on the scene.

10. *Emotional catharsis.* When counselees are unduly upset, it is often desirable as a goal in itself to help them reduce their tensions and even acquire perspective and new learnings from "talking out" their disturbed feelings with a counselor.

11. *Finding at least one understanding, wise, loving and/or empathic significant other person.* Nearly all theorists would agree—at least one, Ellis, would disagree—that adolescent and older human beings *need* contact with at least one other human being who is of great personal importance to them. All theorists, however, appear to agree that such a contact is highly *desirable*, not only because counselees can profit from it but because nearly all human beings, reared and conditioned as they are in an interpersonal world, seem to want it so strongly as an experience in itself.

III. A Theory of Stimulus Conditions Which May Constructively Influence People-in-the-World as a Function of Their Characteristics-in-the-World and What Is Good for Them

Suppose, now, that we know what counselees-in-the-world are like and what is good for them. What shall we do to help them change?

Looking at this problem in perspective, it seems clear that we must not jump to use any particular technique or method, *even though it may appear to work*; but we must review the possible variety of stimulus conditions and select from those the influences which may help us more readily achieve our goals. Such conditions appear to break down into three relatively discrete categories: (a) personal qualities of the counselor, (b) counselor techniques and (c) adjuncts related to counseling.

Some counseling theorists seem to have emphasized either the first or the second of these categories alone, far more than the other two. Rogers and his associates, for example, believe that the personal qualities of the counselor almost entirely are the stimulus conditions required for effecting change. However, in response to one of Rogers' statements (Rogers, 1957) to this effect (with regard to basic personality change, rather than temporary symptom removal), Ellis (1959) has remarked that "The conclusion seems inescapable . . . that although basic constructive personality change . . . seems to require fundamental modification in the ideologies and value systems of disturbed individuals, there is probably *no* single condition which is absolutely necessary for the inducement of such changed attitudes and behavior patterns. Many conditions . . . are highly desirable; but all that seems to be necessary is that the individual *somehow* come up against significant life experiences *or* learn about others' experiences *or* sit down and think for himself *or* enter a relationship with a therapist who is *preferably* congruent, accepting, empathic, rational, forceful, etc. Either/or rather than this-and-that seems to be the only realistic description of necessary conditions for basic personality change that can be made at this time."

Following is a list of stimulus conditions which would seem to be most frequently used by counseling theorists and practitioners. Some counseling systems, of course, draw much more on particular conditions (within as well as among the three categories) than they do on others. Although no one or few conditions may be necessary, it is quite possible that some individually or in combination with other conditions may be *much more likely* to influence desired outcomes than are others.

The problem, therefore, in making counseling more of an applied science and less of a beguiling art is to specify in (a) which circumstances (b) which stimulus conditions are most likely to lead to (c) which outcomes for (d) which counselees. Disservice is done to counselees when any one variable or condition is set forth as absolutely and always being the condition most likely to influence behavior change.

There can be no substitute for competence, knowledge and the continuing search, in the light of increasing research and new thinking, for increasingly effective methods.

A. Counselor Personal Qualities

1. *Non-condemnation of the counselee as a person.* Here the counselor conveys the attitude that the counselee has the right to be wrong, even while he may vigorously attack the counselee's behavior and ideas. He refrains from moralistic judgments, and regards the counselee as a person of intrinsic worth.

2. *Non-possessive warmth.* This is a category developed by Truax and Carkhuff (1967), closely related to the previous category but implying also some other ingredients, such as, apparently, an openness and respect for the counselee, with overtones of the counselor's humanity and personalized caring. The characteristic tends to be a subtle one, and is not well described operationally by these authors. It is related to the attitude of unconditional positive regard which was elaborated by Carl Rogers for many years.

3. *Communicated competence, authoritativeness, confidence and wisdom.* These four aspects of the counselor's professional yet personal attitudes and behavior indicate the importance of communicating to the counselee, by a variety of non-verbal as well as verbal means, the professional strengths of the counselor. Voice tone suggesting confidence in himself and his professional skills, style of talking, general manner, quality and content of advice given, common sense, etc.—these things may subtly, yet effectively, build confidence and trust in the counselee. Communication that the counselor is confident, even optimistic, that the counselee will change is a subtle, yet highly powerful, condition for changing behavior.

4. *Genuineness, humanness, sincerity and openness.* Researched as genuineness by Truax and Carkhuff (1967), and formerly called self-congruence by Rogers, this over-all attitude, when well communicated in the counselor's manner, seems to build the counselee's confidence that the counselor has nothing to hide, is non-punitive, and does indeed wish to help him.

5. *Empathy and understanding.* Another communicated attitude emphasized by Truax and Carkhuff (1967), as well as by Rogers (1951), empathy tends to include understanding, as well as acceptance,

and implicitly the notion "I see how you feel." Understanding, however, may be communicated without empathy.

6. *Sensitivity*. The acuteness to perceive what is taking place in the counseling process from the counselee's verbal and non-verbal cues and from his own internal experience as well. It includes the ability to perceive underlying and obscure content as well as obvious material. To the extent that it exists, it, like the following three counselor traits, will serve as a stimulus condition and be picked up by the counselee without difficulty.

7. *Objectivity*. This means taking a detached, neutral, non-personally involved perspective on the counselee's problems. Along with other counselor qualities, it aids the counselee in feeling free to be himself and express ideas and behavior that differ from the norm.

8. *Flexibility*. The counselor furthers the counseling process when he communicates a willingness and ability to adapt to the ongoing exigencies of the counseling process.

9. *High intelligence*. What happens when a counselor cannot out-think his counselee? It is easy to respond to this desideratum by saying, as a therapist friend of mine once said when she encountered a brilliant, yet emotionally troubled, young man, "It's a good thing that's not what this is all about" (implying emotional reconditioning techniques can entirely bypass intellectual aspects). However, every counseling professional can recall cases he has heard of where counselees "couldn't respect" their counselor, or adolescents derided him to their friends as being "not very smart."

10. *Absence of serious emotional disturbance*. It goes without saying that an emotionally disturbed counselor will bias, distort, or disrupt the effective use of other stimulus conditions to aid the counselee.

11. *Absence of communicated disruptive personal values*. Private values and ideologies (religious, ethical, political, philosophical, etc.), particularly when they are neither shared by the counselee nor shown to be clearly self-benefiting for him, should be carefully screened from the counseling process.

12. *Personal style*. The personal dimension of counseling style is reflected in a great variety of counselor behaviors and may be highly useful or, on the other hand, useless or even detracting, in promoting counseling success. Included here are such aspects as counselor

forcefulness and vigor versus impotence and lack of emphasis in counselor responses; emotional range; sense of humor; and activity versus passivity in manner and speech.

13. *Miscellaneous personal aspects.* This category is designed to include personal aspects of the counselor which might otherwise go unnoticed as positive or negative stimulus conditions. Such characteristics would include, as appropriate for particular counselees in particular circumstances: sex, age, race, appearance and dress, and personal habits.

B. Counselor Techniques

One could list almost an infinite number of counseling techniques, since a "technique" might be classified as anything from a minute bit of behavior by the counselor to a lengthy and/or complex set of behaviors, such as the use of group counseling. For the purpose of this section of the model, however, I believe it would be quite valuable to gather in one place a list of counselor behaviors, although few play more than a small role in the over-all armamentarium of techniques in any particular system of counseling. It is the artful *combination* of a few or many of these techniques in conjunction with the other aspects of the counseling process discussed in this chapter that produces successful counseling. The techniques as stimulus conditions are not necessarily listed in order of their importance.

1. *Questioning, drawing the counselee out and evoking problem-related material.* In interviews which are actively of a problem-solving kind, these kinds of interventions usually predominate during the early portion of the session.

2. *Identifying, labeling, clarifying and reflecting feeling.* These are interventions which expose and make clear for the counselee, not just for the counselor, the counselee's problem-related material. For example, issues may be identified and clarified, cues to anxiety may be labeled, and here-and-now (in the counseling session itself) feeling states may be identified in terms of a "reflection" of their major meaning ("You feel that you really want to . . .").

3. *Summarizing and reviewing important material.* Frequently during the interview it is useful to draw together the large bulk of what the counselee has said, often in a haphazard way, so that he may more usefully focus on it in its most essential aspects. Reviewing what has

been uncovered or worked through from time to time also is a useful way of increasing learning.

4. *Restating*. Often it is useful to put what the counselee has said into different words so that he may find it more meaningful.

5. *Establishing connections*. An important intervention identified by Wolberg (1954), this refers to the counselor's piecing together for the counselee fragments of problem-related material that, due to forgetting, repression and simple unawareness, the counselee cannot see as connected.

6. *Emphasizing, accenting or underscoring*. This refers to placing a stress on an intervention or a counselee response by differing the voice tone, discussing the content further, etc. ("So you really *do* want to graduate, eh?")

7. *Interpreting*. This is a description or reformulation of counselee problem-related material, or of test or other data related to the counselee's material that is put to him in more familiar or meaningful terms. Often it refers to giving to the counselee the underlying meaning of an experience or statement.

8. *Confronting*. Usually used when confronting with reality: reality aspects of the counselee's personality and/or situation. Usually, aspects he wishes to avoid are straightforwardly presented to him, and he is forced to look at them. *Confronting* suggests more onus to do something about the reality aspect than does *interpreting*. Active-directive and cognitive systems of counseling, such as those of Ellis (1962), Phillips (1956), Thorne (1950) and Ellis and Harper (1964) greatly emphasize the use of *persistent confrontation*.

9. *Reassuring, encouraging and supporting*. Counselees frequently need reassurance—that they will change for the better, that they are not too fragile to try out a new experience or receive a counselor confrontation, etc. Encouragement may be extended to motivate the counselee when he has doubts about moving himself ahead. And psychological or emotional support is useful at moments during the interview or during episodes in the counseling sequence when the counselee's anxieties begin to inhibit progress rather than promote it. It is important to note, however, that reassurance, encouragement or support given at the wrong time may disrupt or retard counseling progress.

10. *Creating and maintaining tension*. Frequently it is useful to

create or maintain a degree of tension or anxiety on the part of the counselee during the interview or portions of the counseling sequence for use as motivation to get the counselee to move ahead in his development.

11. *Contrasting and showing alternatives.* Showing the counselee the opposite of his behavior is a useful technique to help him get perspective on it. Similarly, not only does it help the counselee's first behavior option to become more meaningful when alternatives are presented to him, but frequently such alternatives themselves may become the chosen course of action. Helping the counselee find the best alternative course of action is quite clearly one of the most crucial functions of psychological counseling.

12. *Information- and advice-giving.* Another major contribution that the psychological counselor can make is the introduction of information—data about the counselee and/or the world—at the appropriate time in counseling. Advice-giving is usually disparaged by counseling theorists and practitioners. However, when seen not as the most important tool of counseling but as a highly useful intervention, if used appropriately, advice-giving certainly has its place. In this regard, the counselor functions as a wise mentor or consultant. He does not require that the counselee follow his advice; rather, he attempts to help the counselee clearly understand what the consequences of following his advice will be, as compared to following other alternatives.

13. *Using ambiguity and "inability to understand."* Bordin (1955) has developed the importance of ambiguity as a dimension for therapeutic change. The lack of clarity of elements in the counseling process itself creates pressure for counselee change. Along these lines, I have many times found it useful to seem to be "unable to understand" the communications of a counselee. Such a condition forces the counselee to clarify his meaning, and usually results in a highly useful bit of counselee learning.

14. *Using the counseling relationship as leverage for change.* The counseling relationship, in its varied aspects, may be a useful tool to promote counselee change. Prestige suggestion, for example, may result in the counselee embarking more readily upon a certain course of action. Ultimately, of course, the counselee should be doing things for himself, not to secure the counselor's approval or to avoid his displeasure.

15. *Using oneself and others as role models.* Much of traditional counseling theory has had it that if the counselor serves as a warm, understanding, non-punitive person who accepts the counselee unconditionally, the counselee will learn more positive feelings toward other people and accept himself more in their presence. To achieve this it has been held that the counselor should keep under cover most of the personal aspects which define him as a unique human being—for the more unique and unambiguous he is the less generalizable to people-in-general are his positive dimensions. Some theorists and practitioners feel that this view simply does not work in many cases and in others is, at best, inefficient. They propose an alternative view: where the counselor doses the counselee, as appropriate, with aspects of his personal life which are appropriate for influencing the counselee to learn in certain directions. Glasser (1965) holds that the counselor must necessarily tell about himself to the counselee in order to get the kind of involvement—which includes as an important aspect being seen as more human and real—he believes is necessary for maximum change leverage. The counselor may use other persons, fictional or real, as role model examples, too. ("Did I tell you about the time Darwin quit school?")

16. *Using hypothetical situations and examples.* The human being's capacity for imagination may be used profitably to get the counselee to imagine hypothetical future or actual past situations and to reexamine them, challenging his previous assumptions. He may be asked to "imagine the *worst* that can happen if you do that" by a rational-emotive therapist or to vividly attempt to reexperience in his mind the situation about which he is phobic so that he may be counter-conditioned by a behavior therapist (Ullmann and Krasner, 1965). Other kinds of examples may be used as appropriate to make issues more meaningful. The usefulness of these and other techniques depends upon the skill and creativity of the counselor, in conjunction with the counselee's characteristics and other considerations set forth in this chapter.

17. *Communicated focus on the counselee's self-interest.* As noted elsewhere in this chapter, insofar as the counselee believes the counselor is not working to help *him* achieve things that are good for *him*, he will resist counseling. Therefore, the counselor must obviously and consistently work in terms of the counselee's self-interest. To do

this, of course, he must define with the counselee what goals may be in his self-interest. In cases where the counselee's self-interest lies mainly in avoiding short-range negative circumstances (e.g., studying his hated algebra not to get a reward but to avoid being left back in school) or in achieving long-range rewards (e.g., working at his school work now to graduate from college later and live a better life financially) the counselor must be certain that he is communicating this idea.

18. *Using clear, concise, meaningful communications.* It is with reality that the counselee has his great difficulties: he is ignorant of it, confused about it, protests against it, or denies it. Therefore, to the extent that the counselor's communications are unclear—wordy, confused, using vague or meaningless language, etc.—the counselee will be unclear about his problems and what to do about them. Some writers say that it is not the content of what the counselor says but the way that he says it that is most important. In actuality, both aspects are very significant, which reflects the fact that it is the meaning of the communication that is most important, whether this is in the obvious content or in the meaning implied by voice tone, accompanying gestures, etc.

19. *Emotional catharsis and desensitization.* Often, when the counselee is upsetting himself or is highly tense about some issue, it is valuable to encourage him to "talk it out," or reduce his tensions and gain perspective on the issue by pouring out his feelings about it.

20. *Psychological homework.* This technique is used mostly by active-directive counselors who, generally in agreement with the counselee, assign problem-related psychological tasks for the counselee to work on between counseling sessions. Such assignments generally are designed to create problem-related experiences rather than to wait for them to occur of their own accord. For example, a boy might be assigned increasingly longer periods of time to focus on his studying, gradually building up his frustration tolerance. Or a counselee might be set the task of asking three people each day for directions, as a way of overcoming his fear of rejection. Another typical assignment might be to stop at specified times during the day to spend two minutes each time reviewing one's problems and questioning the fear aspects in them. The user of psychological homework recognizes that problem-related experiences are an important ingredient in getting over the problems themselves.

21. *Persuasion, exhortation, pressure and coercion.* There may be times, not only in emergencies, when all counselors may use different degrees and kinds of non-physical force on a counselee.

Intellectual reeducation theorists, such as Ellis, see forceful persuasion and related techniques actually as fundamental to their efforts to achieve behavior change.

C. Counseling-Related Adjuncts

The counseling-related adjuncts listed below are merely suggestive, and undoubtedly do not exhaust the possibilities that the creative counselor might use.

1. *Environmental manipulation.* Behavior may often be changed, temporarily at least, by changing the counselee's reality situation. However, unless the environmental change is sufficient to help the counselee learn permanent new behavior, where this is the goal, such changes must be sought through counseling. For example, two children who are joining to disrupt the classroom procedures may be quieted by putting one of them into a different class, but this in itself is unlikely to teach non-disruptive behavior.

2. *Group counseling.* Seeing many individuals at one time, the use of peers to gain psychological leverage, and here-and-now social learning are merely some of the reasons why group counseling is a useful adjunct to individual counseling.

3. *Simulated experiences.* Psychodrama and problem-related films and filmstrips are examples of useful experiences which may augment individual counseling. In a related vein, formal involvements in activities such as art and recreation, and even relevant programs on teaching machines, also are helpful at times.

4. *Tests and other diagnostic materials and situations.* One important innovation, which should be mentioned here, is the promising use of computers for a variety of counseling functions.

5. *Miscellaneous aids.* Medications (prescribed by and taken in consultation with a physician), eyeglasses, lunches for school children and wearing apparel and transportation costs for indigent counselees, all are examples of aids which may be useful in helping to solve problems encountered in counseling.

References

Bordin, Edward S. *Psychological Counseling.* New York: Appleton-Century-Crofts, 1955.

Dollard, John and Neal E. Miller. *Personality and Psychotherapy.* New York: McGraw-Hill, 1950.

Ellis, Albert. Requisite Conditions for Basic Personality Change. *Journal of Consulting Psychology,* 1959, *23,* 538-549.

Ellis, Albert. *Reason and Emotion in Psychotherapy.* New York: Lyle Stuart, 1962.

Ellis, Albert and Robert A. Harper. *A Guide to Rational Living.* Englewood Cliffs, New Jersey: Prentice-Hall, 1964.

English, Horace B. and Ava C. English. *Comprehensive Dictionary of Psychological and Psychoanalytical Terms.* New York: Longmans, Green, 1958.

Eysenck, Hans J. (Ed.) *Behavior Therapy and the Neuroses.* New York: Pergamon Press, 1960.

Glasser, William. *Reality Therapy.* New York: Harper and Row, 1965.

Harper, Robert A. *Psychoanalysis and Psychotherapy: 36 Systems.* Englewood Cliffs, New Jersey: Prentice-Hall, 1959.

Patterson, C.H. *Theories of Counseling and Psychotherapy.* New York: Harper and Row, 1966.

Phillips, E. Lakin. *Psychotherapy: A Modern Theory and Practice.* Englewood Cliffs, New Jersey: Prentice-Hall, 1956.

Rogers, Carl R. *Client-Centered Therapy.* Boston: Houghton Mifflin Co., 1951.

Rogers, Carl R. The Necessary and Sufficient Conditions for Therapeutic Personality Change. *Journal of Consulting Psychology,* 1957, *21,* 95-103.

Thorne, Frederick C. Principles of Personality Counseling. *Journal of Clinical Psychology,* 1950.

Truax, Charles B. and Robert R. Carkhuff. *Toward Effective Counseling and Psychotherapy: Training and Practice.* Chicago: Aldine, 1967.

Ullmann, Leonard P. and Leonard Krasner. *Case Studies in Behavior Modification.* New York: Holt, Rinehart and Winston, 1965.

Wolberg, Lewis R. *The Technique of Psychotherapy.* New York: Grune and Stratton, 1954.

Wolpe, Joseph. *Psychotherapy by Reciprocal Inhibition.* Palo Alto: Stanford University Press, 1958.

3.
Counseling Technology:
A Needed Conceptualization*

John Vriend

Men can agree readily that a given unit of reality should be known by a common symbol. The referents of polliwog, wart, hammer, tree, or moon cannot be explained away: they exist. There is no question of what such terms signify: the realities behind them are available for observation and measurement, and so justify the need for the names. There is a real world filled with an infinite number of real things: discoverable, tangible, namable things.

There is another world, one which is just as real to man but which has confounded him since the beginning of his tenure on the planet, the world of his mind. It also contains an infinite number of simple and complex units to which he would like to give names, and so he does. Who can deny the existence of law, ego, idea, freedom, or even of an angel? While such abstract symbols do not have referents which can be observed, measured, or painted yellow, they stand for realities in man's mental world.

But all men do not agree to the same existence of what stands behind all abstract terms. Because individual men are so infinitely variable, because each man lives out his own existence in his own way for his own purposes at his own pace, he tends to redefine, to restrict or extend, or otherwise qualify those abstract symbols which are personally important to him; his preferences, his values, his peculiar perceptions, his social roles and relationships, his dreams and his fears all enter his definitions.

The term *technology* has enormous appeal to a wide variety of

*Under the same title, with minor differences, this manuscript first appeared in the March, 1969 issue of *Educational Technology* Magazine.

men for many psychological reasons. (The same may be said of such sister abstractions as *technological, technical, technique* and, to a lesser extent, *technician.*)

In the minds of most men *technology* stands for all that is associated with "progress," one of the secular gods of Western Civilization, and progress is clearly understood to mean man's ever-increasing control over his environment. Primitive man was the victim, the pawn, of the forces of nature: modern man is nature's master. Man's technology has enabled him to abandon cave life, to live in giant cities, to master water and air, to explore the moon. It is only in the technological society and era, when they are feeling some measure of autonomy and control of destiny, that so many men are willing to widely and confidently proclaim that they need neither gods nor God, that God is dead. Technology refers to applied science, the application of accumulated specialized knowledge to age-old problems man has in living. Technology means expertise, technical nomenclature, the existence of a body of tested processes and methods which work every time, and it means machines, mechanization and the elimination of manual operations.

Most men can accept the prominence of technology in the physical sciences and industrial arts with felicity, and they can readily understand how technological advances have contributed to increased productivity in all manufacturing areas, to greater sophistication and efficiency in construction, food gathering and processing, mining, transportation, communication, office management, the practice of medicine, heating, refrigeration, even in most aspects of governmental operation. The multiplied numbers and varieties of technicians, technical training programs and research centers are all an accepted part of the technological age. What many men choose not to see, either because they fear it or because it has not been clearly demonstrated to them, is *how technology can be applied to human behavior.*

If technology is defined in such a way as to include only things and methods, procedures and processes related to things, then, of course, it cannot be applied to human behavior. Such a restricted definition of technology safely limits it to hardware and software, to physical and mechanical aids, to what is environmental rather than human. But if the definition of technology is broadened to include scientific methodology, the application of reliable knowledge to human problems and behaviors, as Robert Gagné has suggested it should be (Gagné, 1968), the implications for those who deal in social and personal services are far-reaching.

If this broader conceptualization of technology is joined to counseling, whether one conceives of counseling as a field of study, a discipline, a profession, or simply as an occupational role, and can be accepted by those who educate, train and supervise counselors, as well as by counseling practitioners, researchers and theorists, then a whole new order of counseling values, emphases and practices is possible.

In the present, counseling is grossly unscientific, and that is what ails it. Competency and incompetency are given equal credence; myths, platitudes and favored delusions are awarded the same attention as facts and tested principles; effective practices are ranked no higher than ineffective ones; problems are solved, and new policies and practices are instituted, by compromise and consensus rather than through the application of scientific knowledge, the establishment of clearly demarcated attainable goals and the employment of objective criteria.

The concept of efficiency in counseling is either scorned or ignored, as though it is somehow antithetical to the very nature of counseling, as though it somehow abrogates that highest of counseling ideals—human freedom. Counselor passivity is prized over counselor activity, as though predetermined counselor behaviors tend to result in client-manipulation, which used to be one of the most universally acknowledged negatives in the field. Diagnosis, evaluation and quality control, both in counselor education and on-the-job functioning of counselors, are the exception rather than the rule.

It is simplistic, of course, to so characterize the present state of affairs in the counseling field, but doing so helps to dramatize the need for reconstruction. The field is comprised of a conglomerate of factions, of a variety of individuals who carry out their professional work in many diverse occupational environments which are shaped by a host of local conditions. If one were to make a national assessment of what counselors are and what they do, assuming such were possible, regardless of what criteria were employed, one would find such a wide range that the practitioners at either end would bear almost no resemblance to each other. While a dentist in downtown Chicago functions in a way predictably similar to one in Panama City, Florida, the same cannot be said of counselors. Universal or even normative truths about the real world of counseling are hard to come by.

But there is a need and an opportunity, more than ever before in human history, for this professional newcomer called a counselor to serve his fellow man. The social, psychological and economic pathology which are conditionally a part of modern domestic life, or the nation's need for an ever-enlarged pool of stable, effective, highly trained and educated human resources, or the way in which it is possible in our time for even our "lowest born" citizens to fulfill their potential: these need no documentation here. The point is that counseling services exist to help human beings, singly and together, to eliminate social and psychological pathology and to enhance individual growth and development. The declared ultimate goal of every counselor worthy of the professional label is to help all of his clients to become as self-directing as their respective capacities and circumstances allow. The extent to which a given counselor is able to accomplish this goal depends upon his knowledge, expertise, professional resources and the conditions which are part of his work setting.

Counseling is a young profession, if profession it can yet be called. It has come into being within the last 50 years almost in spite of itself. Today some 50,000 counselors provide special services to clients in schools and other agencies throughout the nation. The American Personnel and Guidance Association, the parent professional organization to which most counselors belong, has grown from 5,000 to 27,000 members in the last 20 years, and its rate of growth continues to accelerate.

There exist presently: 1) a demonstrated widespread need within our society for counseling services; 2) a recorded history of counseling research, practices and professional activity; and 3) a sizable body of individuals who identify with and work within the counseling culture. Thus, there are sufficient conditions (need, personnel and know-how) at this point in the development of the profession to conceive of and make practical the establishment of a counseling technology. Such a technology would include the following dimensions.

What a Counselor Is

Just as dentistry requires a dentist, counseling requires a counselor. The establishment of a counseling technology depends upon a clear description of the counselor, the embodiment, the guardian, the manifestor of this technology.

Counselor, like dentist, is an occupational title, defined and classified in the *Dictionary of Occupational Titles* (U.S. Department of Labor, 1965) according to the specialized knowledge and occupational behaviors needed (what a counselor knows and does), the purposes such behaviors serve (why and for whom he does it), the work settings in which these behaviors are manifested (where he does it), and the preparation needed to acquire his specialized expertise.

From the point of view of counseling technology, this professional worker can be further described as a social scientist, as a human relations technician, as a behavioral engineer, as a designer and facilitator of positive, healthful behavioral changes, physical, social and mental.

He would be an expert. His professional behavior would exemplify the most effective techniques, methods and practices, the application of the latest scientific knowledge, and a mastery of mechanical and environment aids. He would be pragmatic, concerned with productivity and efficiency, have a scientific attitude, be disciplined in scientific methodology. He would either know or have access to all of the most up-to-date knowledge from the physical, social and behavioral sciences. He would use his person, his being, as an instrumentality in the service of each of his clients, each of whom he would accept completely and regard as equally important, however different from each other or himself. He would understand that human beings are freed to develop not by the absence of restraints, but by the acquisition of knowledge, skills and competencies, by the elimination of self-defeating behaviors and the gaining of self-promoting behaviors, so they are better equipped to handle each new life situation they encounter. He would not serve his own needs at the expense of those of his clients, nor would he engage in any occupational behavior beyond his level of competency.

Such is a description of the general practitioner, and it is overly pat. To conceive of every counselor as the complete expert, proficient in all aspects of counseling technology, able to service every conceivable kind of client, is to dream the impossible dream. Yet too many discussions in the counseling literature predicate only the general practitioner.

Each organized bona fide profession provides a model for what is needed in the burgeoning counseling profession: a division of labor, creation of areas of specialization and established levels of competency. Worker roles and performance criteria in each specialized area and at each level are clearly defined, and training programs have been instituted to produce workers in each classification at each level; the medical field is an obvious example. There is too much to medical technology for any one person to be the carrier of it all. Similarly, there is too much to counseling technology.

The counseling profession is at the developmental stage where the creation of a hierarchy of competency levels in a spectrum of specialized areas is needed. This requires an occupational classification system, with clearly delineated performance criteria and worker roles in each category, and the institution of special training programs. A true counseling technology can hardly be said to exist before such an organizational table of workers is made a reality.

Committed Membership

There is a career aspect to professionalism. The authentic professional has decided on his life-work. He has made a commitment to his specialized discipline and to his own vocational development within it. He continually enlarges his knowledge, improves his skills and competencies, and seeks to qualify himself for more responsible and demanding occupational roles where his professional contribution can be greater. He identifies with and gives his primary allegiance to his profession, and his secondary allegiance to the institution wherein he provides his services. He helps to define his profession through his occupational performance and involvement with colleagues as professional-minded as himself (Pietrofesa and Vriend, 1971).

The counseling profession requires a greatly enlarged complement of such committed members for a true counseling technology to come into existence. Space herein does not permit an airing of all the difficulties involved; suffice it to say that responsible (committed) professionals within concerned A.P.G.A. and A.P.A. Divisions are grappling with these, and that progress continues to be evident. (For a first-rate model of exemplary achievement by one professional group, Division 17 of the American Psychological Association, wherein all the alluded-to difficulties are discussed are dealt with, see *The Professional Preparation of Counseling Psychologists: Report of the 1964 Greystone Conference*, Thompson and Super, 1964.)

Counseling Technology Storehouse

The vast amount of accumulated wisdom and technical lore of counseling is presently scattered, contained in a million different published items, haphazardly brought together here and there in inadequate clusters. The specification, selective organization, codification and storehousing of this lore ought to be a critical concern of committed counseling professionals. To do so requires: 1) substantial financial support; 2) released time, boundless energy, single-minded dedication to the task and the concentrated effort of a variety of officially designated experts; 3) the willingness of formalized and duly authorized professional groups to take responsibility for establishing criteria and evaluating counseling knowledge, techniques, methods, procedures, practices and for officially endorsing and certifying essential learnings; 4) publication in usable forms; and 5) saturation distribution to all training programs, supervisors and practitioners.

While hundreds of "counseling" textbooks exist, few are essential reading or definitive within the counseling field. There is more agreement among professionals on academic course requirements leading to minimal state certification standards or the awarding of graduate degrees than there is on specific textual content of available readings, on a minimal bibliography of vital books. As a result, beginning counseling practitioners are left on their own, and must exercise their own unfortified judgment in countless operational areas, with little recourse to any kind of authoritative professional officialdom. There is no sanctioned "party platform."

Liberalism, diversity, plurality and engaging dialogue on the significance of research, the worth of any given practice or method, the determination of professional ends and means: these make for lively encounters in professional meetings and increase the variety of journal offerings, but they hardly provide the tyro with an occupational compass.

Consider a few specific lacks. There is no text in the field which specifies and describes essential counseling practicum learnings. There is no handbook, no operational manual, cataloguing the variety of ways in which tape recording, one-way mirror laboratories, videotaping, closed circuit television, or other mechanical aids can most effectively be used to develop in interns necessary, and appropriate counseling behaviors. Role-workers (see the contribution in this book wherein the editors discard the term "playing" and substitute "working") is given the nod as being a sometimes effective occupational behavior, yet counselors are seldom trained to be skilled role-workers or helped to understand when and how to incorporate specific role-workers' techniques; nor is a definitive text on role-working (which includes role theory, learnings from psychodrama, significant training knowledge from the dramatic arts) a part of the arsenal of counseling literature. There is no authentic comprehensive history of the counseling profession, basic reading for entrants to the field. These are but a few; there is no shortage of lacks.

To declare or demonstrate a critical need is not to assign culpability. Developing taxonomies, concordances, dictionaries, catalogues, histories, handbooks, manuals and the like is easier in the industrial arts and the physical sciences than in the behavioral sciences. But definitive works can be produced, either through private enterprise publishing (Stevens, 1951; Lindzey and Aronson, 1968), through the backing of professional organizations (Gage, 1963), or through governmental sponsorship (U.S. Department of Labor, 1965).

The development of a storehouse of counseling technology would appear to be an inevitability, coterminous with evolution toward full maturity of the total counseling profession.

Professional Stance

The aforegoing discussion of some of the issues and problems involved in the establishment of a counseling technology represents the position of but a single faction within the counseling field. To members of this "camp," explicit directions in which the profession ought to evolve seem logical and necessary. Counseling is seen by them as applied behavioral science.

There is, of course, an opposing "camp" for whom many of the tenets inherent in the formulation of a counseling technology are objectionable, even repugnant. Their objections are reasonable. A clear and responsible presentation of both positions, as well as a thoughtful attempt at resolving differences between them, is contained in the little book: *Revolution in Counseling: Implications of Behavioral Sciences* (Krumboltz, 1966). A thorough knowledge of its contents ought to be the possession of every person directly or indirectly connected with counseling.

References

Gage, N.L. (Ed.) *Handbook of Research on Teaching*. Chicago: Rand McNally, 1963.

Gagne, Robert M. Educational Technology as Technique. *Educational Technology*, November 15, 1968, 5-13.

Krumboltz, John D. (Ed.) *Revolution in Counseling: Implications of Behavioral Sciences*. Boston: Houghton Mifflin, 1966.

Lindzey, Gardner and Elliot Aronson (Eds.) *Handbook of Social Psychology*, 2nd ed. Reading, Mass.: Addison-Wesley, 1968.

Pietrofesa, John J. and John Vriend. *The School Counselor as a Professional*. Itasca, Ill.: F.E. Peacock, 1971.

Stevens, S.S. (Ed.) *Handbook of Experimental Psychology*. New York: John Wiley and Sons, 1951.

Thompson, Albert S. and Donald E. Super (Eds.) *The Professional Preparation of Counseling Psychologists: Report of the 1964 Greystone Conference*. New York: Teachers College, Columbia University, 1964.

U.S. Department of Labor. *Dictionary of Occupational Titles*, 3rd ed. Washington, D.C.: U.S. Government Printing Office, 1965.

4.
A Case for a Technology of Group Counseling and Delineation of Major Group Categories

John Vriend and
Wayne W. Dyer

In March, 1969, *Educational Technology* published a special issue on "Counseling Technology," an issue which, four years later, is still seen by many professionals in the counseling field as a front-runner—as containing most of the important ideas about how the applied behavioral science called counseling ought to develop as a discipline and as a therapeutic service. Indeed, there have been myriad developments to indicate that counseling is more and more becoming a "pindown-able," teachable, learnable collection of methods, procedures, skills, competencies and knowledge; less of an art or mystery and more of an ordered world of available possibilities. Theorists, researchers and trainers are becoming more pragmatic. Practitioners want more "how to" and fewer exhortations, and have been steadfastly reinforcing producers who have been adding to the technology of counseling as opposed to those who merely ruminate, endlessly chewing seemingly indigestible lumps of favorite counseling cud.

As spelled out in "Counseling Technology: A Needed Conceptualization" (reproduced in this book), a collecting and ordering of the discipline's expertise is demandingly crucial. The need has not diminished. Nor will it do so in the immediately foreseeable future. Rather, society's need for the delivery of more focused, potent, thoroughly effective counseling and educational help continues to accelerate, whether one takes the rising incidence of drug use and abuse as an index for this contention, or all the indices implicit in the rapidly changing, increasingly technological national economy and human environment, and what it is doing in gross ways to people, as Toffler chronicles in *Future Shock* (1970). The need of society for more potent therapeutic and educational services is so much on the upswing, is everywhere so obvious, that in the past few years the cries for accountability from the helping professions sound all but ear-splitting. Purse-string controllers of health, education and welfare public services continue to be more critical of what a dollar may purchase. The need has clearly shifted from supplying numbers of counselors and other professional workers to providing things they can do well. Developing and transmitting the most counseling technology to the largest number of practitioners continues to be the primary thrust of a burgeoning profession.

One would think that a major part of this concern for producing professionals who can function more effectively in more ways would emerge as an all-out profession-wide effort to train all counselors to be competent as group leaders, since group counseling constitutes a potent therapeutic-experiential environment. But this is not yet the case. The reasons for this state of affairs are manifold, but several are more influential than others.

First, people fear groups. (See the Rowe and Winborn chapter in this book.)

Another way of saying the same thing is that people fear people. What most of us do not learn to do effectively is to deal with each other in ways that are meaningful and mutually beneficial. In a group, where the agenda calls for dealing directly with each other over personal content material which arises from the people who are present, a pressure to interact and frequently become the focal center of attention builds up and charges the experience with a voltage which exists in few other human encounters. A mythology about what can happen, usually what can happen that is "bad" or "far out," has permeated the general society. Ask a randomly selected citizen what he knows about groups and he will hardly demonstrate an open-minded or unbiased reaction. If he has no scary anecdotes to lay on his questioner, he will most likely at least produce his personal apprehensions, his reasons why he will not participate in a group experience. As we shall see, not all of his global anxiety about groups is unfounded.

But it is most important here to realize that those who are in positions to make decisions about whether or not a group counseling effort by a particular practitioner or a program of group counseling is to be instituted, or those who can support, provide protective custody and help nurture the growth and development of such a program—whether they be administrators, professional colleagues, boards of trustees, or even lay groups—often are prematurely critical of such a program because they project their own fears about their own fantasized participation onto what they ought to be judging objectively on the basis of other criteria and a track record. This kind of emotional thinking gets in the way of many trainers of counselors, as well.

The second most influential reason why the counseling profession hasn't produced enough responsible and effectively trained group counselors comes precisely from this phenomenon: the trainers are untrained.

While it is certainly true that many counselor trainers back off from becoming involved in teaching themselves, ahead of their students, to be effective group counselors, because they have apprehensions about the effects of such a learning experience upon themselves and their status in their professional settings, this is not true for all those who are unknowledgeable and unskilled, perhaps not even more than a minority. A larger cause for trainers being untrained is that so few group counseling training experiences have been traditionally required or even open to trainers in their own professional development. Nor are there currently. Consequently, trainers who are interested in self-development engage mostly in self-instruction, in trial and error groping, in brain-picking, whether at professional gatherings or through books and articles. As a direct consequence of there being too few trained trainers, too few counselor training programs include the kind of developmental, minimally adequate series of group counseling training experiences which ought to be an integral part of them.

A third reason behind the lack of widespread group counselor effectiveness is the confusion in the ranks. Too few authorities exist who know the differences between group counseling and other forms of therapeutic group work, and many of those who do know have a vested interest in perpetuating the confusion. At least this is true of most writers on the subject. They and their publishers naturally want their works to appeal to the greatest number of readers, so searchers after group work knowledge and expertise are encouraged to come to drink at the same fountain regardless of the paths they have come down to get there or where they are headed upon return "home." A lumping together of group work expertise is done in the name of being all things to all comers. Group characteristics, for example, are presented as if they are true (or at least normative) for all groups, whether one has a counseling group of typical teenagers in mind, or an encounter group of selected adults. (Nor even are all the writers who appear in this book clearly or cleanly speaking only from a group counseling point of view, as distinct from a sensitivity training or group psychotherapy orientation and thrust.) Almost everywhere it is the same: *caveat emptor*.

But the need to delineate and establish workable boundaries ought to have the highest of priorities. This defining and separating out of group counseling from other forms and brands of group work is a significant exercise; for the multiple confusions in the minds of different populations, both lay and professional, to a large extent determine how clients arrive in counseling groups, how group counselors get trained, indeed, how group counseling is effectively prohibited from existing in most environments where it could be the most powerful guidance service delivered. There are too many cases of well-meaning counselors attempting to translate their own week-end encounter group experiences into something which they later call "group counseling" when they involve their counselees. And there are too few cases of counselors actually spelling out what they will do, what is expected of group members, how the process will work, what the expected outcomes are, what kinds of behaviors will not take place in the group counseling experience. When counselors are not clear about a rationale for setting up a counseling group in the first place, about operating procedures, about how behavior changes occur as a result of what goes on in the group, about the kinds and range of their own counseling behaviors, they can hardly be expected to communicate their intentions with clarity to parents, administrators, or other interested parties who want to know what is going on and are in a position to prevent or endorse a group counseling experience.

A corollary of the confusion surrounding the separating out of group counseling from other forms of group work is the systematic explication of what constitutes the specialized technology of group counseling and what technology it shares with other forms of group work. Certainly if practitioners are confused about the whole, they must be confused about some of the parts.

If the technology of group counseling consists of all those human interaction principles and practices which can be employed in counseling groups to help people successfully bring about positive behavioral changes in their personal worlds, then there most certainly is a technology of group counseling, however scattered and disorganized the bits and pieces might happen to appear. The uncollected collection of specialized knowledge, workable methods, dynamic principles and expertise which comprise the young technology of counseling in groups presently reside in differential amounts within largely self-trained individuals doing their professional work in isolation and in writings—books and articles. But there is a need to bring it all together. There is a need to assemble the technology of group counseling in order that responsible leaders in the profession can agree on what group counseling is and is not, how group counselors are to be trained, and under what circumstances and in what settings counseling in groups ought to be institutionalized.

Currently there is no central core of group counseling technology which is agreed upon by any authoritative body, and this retards wider use of group counseling as a helping force, particularly in the schools—where the "safety" of a practice is so necessary to its broad adoption. Ultimately, it is thus the youth of America who are being denied the richness of a significant growth experience in their formative years, an experience which may enable them to develop personal and social skills and competencies of life-long value; and, for this reason, if for no other, advocates need to build a case for institutionalization, whether in professional organizations, state certification programs, university and other (such as governmental) training programs, or counselor inservice training in school districts, large and small—a case for the institutionalization of group counseling as distinct from group psychotherapy and sensitivity training.

Groups, Groups, Groups

The growing popularity of quasi-therapeutic group activities has left educational decision-makers in a quandary as to how "group counseling" fits into the school curriculum or into a special services category. One reads about t-groups, sensitivity groups, encounter groups, therapy groups and a host of other appellations. For each of these practices there are proponents who argue for their inclusion, directly or indirectly, into the school's program of studies; and yet there are no firm guidelines to aid the decision-makers in deciding upon the appropriateness of this or that brand of group experience. What follows is a description of group psychotherapy, encounter groups and group guidance; and an explication of how group counseling is in a category of its own, with special characteristics.

Group Psychotherapy

The tag group psychotherapy ought not to label any intraschool group activity. Group therapy is generally practiced in a hospital, clinic, or private psychotherapeutic office. It is conducted by licensed therapists, and is available to patients with observable pathology, which has been diagnosed by the therapist or the referral agent as being remediable as a result of the group treatment. In a hospital setting, group therapy is a useful treatment for working with patients who fall anywhere within the entire spectrum of psychological imbalance, from institutionalized psychotics to mildly disturbed neurotics seen on an outpatient basis. It is usually a major part of a psychological restoration program, which may include individual therapy sessions and medicinal or other kinds of help.

The process of group psychotherapy involves a number of patients in combination with a therapist (or a team working together) agreeing to present problem areas and work on strategies for improvement of the pathology. Patients usually present their problem to the group, and the group members attempt to help by confrontation and challenge in an atmosphere of safety and acceptance. The therapist's role varies, depending on his own orientation. Often the therapist will serve as a moderator and explainer. He will protect the rights of each member of the group and aid in drawing out and evoking problem-related material. The therapist who conducts the group usually works on a one-to-one basis outside of the group with each of the members. He is aware of at least some of the etiology and extent of the existing pathology of each patient before the group convenes, and in the group he helps his patients to freely discuss their problems with others who are working on their own psychological difficulties.

Group therapy is not an appropriate activity for the schools. It is generally conducted with individuals who have admitted their own pathology, who are not in control of their own behavior in some or all areas of their lives, and who are participating in the group as part of a physical and psychological health-restoring plan. There are hundreds of specific approaches to group psychotherapy, many experimental and innovative practices, and as much confusion in the literature on group therapy about what constitutes the most effective practices and procedures as there is in what has been published about group counseling—not the least of which is that too many writers don't distinguish between the two forms of therapeutic group work.

Encounter Groups

Outside of the category of group psychotherapy in what has come to be called the "group movement," a melange of titles signifies group experiences that are available to the general public. It is impossible to be totally up to date, since fresh labels appear in each new journal article, in each new brochure arriving in the mails announcing special conferences and workshops. While the list seems all but inexhaustive, the front-runners appear to be: Encounter, T-, Sensitivity, Marathon, Human Awareness, Human Potential, Human Relation, Sensory Awareness and Interpersonal Growth groups.

While the labels are not all synonymous, and for each of these groups there are some differences, unique overtones and special techniques, they tend to be more alike than unalike. There is a whole encounter group service industry which has come into being. Indeed, handbooks of copyrighted exercises and group leader instructions are on the market, games are available, kits containing tape-recorded instructions from a leader in absentia can be bought, and a number of corporations have been created which have as their end-product group experiences for the public.

Promoters of these special groups generally state their purposes in global terms, such as learning more about one's self, receiving feedback from others, maximizing one's human potential, improving one's self-concept, tuning in on one's own feelings, and other hard-to-pin-down goals for the participants. Often there is a focus on everyone gaining a feeling of "we-ness" in the group, cohesiveness being stated as an end rather than as a means to an end. With few exceptions the emphasis in these special groups is on feelings. Statements such as: "But how do you feel?," "Gut-level feelings" and "Get your feelings out!" are hallmarks, and intellectualizing about one's self is considered a "cop-out" by proponents of these affect-centered groups. The sharing of feelings is utmost in the minds of the group members, and distinctions are made (although not always clearly) between feelings and thoughts, or to use the more modish dichotomous cliche, between the affective and cognitive domains.

Perhaps one thread which winds through all of these special groups is the idea of intimacy. This takes the form of becoming closer together as human beings, learning to share feelings by breaking down debilitating inhibitions and defenses, learning to love one another without shame or fear, and removing the handcuffs of apprehension and anxiety which stultify warm human relationships. The leaders of these groups talk of becoming free, of obtaining joy, of learning how to touch and be in tune with one's body and one's senses, of becoming more intimate with one's fellow man, one's environments and, indeed, one's self.

These special groups are generally conducted by a trained (or semi-trained but zealous and true-believing) "facilitator," who often considers himself to be a member of the group, or, at the least, a player/coach, one who assumes low or no responsibility for what occurs; it is the group itself that is responsible and members are encouraged to share their feelings about each other. The "here-and-now" is emphasized. Facilitators regularly point out to members that "we should stay with the here-and-now" and that "none of us will grow unless we learn to be honest with our feelings." Being "real" is praised and prized, as though one could be and usually is something other than so.

The facilitators of these special groups commonly have a repertoire of exercises, drills and techniques that are used at various stages of the group's development. These include activities which build trust and permit the expression of various emotions. The exercises are often physical in nature, and they involve group members in touching experiences which run the gamut from simple facial explorations and hand-holding to collective group groping and nude hydrotherapy. In addition to the physical exercises programmed for the expression of a multitude of emotions, props are often employed to help members get down to the "feeling level." Such devices as flowers for talking to (Finney, 1968), pillows for hitting to release sublimated anger, and masks for assuming new and varied identities are all part of the equipment used by different segments of the special group world.

It should be pointed out that the training of the leaders of these special groups is as varied as the kinds of available experiences. While some organizations maintain exceptionally high standards of training for the group facilitators, others come under the general heading of untrained manipulators of human behavior, the "Sally-Psychologists" of the group world.

The authors take the position that membership in any of the special groups described in this section should be limited to volunteering adults whose eyes are open as a result of having personally investigated the background and purposes of the institutional machinery behind the group, as well as the training and orientation of the group facilitators. Groups which have as their stated or unstated goal the advancement of intimacy between human beings should not be made available to school-age youth, who are not yet into the early adult developmental stage of reconciling the problems of intimacy versus isolation, as that stage is understood in Erik Erikson's scheme of personality development in human growth. Untrained teachers or other school officials should be wary of experimenting with exercises which produce emotional or physical reactions in students. Parents are beginning to sound the gong against using group procedures for the purpose of fostering emotional expression or creating physical contact. Although membership in a counseling group is certainly a most powerful and fruitful experience for helping young people, the present orientation and flavor of the flourishing special groups is hardly the appropriate character for such counseling groups to adopt.

Guidance Groups

The term "group guidance" is essentially one referring to those activities and services usually but not necessarily delivered by the counseling staff in a school setting. These services are adjuncts to the regular educational program, and include such areas as testing, advising, scheduling and providing post high school educational and occupational information. Groups convened either on an *ad hoc* or long-term basis for the purposes of accomplishing guidance tasks or for disseminating guidance information are what is meant by guidance groups. School counselors who carry out their guidance functions most efficiently are those who can think in terms of various group constellations and designs for accomplishing differential ends, and adapting suitable styles, structures, procedures and techniques appropriately to the student population to be served.

Group Counseling

Group psychotherapy seeks to eradicate pathology, and is predicated on the notion that members are sick, where such members are even designated as patients—people who are professionally diagnosed as less than whole. In contrast, group counseling seeks to develop people, to aid any and all individuals in adding to their repertoire of behaviors mustered to work in their behalf, to help them cope better or to develop mastery over their own mental, emotional, social and physical behaving. They are called clients or counselees, folks seeking a service. They have no reason to admit to being inadequate, for they are not. Like all people everywhere, they have a range of behaviors, some of which are self-defeating, unproductive, inappropriate, even wacky, and most of which are self-enhancing and totally serviceable, given the circumstances of their lives. Group counseling is predicated on the notion that everyone is normal, but that normality in each of us includes areas of aberrant behavior, as well as areas of pluperfect adjustment. "All the world is queer save thee and me, and even thou art a little queer."

We contend that group counseling is the most appropriate group experience for the educational setting. Group counseling is viewed as a process that can be useful to all individuals. It is in no way to be considered the exclusive domain of the schools. Group counseling is not designed for individuals with highly compartmentalized problems, nor should membership in a counseling group be restricted to any category of people. To the extent that people display self-defeating behaviors, or engage in self-crippling thinking, they can benefit from participation in a counseling group. To the extent that people can learn new ways of behaving, even if they have never imagined or encountered them before, they can benefit from group counseling. The counseling group is a selectively enriched, stimulatingly beneficial environment. The group counselor is not overly taken up with the kinds of problems, concerns, or difficulties that counselees may exhibit. He is more interested in helping group members to identify the areas in their lives in which they are not functioning at the optimal measure that they would prefer, and then helping them to work hard to use the group counseling opportunity as an arena for maximizing their own personal effectiveness.

Group Counseling Works

We can make the assertion that group counseling works because we have seen people of all age groups, including students in elementary and secondary schools, participate in planned group counseling programs and leave the experience with whole new assemblages of behaviors and fresh ways of thinking about situations and conditions in their lives which helped these individuals to be more effective. By works we mean very explicitly that people who participate in the counseling group develop new ways of thinking about their self-defeating behaviors, and develop alternate ways of thinking or behaving when the problem arises. It is one thing to be able to talk about changing, and something quite different to actually change when the temptation to remain the same is so dominating. Effectiveness in group counseling is measured on the basis of how well the group member is able to change a behavior (including mental behaviors or thought patterns) outside of the group where it really counts for that person.

Here is an example of how group counseling works by this definition: Johnny can talk in the group about how his father's drunkenness bothers him, and how he always gets upset when his father nags him while in a drunken stupor. He can agree that his reaction to his father's drunkenness, which is usually anger and being agitatedly upset, hurts him and even interferes with his school work, his having his friends over, and his omnipresent irritability toward everyone. Yet Johnny has not been helped in the group unless he first of all recognizes that the problem is Johnny's rather than his father's, that he must learn alternate ways of reacting to his father's dipsomania, and that his being angry and upset and having his school work suffer are essentially self-defeating ways of thinking and behaving. If Johnny just agrees to this, it is not enough; he must learn to act differently at the time of his father's nagging behavior in order for the counseling to have worked. But the group counseling environment is the place in which Johnny can learn to reorder his thinking, and subsequently, his self-defeating reactions.

The above example illustrates how a shift in thinking can result from participation in a counseling group. Yet the dynamics of precisely what takes place in the group to bring about more healthy thinking must be carefully examined. Basically the group counselor (or co-counselors, if possible) is the key person in helping group members to change in a direction of mastery over their own environment, over their own mental, physical and social behaviors. It should be remembered that each individual within the group is unique, comes from and spends his life in his own set of circumstances and relationships, and therefore has a unique set of goals for himself. The group as a separate entity is essentially an irrelevant concept, for the only "group" goal is for each member to emerge from the counseling experience as a more effectively functioning person in his own life. In that sense, group goals do not exist. There can only be a collection of individual goals. In order for the group counselor to "help" the "individuals" within the group, he must of necessity treat them as individuals rather than as members of an enclave which will cease to exist at the termination of the group's life.

An entire literature of group work has built up which addresses itself to the concept of the group as a totality. Thus we hear of group norms, group stages, group goals, as though the group has a life of its own independent of the people who make it up. From a counseling point of view this is sheer claptrap, only more dangerous, for it subordinates the individual to the collectivity. While a counseling group is composed of many people, it continues to superordinate the individual members: the one plus one plus one plus one plus . . . never adds up to two or a larger sum; each member is who counts, one at a time, and each is given the attention and help of the others. Teams win ballgames, committees accomplish tasks, mobs riot and counseling groups do nothing except to be a name and place for individuals to work on their own growth and development.

Group counseling is a process involving interpersonal interaction, wherein the leader's role and only reason for being is to counsel and help the counselees in the group. He is not himself a group member, nor does he ever use the group for the resolution of his own problems. Nor should he use the group process to service any of his own needs in any way. The hallmark of an effective group counselor is that he has taught the membership to "call him" on any intervention he makes, if it is unclear to any one of them, in order that they can assess his rationale for so functioning; this keeps him honest and helps him to work on the only legitimate goal he can have for himself: to become more professionally effective in the delivery of his skills and competencies. He continually seeks to be the better and better qualified expert who assumes responsibility for his own actions and whatever happens in the group.

The process of group counseling includes (a) labeling behavior of group members that is self-defeating; (b) helping individuals to identify their goals, stating them clearly and publicly in behavioral terms, and expressing a commitment to work on goal attainment; (c) assisting each group member to understand himself and the motivations for his behavior; (d) creating alternatives to the debilitating behavior; and (e) trying out new modes of behavior both within and without the group. The interaction between group leader and group members is always verbal. The counselor clarifies thinking, confronts discrepancies between thought and action when they appear, helps to interpret behavior (or the lack of behavior) and serves as a model of helping effectiveness.

Group members share their feelings with each other related to specific problem areas. They learn to read their own feelings and those of others as physiological reactions to mental formulations. Psychophysical feeling states exist because thinking has made them so, and group members learn that such mental behavior can be changed. The social atmosphere in the group is such that a helping climate always permeates it. Discussions about people or events outside of the group are discouraged, since each member is there to work on specific goals rather than engage in non-helping conversation.

Group members are consistently encouraged to work on their goals both in and out of the group. Specific homework assignments are suggested by group members and the group leader, and individual reports are strongly recommended at the beginning of subsequent group sessions. These reports serve to reinforce positive behaviors of group members once they have returned to the group, while simultaneously providing an opportunity to share with their peers the struggles they are going through on the road to becoming more effective. Role-working techniques are a vital part of group counseling, and are used regularly to aid group members in working out their problems in simulation prior to taking on the task for "real" outside the group. Free and spontaneous participation is constantly evoked by the leader. Providing an environment in which group members can work on their own personal areas of ineffectiveness in safety is essential. Yet the group counselor knows that in order for change to take place, the group members must somehow become uncomfortable with their own self-defeating behavior in order to work at eliminating it.

The notion of the "accepting confronter" is the vision of the skillful group counselor, being non-condemning, non-judgmental of the person while still fearlessly labeling discrepant behaviors as they arise. The accomplished group counselor must also have masterful control of himself and his ego and be intellectually sharp; that is to say, the members must not steadily out-think him or diagnose the dynamics of group process and individual behavior ahead of him with any degree of consistency, or he will thereby have his authority discredited and lose his effectiveness as the potent professional helper. He must have a thorough knowledge of human behavior, the faulty circuitous logic of the self-defeating thinker, and must know how to intervene in such a way that the group member will begin to reassess his behavior and be motivated to change in a positive direction for self-improvement.

Among all the available group experiences in the helping world, group counseling holds the most promise for the educational setting, though it should not be construed here that group counseling is inappropriate for other settings (i.e., prisons, vocational workshops and other agencies, even for private practice). It is an experience that should be made available to as many people as is humanly feasible. Group counseling, when practiced at the professional level advocated by the authors, is a powerful force toward helping people move toward functioning at optimal limits. The human concerns and problem areas which can be effectively worked on in group counseling are endless. From academic difficulties to problems in social and family interaction to being addicted: the list cannot be exhausted.

Group Counseling Technology

Primarily because we see the widespread institutionalization of group counseling in the schools as a necessary concomitant of effective education for all children, and because there are presently too few trained counselors who could bring this about even if they were tenaciously impelled to do so, we have tried to make a case for group counseling as a preferred counseling modality, with all that this entails. What it chiefly entails is the establishment of a technology of group counseling—a collected depository of all the group counseling know-how that exists, the creation of reliable and effective means to transmit that know-how to practitioners and trainees, and a broad body of competent professionals to lead the field in both undertakings.

References

Finney, Ben C. The Flower Turn-on: A Group Facilitating Technique. Paper read at the American Psychological Association meeting, San Francisco, California, 1968. (Mimeo.)

Toffler, Alvin. *Future Shock.* New York: Random House, 1970.

5.
Goal-Setting in Group Counseling

T. Antoinette Ryan

Mission of Group Counseling

Counseling is a helpful process aimed at aiding individuals to increase understanding of themselves and their relationships to other people. One of the primary ways in which guidance services seek to enhance the realization of healthy growth and development of all individuals is through a counseling process, in which professionally trained persons employing specialized techniques relate in systematic ways to other persons to help these individuals deal realistically and successfully with developmental tasks appropriate to their ages, leading to full realization of a total personality. Through counseling, the individual comes to an awareness of his weaknesses and strengths, recognition of his skills and knowledge, and appreciation for his values and attitudes. At the same time, he learns how to make viable decisions, achieve self-direction, and become self-actualized (Perrone, Ryan and Zeran, 1970).

The counseling process is implemented in one-to-one and group settings. In the one-to-one setting, the counselor engages in face-to-face interaction with one client. In the group setting, a counselor meets with several counselees, usually six to ten, to assist them in exploring problems and feelings, developing decision-making and self-directing competencies, and meeting and coping with developmental tasks. One-to-one and group counseling processes are implemented in a number of environments—school, employment office, welfare office, correctional institution, rehabilitation center, Veterans Administration office, military installation. Regardless of the environment in which the counseling takes place, and regardless of whether counseling is one-to-one or group, the overriding purpose is the same—to help the individual become the person he is capable of becoming. This calls for ameliorating and repairing malfunctioning systems, while stimulating growth toward self-actualizing and self-fulfilling personalities.

Group counseling is designed to accomplish its mission—that is, helping individuals become the persons they are capable of being— through a process of group thinking about common problems and experiences. In group counseling, a therapeutic dimension is given to group discussion and thinking, and opportunity is provided for clarification of values and resolution of conflicts in a group of peers. Group counseling is accomplished when activities specifically selected and empirically assessed are used to help two or more individuals realize mutually agreed upon changes in behaviors. Evaluation of group counseling has failed to provide the kind of data that are needed to document unequivocally the effectiveness of this approach. Gazda and Larsen (1968) found on the basis of a comprehensive appraisal of group counseling research covering 100 studies from 1938 to 1968, that goal-setting was a major weakness. They reported that outcome variables were too global to be tied down to treatment; specific goals were not stated in measurable terms; specific outcome goals for each member of the group were lacking.

The demand for attention to goal-setting in evaluating group counseling has implications that are far-reaching. The goal-setting function is one of the most critical elements in group counseling, bearing either directly or indirectly on every other element in the system.

Goal-Setting in the Group
Counseling Setting

Goal-setting in group counseling is the process of setting goals to implement the group counseling process. Goal-setting is accomplished by defining group goals and subgoals, which are implemented in individual behavioral objectives, and ordering the objectives according to priority needs and contribution to the group goals. To be of value for group counseling the goals must be operational. When group counseling is implemented in non-operational goals, there is a tendency to experience member apathy and intra-group conflict. There is difficulty in mobilizing resources of the group. There is no way of knowing the extent to which the counseling process has been successful. *Counseling goals are operationalized when the group goals and subgoals are translated into behavioral objectives for individual members of the group.*

Definitions of Goals, Subgoals and Objectives

Goals are collections of words or symbols describing general intents. These broadly defined statements of intent, such as, "achieving self-fulfillment" or "developing self-actualization" set the direction and indicate the general nature of the desired outcome, but do not specify the characteristics of the expected products. Counseling goals refer to the general intentions or desired outcomes of the counseling process. These intentions relate to the desired changes that will take place in counselees as a result of the counseling intervention. Analysis of counseling goals reveals three kinds of changes which can be anticipated as a result of counseling intervention. These changes are defined as cognitive, affective or psychomotor. The collections of words or symbols describing the cognitive, affective or psychomotor elements implementing a given goal are called *subgoals*. These subgoals are expressed in broad terms, but are less global than goal statements. The referrent of a counseling goal is the total person. The referrents of subgoals are cognitive, affective or psychomotor dimensions of the total person. The goal "self-actualization" might be implemented in subgoals, "increased understanding of the self," "increased capability for self-directing behaviors" and "enhanced feelings of self worth."

Behavioral objectives are descriptions of specific, pertinent, attainable, measurable and observable behaviors that will result from planned intervention. The collection of words or symbols describing the desired outcome must identify and name the behavioral act, define the important conditions under which the behavior will occur, describe the restrictions, limitations and constraints, and define the criterion of acceptable performance (Mager, 1962). The broad goal can be expected to hold for all members in a group Krumboltz (1966a, 1966b) repeatedly has pointed out the fallacy ... expecting that one set of objective statements would apply to all individuals in a group. The mere fact that 10 or 20 persons in a counseling group might share the need for increased self-actualization does not mean that each of the group members desires the same behavioral change in attitudes, skills and understandings.

Importance of Operationalizing
Group Counseling Goals

Group goals are operationalized when the broad statement of intent for the group is analyzed into cognitive, affective and psycho-motor dimensions expressed as subgoals, which in turn are described as behavioral objectives for individual members of the group. There are four advantages from operationalizing group counseling goals, which, taken together, work to increase the likelihood of counseling success.

1. Operationalized goals make for a homogeneous group. When a group is structured to implement clearly defined outcomes, the individuals who elect to participate in the group share common interests which support the group goal.

2. Operationalized goals contribute to realistic expectations. Krumboltz (1966a) feels that one advantage to having behavioral objectives is that counselors and counselees can anticipate more clearly what the counseling process can and cannot be expected to accomplish.

3. Operationalized goals lead to more highly motivated group members. When individuals are in a group which implements clearly defined objectives that have meaning for them, there is individual motivation to move the group toward the goal. This has been demonstrated in a number of studies. Katahn, Strenger and Cherry (1966), reporting on effectiveness of systematic desensitization coupled with behavior oriented discussion in a group setting to alleviate test anxiety, observed that a number of other factors probably influenced the outcome, including the fact that participants were highly motivated volunteers who entered with a specific purpose in mind. In two studies in which effectiveness of group counseling was reported for improving decision-making behaviors and increasing study behaviors, the success of the group counseling process was attributed in part to the fact that clearly defined objectives had been set in advance (Ryan, 1968, 1969b).

4. Operationalized goals make the group more interdependent. When the goals are explicated in advance and members of a group are able to see the goal operationalized in objectives that have meaning for them, they experience satisfaction—and this makes the group more interdependent and builds group belongingness. The cooperative situation created by existence of clearly defined outcomes tends to promote cathexis, that is, attraction of members for one another, since each one contributes to the progress of others toward the accepted goals and objectives.

Place of Goal-Setting in the
Group Counseling System

Group counseling is a system, comprised of seven basic functions: (1) study of the real life environment; (2) establishment of a counseling philosophy; (3) assessment of needs; (4) setting of goals; (5) formulation of a plan to achieve the goals; (6) implementation of the group counseling plan; and (7) evaluation of group counseling effectiveness. A flowchart model of the group counseling system is shown in Figure 1.

The first step in the development and implementation of a group counseling system is to look at the situation as it is. This means making a careful analysis of the environment and systematic processing of information about the individuals in the environment. This is a key function, since it is from the synthesis of information describing the real life world that the counseling mission can be determined. The (1.0) function, STUDY REAL LIFE ENVIRONMENT, is implemented as analysis is made of the environment and the individuals who are in the environment. In a school situation, this would involve analysis of information about the learner population, and would provide the basis for determining at a later time the extent to which generally accepted goals of counseling are being realized. The (2.0) function, ESTABLISH PHILOSOPHY, serves the purpose of establishing a rationale or theoretical framework within which the counseling function will be carried out. The statement of philosophy provides the basis for synthesizing a picture of the ideal, as opposed to the real which was described in (1.0). ASSESSMENT OF NEED (3.0) is made by determining discrepancies between the real life world (1.0) and the ideal (2.0). The needs identified in (3.0) are considered again in (4.0), SET GOALS, as the question is asked, "What changes must take place in order for these needs to be met?" The process of setting goals (4.0) involves operationalizing the goals by converting them into sub-goals and behavioral objectives, establishing priorities among the objectives, and determining the contribution of each to the group goal. Once the goals have been set, the task becomes one of developing and implementing strategies to achieve these goals. The development of counseling interventions in the group setting is accomplished in (5.0) FORMULATE PLAN, and the plan is put into operation in (6.0) IMPLEMENT PLAN. Finally, the counseling intervention developed in (5.0) and implemented in (6.0) must be evaluated. This is accomplished

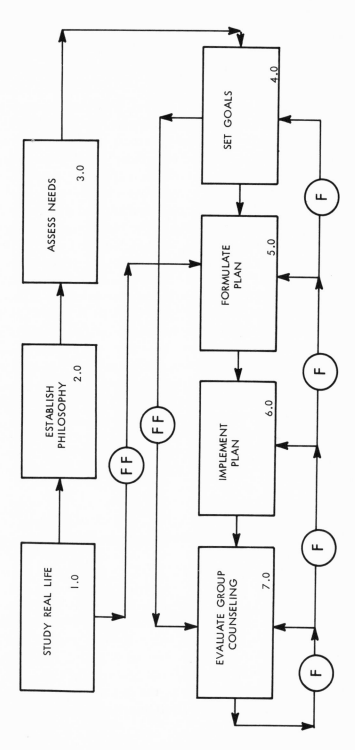

Figure 1

Group Counseling System

in (7.0), EVALUATE GROUP COUNSELING when outcomes are compared against the objectives which were defined in (4.0) SET GOALS.

In this model, the function of goal-setting is one of the most critical elements in the system because of the relationships that goal-setting has to the other elements in the group counseling process.

Goal-setting relates to the study of the real life environment (1.0). The goals which are set in (4.0) must be operationalized in behavioral objectives which are pertinent to and have meaning for the individuals who make up the population in the real life environment.

Goal-setting relates to the philosophy established in (2.0). Krumboltz (1966a) states that goals of counseling must be compatible with values of the counselor. Delaney and Eisenberg (1971) hold that outcome goals must be consistent with the counselor's professional ethics. It is from the theoretical frame of reference defined by the statement of philosophy that assessment is made to see if the objectives are compatible with the personal values and professional ethics of the counselor.

Goal-setting relates to the assessment of needs (3.0). The setting of goals (4.0) derives from the assessment of needs. Typically the needs point to broad goal statements, such as "achievement of self-actualization." One of the standards against which assessment of the group counseling process in any given setting is made is the strength in relationship between needs and goals. The goals which are set in (4.0) *must* relate to the needs stated in (3.0).

Goal-setting determines the nature of the counseling plan (5.0). The counselor has responsibility to develop a strategy, or plan, to facilitate growth and development of the counselees. This formulation of a counseling plan (5.0) cannot be made without attending to the nature of the goals set in (4.0). The counselor must develop a plan which will offer the greatest chance for realizing the outcomes specified in (4.0). Courses of action which will contribute to attainment of the desired outcomes must be identified. Actions on the part of counselor and counselee which will contribute to achievement of desired outcomes must be determined.

The plan for group counseling must explicate the way in which process dimensions will be implemented. This means specification of a number of process variables: group size, focus of the session, member responsibilities, leader techniques and group duration. The counseling goals, subgoals and objectives relate directly to each of the process variables. In fact, the goals determine the way in which the variables are implemented. For some objectives, it is important to have a group made up of no more than two individuals. For other objectives, a group of eight or ten would be advisable. The focus of each group session is determined by the goals and objectives. A counseling group concerned with overcoming shyness and withdrawal tendencies will have a different topical focus from a group concerned primarily with the problem of scholastic failure. The duration of counseling will be suggested by goals. Mahler (1969, 1971) suggests that setting the number of counseling sessions in advance, based on the nature of counseling goals, holds on sound theoretical grounds. A clear statement of goals and objectives will go a long way toward deciding on the kind of experiences most likely to help members of the group.

Goal-setting determines the way in which the counseling plan is implemented (6.0). The plan developed in (5.0) must be put into action. This means conducting the group counseling sessions. The way in which the sessions are conducted depends on the goals set in (4.0).

Goal-setting determines evaluation of group counseling process (7.0). When a group has clearly stated and generally accepted operational goals, a basis is provided for evaluating group effectiveness. If groups are lacking in operational goals, evaluation tends to be based on irrelevant criteria. Group goals affect evaluations made by members of one another, and these evaluations in turn affect selection of group goals. The failure to develop operational goals, that is, behavioral objectives, for the group will result in the use of global and irrelevant criterion measures. Krumboltz (1966c) takes a strong stand that counselors have a responsibility for evaluating the success of their work. This means being able to determine which kinds of counseling techniques and which group counseling variables work best with which kinds of counselees to bring about specific kinds of behavioral change.

Evaluation of the group counseling process entails identifying the process variables which contribute to or militate against achievement of the goals. When it can be shown that the group has defined goals and objectives, then it is possible to ask what conditions facilitated or hindered the group locomotion toward the goals. Determination of group counseling effectiveness must take into account the extent to which clearly stated objectives were defined, the degree to which the group goal mobilized the energies of the group members, the degree to which there was conflict among members of the group concerning which of several possible goals should control activities of the group, and the degree to which there was conflict among members concerning means that the group should employ in reaching the goals.

Process of Goal-Setting
in Group Counseling
Problems in Goal-Setting

There are problems inherent in the process of goal-setting for group counseling, by virtue of the fact that a group is made up of two or more individuals, each of whom has a unique set of needs and personal goals. The extent to which personal goals implement group goals varies from time to time and place to place. There is a constant reordering of goal priorities within and among individuals in the group. The valence of a particular goal for any individual in the group may be influenced by the nature of his individual motives, and his evaluation of the rewards and costs involved in activities related to the goal.

Despite the problems attendant upon the goal-setting process in group counseling, the fact is that this function remains one of the most important to the success of the counseling process. The challenge—to counselor and counselee alike—becomes one of finding ways to overcome and circumvent the problems in the interest of achieving a viable approach to goal-setting which will enhance the potential of this element for contributing to the total system of group counseling. The best way to accomplish this end is through a systematic procedure for setting goals.

Systematic Procedure for Goal-Setting

The process of goal-setting for group counseling (4.0) involves specification of goals (4.1), operationalizing goals (4.2) and ordering of goal priorities (4.3). These three activities are required to accomplish goal-setting for group counseling. The relationships among the goal-setting elements are shown in Figure 2.

The SPECIFY GROUP GOALS function (4.1) is a part of the counseling process which is accomplished jointly by counselor and group members. The counselor must have available the results of

Figure 2

Goal-Setting in Group Counseling

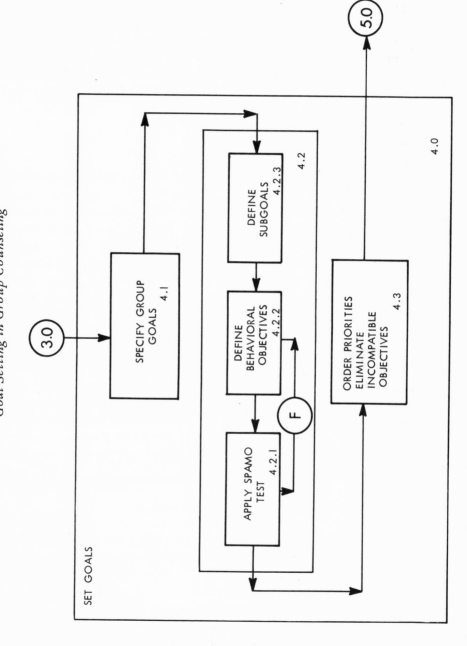

analyzing the real life environment, with a clear picture in mind of the overriding needs which are to be met. This information should set the outside limits for the group counseling mission. If analysis of the real life environment points up needs related primarily to the self-actualization goal, implemented for the most part in deficiencies in the cognitive, affective and psychomotor domains relating to knowledge about, feelings about, and use of drugs, then, the major goal area supporting subgoals will have been indicated. The explication of the goal and supporting subgoals, at the onset of the group counseling, should serve the purpose of bringing together a group of individuals sharing a common concern, and interested in accomplishing a goal of mutual interest.

The OPERATIONALIZE GOALS function (4.2) is crucial to system effectiveness (Ryan, 1969a). Operationalizing the goals and subgoals into behavioral objectives for individual members of the group takes place as part of the counseling process. It is up to the counselor to provide cues which will eventuate in getting group members to express the outcomes they desire in behavioral terms. The operationalizing of group goals calls for translating the needs of a group of individuals in a given setting into major goal areas, such as "self-fulfillment," "self-actualization," or "self-realization." Each goal is analyzed to determine its component subgoals. Each subgoal is analyzed to determine the behavioral objectives which support it. After breakdown of counseling goals into behaviorally defined objectives, the quality of objectives must be tested. Behavioral objectives should be characterized by five attributes: specificity, pertinence, attainability, measurability and observability (SPAMO) (Ryan and Zeran, 1972). The quality of objectives is reflected in the degree to which these attributes characterize the objectives.

Specificity of objectives. Behavioral objectives for the individual should be stated with as much specificity as needed for the decision-making task at hand. Objectives that are vague and ambiguous can result in meaningless and ambiguous plans to implement the objectives. Vague objectives do not generate sound criteria of effectiveness. Goals can be presented as abstractions. Objectives must be described by the operations that define them. Two tests of specificity can be implemented: (1) degree of concreteness of meaning; and (2) degree of agreement among observers on meaning. The relative position on a continuum of abstraction, the degree of operationalism and the extent of agreement among observers can be shown on a ladder of abstraction (Korzybski, 1933). In constructing the abstraction ladder, the more abstract the concept the higher it is on the ladder.

In using the abstraction ladder (Figure 3), the aim is to generate objectives which satisfy criteria for location on the dimension of abstraction as near the OPERATIONAL end of the continuum as possible.

Pertinence of objectives. In group counseling it is essential that all individual objectives implement the group goal. This is a critical aspect of operationalizing the counseling goals. It does little if any good to have carefully conceived and precisely stated objectives which do not support the group goal, and upon which it is not possible to gain group consensus concerning the value or worth of the objective.

Measurability of objectives. The test of measurability is to determine whether or not the statements of objectives describe behaviors which can be quantified. The concern is with the relationship between product and purpose, outcome and objective. The amount of precision in measurement that is required depends on the situation. Whether objectives describe outcomes that are cognitive, affective or psychomotor, there must be some way of assessing the extent to which the desired behaviors have been achieved. The results of measurement provide the basis for evaluation. It will not be possible to determine effectiveness of the counseling process without some indication of the extent to which the counseling goals have been realized. This is provided through measurement of the degree to which objectives have been reached by individuals in the group.

Observability of objectives. The anticipated outcomes from the group counseling must be observable. There must be something which the person will be doing which can be observed to indicate that the objective has been achieved. Observation of the behavior must be capable of being made directly, or there must be behaviors which can be observed from which it can be inferred that the desired outcomes have been achieved.

The ORDER PRIORITIES/ELIMINATE INCOMPATIBLE OBJECTIVES function (4.3) helps to provide a structure for counseling, and cuts down on the dissipation of group resources on non-goal oriented activities and issues. The ordering of goal priorities and elimination of incompatible objectives (4.3) are accomplished after the

Figure 3

*Abstraction Ladder for Translating Goals
into Behavioral Objectives*

Dimension of Abstraction	Statement of Objective	Behaviors Demonstrated	Extent Observable	Extent of Observer Agreement
very abstract	acquire knowledge			very little agreement
less abstract	acquire knowledge of counseling	talks about counseling	observable	slight agreement
more specific	use terms re: counseling in meaningful sentences	discusses with others counseling concepts	observable	little agreement
very specific	differentiate between counseling and guidance	demonstrates, selects correct concept term	observable	authorities generally agree

ABSTRACT ←————————————————————————→ OPERATIONAL

goals have been specified and operationalized. Priority-ordering of individual objectives (4.3) is accomplished as a part of the group counseling process in the initial sessions. It is at this time that the group must attend to the objectives set by the individuals, and come to some conclusions concerning the priority needs within the group. At the same time, the question of individual motives in relation to group welfare must be answered, and group decisions must be made to determine the extent to which individual objectives support the group goal.

With the priority of individual objectives accomplished, and consensus reached concerning the worth and value of each objective in terms of supporting the group goal, the task is one of formulating the plan for achieving the desired outcomes (5.0) then implementing this plan in the group counseling environment (6.0) and, finally, determining the effectiveness of the process for achieving the counseling goals (7.0).

Conclusion

The mission of group counseling is to help individuals achieve their optimum growth and development. When a group is comprised of individuals sharing a common concern for reaching the same general destination, and members of the group, under guidance of a competent counselor implementing a systematic plan, are motivated to work together to help realize the behavioral objectives which for each one represent attainment of the group goal, then, there is every reason to expect success from the group counseling process. The crux of the matter lies in the goal-setting function. Without viable goals, operationalized in individual behavioral objectives which meet the SPAMO test (Ryan and Zeran, 1972), the potential for realizing the mission of group counseling will be attained only by chance, and the individuals participating in the group process will be denied the opportunity for achieving positive growth and development.

References

Delaney, D.J. and S. Eisenberg. *The Counseling Process.* Chicago: Rand McNally, 1971.

Gazda, G.M. and M.J. Larsen. A Comprehensive Appraisal of Group and Multiple Counseling. *Journal of Research and Development in Education,* 1968, *1,* 57-132.

Katahn, M., S. Strenger and N. Cherry. Group Counseling and Behavior Therapy with Test-Anxious College Students. *Journal of Counseling Psychology,* 1966, *30,* 544-549.

Korzybski, A. *Science and Sanity: An Introduction to Non-Aristotelian Systems and General Semantics.* Lancaster, Pennsylvania: Science Press, 1933.

Krumboltz, J.D. Behavioral Goals for Counseling. *Journal of Counseling Psychology,* 1966a, *13,* 153-159.

Krumboltz, J.D. Promoting Adaptive Behavior. In J.D. Krumboltz (Ed.) *Revolution in Counseling.* Boston: Houghton Mifflin Co., 1966b.

Krumboltz, J.D. Stating the Goals of Counseling. Monograph No. 1, Fullerton, California: California Personnel and Guidance Association, 1966c.

Mager, R.F. *Preparing Objectives for Programmed Instruction.* San Francisco: Fearon, 1962.

Mahler, C.A. *Group Counseling in the Schools.* Boston: Houghton Mifflin, 1969.

Mahler, C.A. Group Counseling. *Personnel and Guidance Journal,* 1971, *49,* 601-608.

Perrone, P.A., T.A. Ryan and F.R. Zeran. *Guidance and Emerging Adolescents.* Scranton, Pennsylvania: International Textbook Inc., 1970.

Ryan, T.A. *Effect of an Integrated Instructional-Counseling Program to Improve Vocational Decision-Making of Community College Youth.* Final Report. OE 413-65-5-0154-6-85-065. Corvallis, Oregon: Oregon State University, 1968.

Ryan, T.A. Systems Techniques for Programs of Counseling and Counselor Education. *Educational Technology,* 1969a, *9,* 7-17.

Ryan, T.A. Formulating Educational Goals. In J.D. Krumboltz and C.E. Thoresen (Eds.) *Behavioral Counseling: Cases and Techniques.* New York: Holt, Rinehart and Winston, 1969b, 70-73.

Ryan, T.A. and F.R. Zeran. *Organization and Administration of Guidance Services.* Danville, Illinois: Interstate Printers and Publishers, 1972.

6.
Behavioral Techniques for Developing Trust, Cohesiveness and Goal Accomplishment

John D. Krumboltz and
Beverly Potter

Group members must learn to trust each other and work together to help each member accomplish his own goals. But what specific leader actions develop trust and openness among group members? How can the leader behave to facilitate group cohesiveness?

Krumboltz (1968) and Varenhorst (1969) have described the use of behavior modification in groups to maximize client change. However, advocates of behavioral counseling have not spoken much of concepts like trust and cohesiveness, even though such concepts can be behaviorally defined as readily as information-seeking.

If two people trust each other, we can observe words and actions indicative of that trust. If they do not trust each other, quite different behaviors can be observed. Here we shall suggest a non-exhaustive list of behaviors indicative of trust and openness, group cohesiveness and goal accomplishment, and propose some illustrative leader activities likely to promote such behaviors.

Liberman (1970) has demonstrated that the systematic use of social reinforcement can be used to increase group cohesiveness. Groups socially reinforced for intermember cohesiveness behaviors also showed earlier "symptomatic" improvement and developed more independence from the therapists than did members of a comparison group. Once a specific observable category of behavior has been identified, behavioral techniques can be applied to either increase or decrease the frequency of that behavior.

The first step is to define operationally exactly what behaviors indicate the presence of trust, openness and cohesiveness. In this way the counselor knows precisely what behaviors he wants to increase or decrease. Table 1 presents the beginnings of such a behavioral definition. Each counselor would need to adapt the suggested list of behaviors to the unique characteristics of his particular clients.

The second step is to diagnose the level of trust, openness, cohesiveness and goal-directed activity in the group. One simple way to do this is to tape-record a group session, select at random one or more 10-15 minute segments, and count the frequency of those behaviors selected from Table 1. From this the counselor can develop clear goals as to what behaviors he wants to increase or decrease. For example, the counselor may find that members make very few here-and-now statements, members rarely talk directly to one another, and the frequency of goal-directed statements is very low.

The third step is to intervene. Table 2 lists some possible interventions a counselor might employ. He may decide to use a group technique which elicits here-and-now statements which he can then reinforce. He may redirect to other members all statements made to him and reinforce any spontaneous member-to-member talk. He may cue and shape goal-directed statements.*

The fourth and final step in this process is to assess the impact of his intervention. The same behaviors counted earlier must be counted in later sessions to see if the hoped for increase or decrease occurred. If the frequency of here-and-now statements, member-to-member talk and goal-directed statements has increased, the counselor can conclude that the intervention was working. If not, he can diagnose the problem again and vary his intervention. The counselor can continuously recycle through the steps of defining, diagnosing, intervening and evaluating to promote the behaviors of trust, openness, cohesiveness and goal-accomplishment.

How can the counselor monitor his own effectiveness? From a taped segment the counselor can count the frequency and type of response he made before and after each member statement. For example, he may find that he is inadvertently reinforcing irrelevant talking by responding to it; or he may find he provides few cues for goal-directed statements. He can then change the frequency of his own

---

*Ideas for possibly effective interventions have been suggested from diverse sources, such as Anderson, Shaffer and Harris (1970) and Schutz (1967) as well as our own experiences. As always, effectiveness is assessed by the extent to which the intervention helped each client change in the direction he desired.

interventions and evaluate his effectiveness by observing the consequent change in the target behaviors of group members.

References

Anderson, A., W. Shaffer and C. Harris. Practicum in Group Counseling. Unpublished course outline from the Department of Educational Psychology, University of Minnesota, 1970.

Krumboltz, J. A Behavioral Approach to Group Counseling and Therapy. *Journal of Research and Development in Education,* 1968, *1* (2), 3-18.

Liberman, R. A Behavioral Approach to Group Dynamics: 1. Reinforcement and Prompting of Cohesiveness in Group Therapy. *Behavior Therapy,* 1970, *1,* 141-175.

Schutz, W. *Joy: Expanding Human Awareness.* New York: Grove, 1967.

Varenhorst, B. Behavioral Group Counseling. In G.M. Gazda (Ed.) *Theories and Methods of Group Counseling in the Schools.* Springfield, Illinois: Charles C. Thomas, 1969, 119-156.

Table 1

Behaviors Defining Trust and Openness, Cohesiveness and Task Accomplishment

Trust and Openness

A high frequency of:
Making here-and-now statements
Making self-disclosing statements
  Members request and reinforce self-disclosing statements
  Members make self-disclosing statements
  Members ask for and give feedback to other members
  Members ask for help with problem
Spontaneous unprompted participation
Members reinforce each other

A low frequency of:
Anecdotes
Making non-self-disclosing statements
  Self-disclosing statements cut off, rejected, ignored
  Irrelevant talk about other people or things
  Members cut off or reject feedback
  Members minimize problem
Silence
Defensive statements

(continued)

Cohesiveness

A high frequency of:

"We" statements (referring to the whole group)

Statements expressing liking for group

Statements expressing desire to continue group

Attention directed to speaker

Talk directed to other group members

Equal participation of members

Talk relevant to previous members' statements

Cooperative statements ("Here's a way we could do this . . . ")

A low frequency of:

Negative statements about whole group with positive remarks about a subgroup (clique)

Statements expressing dissatisfaction with group

Statements expressing desire to terminate group

Absenteeism

Tardiness

Distracting behavior (yawns, horseplay)

Statements directed to leader only

Time monopolized by leader or one or two members

Statements cutting off others by referring to self prematurely ("The same thing happened to me . . . ")

Statements changing the subject

Competitive statements ("That's nothing . . . ")

Task Accomplishment

A high frequency of:

Statements to develop agenda

Statements to describe problem

Statements to develop goals

Statements proposing course of action

Statements to evaluate progress

Reinforcement for others' task-oriented statements

Statements that initiate and implement problem-solving actions

Reports of relevant actions taken between meetings

A low frequency of:

Social conversation

Critical statements in reference to other members' task-oriented statements

Table 2

Illustrations of Leader's Intervention Behaviors Which Facilitate Trust and Openness, Cohesiveness and Task Accomplishment

	Trust and Openness	Cohesiveness	Task Accomplishment
A. Leader behaviors which facilitate:			
Model desired behavior	"I feel sad when I listen to your experiences with your parents."	"I was upset when we moved away from John."	"We can start by deciding what we would like to work on today."
Reinforce desired behavior	"John, I am pleased that you can talk about how this discussion makes you feel."	"Cecil, I am pleased you look forward to coming to our group."	"Rachel, that is an excellent idea!"
Cue (use questions or comments) to elicit small steps which can be reinforced toward the desired behavior	"Sue, can you tell me how you feel right now talking to new people about personal things?"	"Sid, I noticed you said 'we'—you must feel you belong here."	"Frank, you are doing pretty well at trying to get to the problem with your study habits. What do you think you can do to find out exactly how you use your time?"
Reinforce the reinforcer—reinforce group members for reinforcing (following-up, supporting, making suggestions to) each other	"Sharon, you were very sensitive to pick up on how hard it is for Claire to talk about herself."	"Jose, I am glad that you told Jeff how good it makes you feel when he said he likes our meetings."	"Jody, I imagine Jack appreciates the support you gave him on his new objectives."

(continued)	Trust and Openness	Cohesiveness	Task Accomplishment
A. Leader behaviors which facilitate:			
Extinguish by ignoring or cutting off inappropriate talk and behavior	"Excuse me, Sally, but that is not relevant yet. Mary, how do you feel telling us about that embarrassing experience?"	After completely ignoring another member's inappropriate comments, focus on member who is behaving appropriately: "Steve, you got here right on time today—great!"	"Peggy, your talking about what a good time you had at the dance last night is getting us off Tom's problem of being afraid to ask a girl to dance. Tom, what did you do at the dance last night?"
Set norms by defining desired behavior			
Explicitly	"We are here to learn to share our feelings with other people."	"The reason we are here is to work together as a group to help each one of us become more assertive."	"The purpose of our group is to help each other decide how he wants to behave differently and then give him positive support as he begins to change."
Implicitly	"It is a lot easier to talk about other people than it is to talk about your own fears of approaching new people."	"I wonder if we can discover what we have in common?"	"We are having a lot of trouble deciding on what goals we want to achieve."
Confront by calling attention to inappropriate behavior	"Jenny, the last three times anyone suggested an idea to you, you defended your previous way of acting."	"Marci, I notice you always approve of what your friends, Judy and Mary, say, but you ignore the comments of others."	"Mike, you have found a reason not to act on every suggestion made to you so far."

(continued)

A. Leader behaviors which facilitate:

	Trust and Openness	Cohesiveness	Task Accomplishment
Reflect: if said prior to desired behavior it is *implicit norming*; if it follows desired behavior it is *reinforcement*	"It is very difficult to share our fears with each other."	"I sense a feeling of warmth and closeness among us today."	"I sense a feeling of not wanting to set goals because it is a commitment that may be hard to keep."
Restate harsh and negative statements to point out positive implications	"What Mildred said may have hurt—but sometimes saying something negative is a sign of caring."	"Perhaps what you mean when you say you are frustrated with this group is that you want to get through the barrier keeping us strangers from each other."	"I am glad you mentioned how Jim rambles. It helps him to know what he needs to change so that others will like him more."
Redirect statements from leader to other members	"Ann, would you tell Herb directly how you feel about his relationship with his mother?"	"Barbara, tell Carol directly that it is easier for you to talk if she is attentive."	"I think Jim would like to hear that proposal from you."
Make optimistic expectation statements	"If we practice we can learn how to be more open with each other."	"As we get to know each other better, we will learn how to work together as a team."	"Some of these problems may seem insurmountable today–but if we keep working on small steps as we have been doing, we will be able to solve them."

(continued)	Trust and Openness	Cohesiveness	Task Accomplishment
A. Leader behaviors which facilitate:			
Redirect attention to important content that was avoided or unnoticed	"Do you really think that Susan was saying that she dislikes school or might she have been talking about being afraid that she might fail?"	"I do not think Richard was saying he dislikes this group. I think he was saying he is afraid he might be rejected."	"Eric made an important suggestion which no one noticed. Eric, would you repeat it, please?"
Set definite agenda and redirect members when they deviate	"Today let's each of us share something that we find difficult to talk about."	"Today let's see how many things we have in common—this will help us to feel closer."	"We are getting off our agenda for today. We decided to explore ways of preparing for tests. What ideas do you have, Betsy?"
Remain silent	Silence may be used to help members learn that good friends can enjoy being with each other without pressure to communicate in words.	Silence after an especially warm moment of sharing may enable group members to appreciate their feelings of belonging.	Silence may be used to force group members to take initiative for problem-solving and reduce dependence on the leader.
B. Group exercises that facilitate:	Trust and Openness	Cohesiveness	Task Accomplishment
Group exercises are used to elicit the desired behaviors; then leader uses techniques above to maintain or modify			

B. Group exercises that facilitate:

	Trust and Openness	**Cohesiveness**	**Task Accomplishment**
Fantasy	*Favorite Fantasy.* Each member tells fantasy, (a) when lonely, (b) if I had a million dollars, (c) for future, (d) when wronged, or (e) if famous. Discuss.	*Shared Fantasy.* One member starts fantasy on specified topic; each member in turn adds on a new element. Discuss.	*Idealized Self.* Each member tells fantasy of self without specified problem. Discuss.
Dyads	*Self-Disclosure Dyads.* Arrange group in dyads. Give definite topic: e.g., "what no one has ever understood about me." Each talks 5 minutes on topic to listening partner. Alternate roles 6-8 times.	*Clique Breaker.* Arrange dyads with one member from each subgroup. Assign task: discover similarities. Regroup and discuss.	*Mutual Aid.* Pair members with common problem to carry out definite practice assignment in natural environment, e.g., stutterers ask for ping pong balls.
Movement	*Trust Exercise.* Group in small circle, one member in center who makes himself rigid and falls backward and is caught and bounced gently back and forth by group.	*Group Sculpture.* Group arranges one another according to roles they assume in group, i.e., dominant one stands on chair, shy one sits in corner alone. Variation: member trying to control group determines positions. Discuss.	*Role Play.* Reenact problem situations with members taking various parts. Can role play alternative behaviors that might have helped in situation.

(continued)

B. Group exercises that facilitate:

	Trust and Openness	Cohesiveness	Task Accomplishment
Perception	*First Impressions—First Names.* Each member gives name and few facts about self. Group turns backs to each other. Each member writes down all names he can remember. Discuss names, feelings attached, feelings about meeting new people and behaviors that generate first impressions.	*Directed Responding.* To improve listening and increase member-to-member talk, instruct group that when a member wants to say something, he must first respond directly to previous comment, then make his own comment.	*Role Reversal.* Have members play role of person with whom they have difficulty and argue antagonist's position convincingly to learn how other person feels.
Homework	*Helping Pairs.* Select partners and meet before next session to discuss a specific problem, e.g., "what is my objective in this group." Next session discuss what happened.	*Group Trip.* Develop common problem or task requiring cooperation and travel somewhere to work on it, e.g., visit to college campus to learn appropriate questions to ask; or in learning to approach new people, go to dance to observe and practice interacting.	*Individual Assignments.* Give each member a task to practice each day during week, e.g., ask one question in each class.

7.
A Human Technology for Group Helping Processes

Robert R. Carkhuff

The Andersons, middle-aged parents of boys, were visibly upset by the boys' development. To be sure, they were distressed by the dysfunctional development of both of their children. While the older child was "acting out" his problems with greater intensity, the younger one seemed to be following in his brother's "footsteps." With each year of living it seemed as if the children were "catching up" with their parents, challenging their authority, rebelling against their "way of life." Indeed, however limited their emotional age, the children did appear to be "closing the gap" with the parents' emotional age. Finally, the parents became so desperate that they sought professional help.

They met with three other sets of parents twice a week for several months. The group leader seemed to be "warm" enough and concerned enough for their welfare. Mainly, they talked about their problems. Once in a while, the group leader shared an insight concerning child-rearing with the group. It was as if the leader did not seem that different from the rest of the parents. Sometimes he really did not understand what the individual group members were trying to express. It made them wonder how well his own children were doing. But mostly they kept plodding along, held together by their mutual plights. For a while that was enough. Things even seemed to be getting better at home. But, ultimately the parents—and leader as well—were left at the end of treatment no different from the way that they were at the beginning. They had learned no effective ways of dealing with each other and their children. They could only emulate the behavior of the group leader, and that was found wanting in their home situation. In a very real sense, things seemed to be worse because they had been promised hope and received only failure.

This experience of a "helping" program is typical of group treatment programs: 1) people have problems; 2) they meet together in groups to discuss mutual problems; 3) the group leader shares an occasional insight into the problems; 4) the people return to face their problems. There is no demonstration on the part of the leader that he has specific skills in the problem areas. There are no systematic programs to develop the skills on the part of the participants. There are no systematic action programs flowing from the insights developed. There is no translation of the group processes to skills with which the participants can service themselves. In short, *there is no technology for human resource development.*

Principles of a Helping Technology

Only a human technology allows helping programs to rise above the forms of "self-taught art." Only a human technology translates the helping effort to tangible human benefits. Only a human technology provides the means to systematically regenerate itself in useful, new programs to meet the new and demanding conditions of human existence.

What differentiates a human technology from all other technologies is that it begins and ends with a human product. An individual with a limited range of functioning (the person being helped) is moved systematically toward a more extensive range of functioning. In addition, a human product, the helper, is the source of the means to this movement, the helping program. Not only is the human not left out of the human equation, in the form of the helper it is the necessary and effective ingredient in the helping program.

The model for a human technology for group helping processes is an empirically-based model that is developed in greater detail in more extensive writings (Carkhuff, 1969a, 1969b, 1972a, 1972b). For the present, this discussion will develop the propositions concerning the behaviors upon which the human technology is based.

There are three basic principles that dominate the development of an effective human technology. The first involves the helper as the primary source of helping effectiveness.

The first principle of effective helping is that the helper is able to do things that the helpee is unable to do.

Behaviorally, the helper (parent, teacher, counselor, therapist) must be equipped with an extensive repertoire of responses in the area that is of concern to the helpee (child, student, client, patient). (See Figure 1.) In other terms, the helper must have responses which the helpee does not have. It is precisely this discrepancy in response repertoire that defines the helping relationship. It is precisely the absence of this response differential between leader and group members that limits the counseling effects of the Andersons and other participants in group helping of all kinds. Unless the helper had responses available to him to cope with conditions that the helpee cannot cope with, there is no legitimate basis for helping.

Figure 1

Extensive Response Repertoire of the Helper

Helper

Extensive Response Repertoire

The helper does not, to be sure, operate in vacuuo. Among other things, then, the helper attends to the helpee as a source of helping effectiveness.

The second principle of effective helping is that helping begins with the helpee's frame of reference.

The helpee must be aware of the discrepancy in functioning between himself and the helper. (See Figure 2.) Phenomenologically, he must view the helper as having something that he, the helpee, wants and, therefore, is motivated to attain through the helping process. Simply stated, the helpee wants to be able to do things that previously he was unable to do and the helper is able to do. In turn, the helper must be aware that, just as the helpee's perception of him initiates the helping process, so will all learning that takes place in helping begin with the helpee's frame of reference. It is the absence of the group leader's ability to discriminate and communicate accurately the experience of the Andersons and other participants that limits the effects of most group counseling.

Figure 2

*Differential Response Repertoires of
Helper and Helpee*

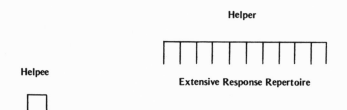

Obviously, it is not enough that helper and helpee interact or even that the helper attend to the helpee's frame of reference. The helper must also develop a program that moves the helpee from where he is toward where the helper is.

> *The third principle of effective helping is that a helping program must be developed to move from the helpee's frame of reference toward the helper's level of functioning.*

The helper must have the repertoire of interpersonal and program development skills that enable him to develop a step-by-step program that begins with the helpee's frame of reference and moves toward or (perhaps ultimately) even beyond the helper's level of functioning. (See Figure 3.) It is the program that is the link between helpee and helper. It is the program that enables the helpee to develop the extensive repertoire of responses that will, in turn, enable the helpee to live effectively in his world. It is the absence of systematic helping programs that places a lid on the development of the skills that the Andersons and other similar helpees need to service themselves.

Figure 3

Program

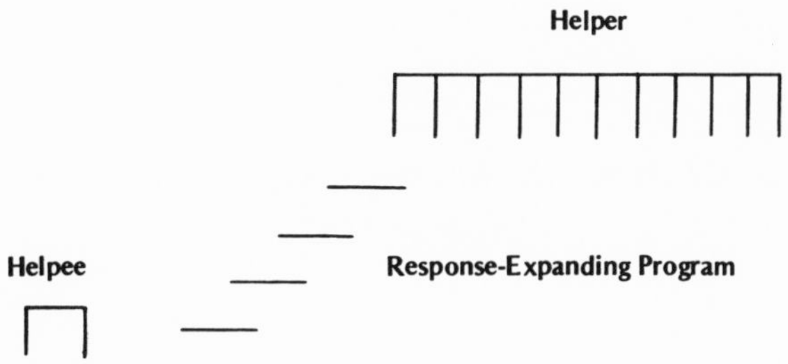

Helper

Response-Expanding Program

Helpee

The three principal ingredients in a human technology, then, are the helper, the helpee and the helping program. As can be seen in Figure 3, it is the helping program that provides the technological link between the limited human functioning of the helpee and the full human functioning of the helper. It is this human technology that offers the helpee hope for movement from his now desperate level of functioning toward the helper's fully functioning model.

Phases of a Helping Technology

With the goal in helping of some kind of a change or gain in the helpee's behavior, the processes by which the helpee arrives at this increment in behavior must be determined. First, before behavior change can occur, an action program must be developed. Second, before an action program can be developed, there must be an understanding of the helpee's frame of reference. Third, before there is an *understanding* of the helpee's frame of reference, there must be an *exploration* of his frame of reference. Helpee exploration. Helpee understanding. Helpee action. The processes leading to change or gain in helpee behavior, then, will emphasize the activities of the helpee as well as those of the helper who influences the activities of the helpee. The processes provide us with criteria by which we can judge our movement toward the goal of helpee change or gain. In this context, they are testable from both an empirical and an experiential frame of reference (Carkhuff, 1969a, 1969b, 1971a).

The first phase of helping emphasizes helpee self-exploratory behavior in relation to his areas of concern.

Self-exploration involves the helpee exploring personally relevant material with the appropriate emotional intensity. (See Figure 4.) In the educative processes of child-rearing and teaching, this means that the helpee must explore himself in relation to the learning material being presented. In the rehabilitation processes of counseling and psychotherapy, this means that the helpee must explore himself in relation to his problem areas. For example, the Andersons explored themselves in relation to each other and their children.

Figure 4

First Phase of Helping

Phases

I

HELPEE BEHAVIOR: **Exploration**

The helpee's exploration of himself in relation to the areas of his concern leads readily to the helpee's need to understand himself in relation to those areas of concern.

The second phase of helping emphasizes helpee self-understanding behaviors in relation to the areas of his concern.

Having explored the pieces of his experience, the helpee must now attempt to come to some level of understanding of his experience, however tentative. (See Figure 5.) Self-understanding involves the helpee's being able to respond accurately to the feeling and meaning of his expressions. In conjunction with the helper, the helpee will put the pieces of his experience together in an emerging pattern or picture of his behavior. For example, in an effective helping program, the Andersons, individually and together, might come to understand themselves as the source of their children's difficulties.

Figure 5

First and Second Phases of Helping

Phases

I   **II**

HELPEE: **Exploration** ⟶ **Understanding**

The helpee's understanding of himself in relation to the areas of his concern leads readily to the helpee's need to develop an action program to produce a change or gain in his behavior.

> *The third phase of helping emphasizes helpee action behavior*
> *in relation to the areas of his concern.*

Having understood his experience in the areas of his concern, the helpee must now attempt to develop some kind of an action program leading to the desired change or gain. (See Figure 6.) Action behavior involves the helpee taking the steps necessary to move toward his goal. In conjunction with the helper, the helpee will choose and develop a preferred course of action. For example, in an effective helping program, the Andersons, individually and together, might attempt to change the behavior which is contributing to the difficulties which they are having with their children.

Figure 6

Three Phases of Helping

Phases

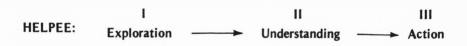

| | **I** | | **II** | | **III** |
| **HELPEE:** | **Exploration** | ⟶ | **Understanding** | ⟶ | **Action** |

There is no effective action without accurate understanding. There is no accurate understanding without relevant exploration. These are the phases of effective helping. Exploration leads to understanding. Understanding leads to action. These phases recycle themselves in an ongoing learning process. (See Figure 7.) Action leads to feedback from the environment. The feedback stimulates further exploration. Exploration facilitates more accurate understanding. Understanding leads to more effective action.

Figure 7

Recycling the Phases of Helping

Phases

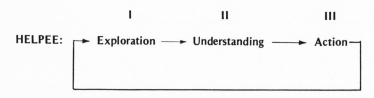

Helper Behaviors in a Helping Technology

To be sure, there are helper behaviors which serve to facilitate helpee movement to action behavior (Carkhuff, 1972a). First, the helper must attend to the helpee in ways that will enable the helpee to attend to himself and express himself. Second, the helper must respond to the helpee's expressions in ways that elicit the helpee's self-exploration. Third, the helper must respond to the helpee's exploration in ways that facilitate the helpee's self-understanding. Finally, the helper must initiate interaction with the helpee in ways that develop the helpee's action program. Each helper behavior facilitates the helpee behavior which leads directly to the next helper behavior.

The first set of helper behaviors emphasizes attending to the helpee at a physical and psychological level.

Attending involves meeting the helpee's physical and psychological needs. (See Figure 8.) Attending is really a pre-helping behavior. It involves "setting the stage" to meet the helpee's needs for security and comfort. It involves preparing and positioning the helper to observe and listen to the helpee. In this manner, the helpee is freed to experience and express himself in a helpful atmosphere. For example, the Andersons came to feel that they were in a helpful environment where people were concerned about their welfare.

When the helpee expresses himself, behaviorally as well as verbally, the helper will have the opportunity to respond to the helpee in a way that will facilitate helpee exploration.

Figure 8

Helper Attending Behaviors in
Pre-Helping Phase

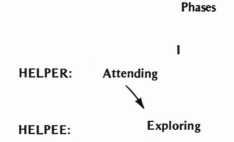

Phases

I

HELPER: Attending

HELPEE: **Exploring**

The second set of helper behaviors emphasizes responding to
the helpee at the level that the helpee expresses himself.

Responding to the feeling and meaning expressed by the helpee at the level that the helpee expresses himself facilitates helpee self-exploration. (See Figure 9.) Responding in such a manner insures the helpee that the helper has understood him accurately at the level that the helpee has expressed himself. This process communicates respect for the helpee and leaves the progression of the helping process under the helpee's control. For example, the Andersons and other couples would have the experience of "controlling" their level of self-exploration and, thus, the pace of the helping program.

Figure 9

*Helper Responsive Behaviors in
Phase I of Helping*

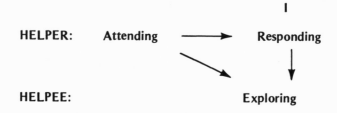

When the helpee can respond to himself at the levels he is expressing himself, he signals the helper of his readiness for movement to the understanding phase of helping, where he can find some of the answers for which he is searching.

> *The third set of helper behaviors emphasizes responding to the helpee at deeper levels beyond which he has expressed himself.*

Responding to the common themes about self which the helpee is expressing facilitates helpee self-understanding. (See Figure 10.) In conjunction with the helper, the pattern of the helpee's behavior will be developed. An analysis of the common themes about self will yield the areas in which the helpee is deficient in his response repertoire. For example, through the helper's efforts to develop a deeper understanding, Mr. Anderson might learn that he is not at all responsive to his wife or his children's perceptions of the world while Mrs. Anderson learns that she does not assume enough initiative in relation to her husband or her children.

When the helpee not only understands the helper's analysis of his behavior but is able to analyze his own behavior at levels beyond which he has originally expressed himself, he signals the helper of his readiness to move to the action phase of helping where he can do something about his understanding.

Figure 10

*Helper Responsive Behaviors in
Phase II of Helping*

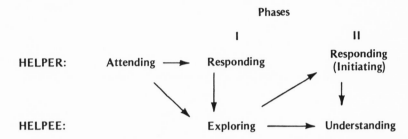

The fourth set of helper behaviors emphasizes initiating courses of action in conjunction with the helpee.

Based upon the understanding which they have developed, the helper and helpee proceed to act upon this understanding. (See Figure 11.) Together, they develop a course of action that will lead to the behavior change or gain of the helpee. That is, understanding the deficiencies in the helpee's behavior, they will develop an action course that will develop these behaviors. For example, in the instance of the Andersons, they might work to develop programs in which Mr. Anderson learns to respond more effectively to his wife and his children and Mrs. Anderson learns to assert herself more effectively with her husband and her children.

Figure 11

*Helper Initiative Behaviors in
Phase III of Helping*

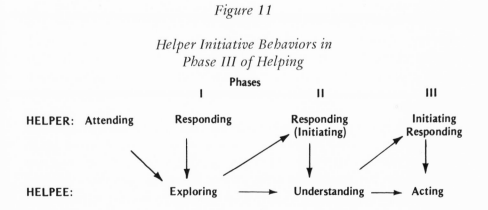

When the helpee has developed his action program and acted upon it, he will receive the feedback from his world that will stimulate exploration, understanding and action. (See Figure 12.) By way of illustration, each of the Andersons will receive behavioral feedback from the other and their children concerning the effectiveness of their new behavior. Alone or in conjunction with the helper, the helpee will work toward more relevant exploration, more accurate understanding and more effective action as a consequence of this feedback. In an on-going process, the helpee will find himself constantly modifying his behavior to become a more effective human being.

Figure 12

Helper Behaviors in Phases of Helping

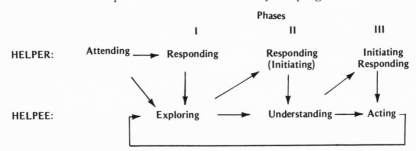

A Training Technology for Helping

In order for the helpers to demonstrate the helping behaviors that facilitate helpee exploration, understanding and action, they must be trained systematically in the specific skills involved (Carkhuff, 1972a, 1972c). First, the prospective helper must learn the skills involved in attending effectively to the helpee. Second, he must learn the skills involved in responding to the helpee at the level that the helpee presents himself. Third, he must learn the skills involved in responding to the helpee at levels beyond which the helpee presents himself. Fourth, he must learn the skills involved in initiating with the helpee.

The first set of training behaviors emphasizes attending to the helpee at a physical and psychological level.

Training in attending behaviors involves at least four sets of variables: (1) contextual; (2) presentation; (3) postural; (4) visual. (See

Figure 13.) With regard to contextual variables, the helper must emphasize the accessibility and attractiveness of the external setting and the comfort, security and functionality of the internal setting in order to attract and hold the helpee in helping. With regard to presentation variables, the helper must present himself as the model of what it is he is offering in order to motivate the helpee for helping. With regard to postural variables, the helper must emphasize addressing fully, moving toward and leaning forward in order to communicate an interest in the helpee. With regard to visual variables, the helper must emphasize eye contact with the helpee in order to fully observe the behavior of the helpee. In relation to the Andersons, then, an effective helper would meet with them in an organized and functional setting that will be attractive to them; present himself sensitively yet with strength as someone who has something that they want; posture himself for the intensity and intimacy necessary to involve them in the helping process; and use his eyes to make contact with them and, above all, to observe their behavior, alone and in interaction with each other and their children.

Figure 13

*Levels of Helper Attending Behaviors in
Pre-Helping Phase*

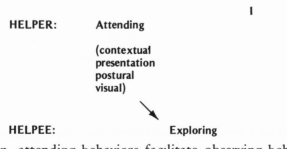

In turn, attending behaviors facilitate observing behaviors which lay the groundwork for the helper responsiveness that facilitates helpee exploration.

The second set of training behaviors emphasizes responding to the helpee at interchangeable levels.

Training in formulating responses that are interchangeable with the expressions of the helpee involves at least three stages: (1) responding interchangeably to content; (2) responding interchangeably to feeling; (3) responding interchangeably to feeling and meaning. (See Figure 14.) Responding interchangeably to content simply involves repeating verbatim in the first person the expression of the helpee. Responding interchangeably to feeling involves discriminating and communicating the feeling attendant to the content. Responding interchangeably to feeling and meaning involves utilizing the content as the reason for the feeling response. Interchangeable responses are considered minimally effective responses and are rated at level 3 on 5-point scales. (See Figure 14.) In relation to the Andersons, then, the helper would respond to the feeling and meaning of their expressions. For example, in response to their agitated helplessness that often translates to the withdrawal of their affection from the children, the helper might offer: "You feel agitated because the children never do what you want them to do."

Figure 14

Levels of Helper Responsive Behaviors in
Phase I of Helping

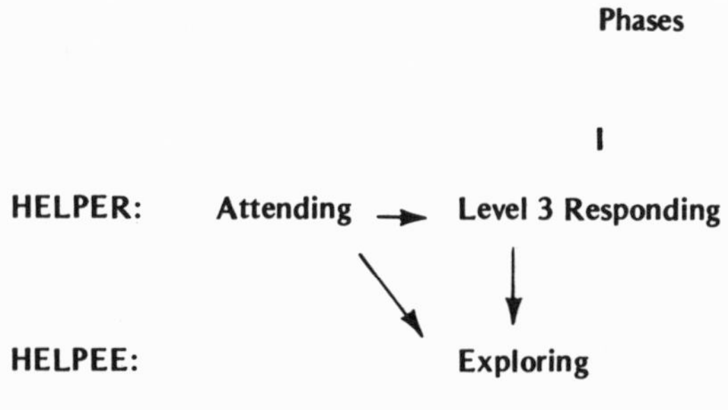

Phases

I

HELPER: Attending → Level 3 Responding

HELPEE: Exploring

Responding at levels that are interchangeable with the feeling and meaning expressed by the helpee lays the base for formulating responses that go beyond the helpee's expression and thereby facilitate helpee understanding.

The third set of training behaviors emphasizes responding to the helpee at additive levels.

Additive responses are responses that facilitate helpee self-understanding. If a response is not interchangeable, it must be additive (in terms of facilitating understanding) or subtractive (in terms of retarding understanding). Training in formulating additive responses involves at least three stages: (1) discriminating common themes about self; (2) discriminating dominant themes about self; (3) discriminating the behavioral deficiencies in the themes about self. (See Figure 15.) Discriminating common themes about self expressed by the helpee simply involves taking frequency tabulations of the different self-themes. Discriminating the dominant theme about self simply involves determining the theme that appears with the greatest frequency. Discriminating the behavioral deficiency in the themes about self involves determining the presence or absence of helpee behavior which leads repeatedly to those kinds of situations described in the themes about self. Responding at additive levels is rated at levels 4 and 5 according to the degree to which the helper's response facilitates helpee understanding. In addition, responding at additive levels automatically introduces initiative behavior at minimal levels (level 3). (See Figure 3.) In relation to the Andersons, the helper might formulate additive responses as follows: "What I really hear you saying, Mr. (Mrs.) Anderson, is that you really are unable to bring yourself to understand (discipline) your child because you never learned how to do that."

Figure 15

*Levels of Helper Responsive Behaviors in
Phase II of Helping*

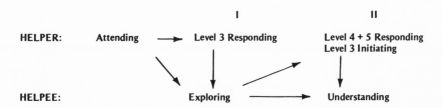

Discriminating the behaviors in which the helpee is deficient dictates the development of initiative behaviors to do something about that deficiency.

*The fourth set of training behaviors emphasizes initiating
with the helpee to develop an effective course of action.*

Initiative behaviors involve action-oriented behaviors on the part
of the helper. Training in initiative behaviors involves at least three
stages: (1) the development of those personal expressions that are
self-assertive; (2) the development of those personal expressions that
are assertive with relation to the helpee; (3) the development of
problem-solving behaviors that culminate in an effective course of
action. (See Figure 16.) Self-assertive personal expressions revolve
primarily around the dimensions of helper genuineness and immediacy
and serve as a model for helpee development of effective initiative
behavior. Other-assertive expressions by the helper involve the helper's
confrontation of discrepancies in the helpee's behavior and, in the
context of understanding, serve as the basis for motivating the helpee to
develop an action course. Problem-solving behaviors involve operationalizing goals, considering alternative courses of action in interaction
with the helpee's value criteria in order to choose a preferred course of
action, and developing a program to implement the course of action
(Carkhuff, 1972b). In relation to the Andersons, the helper might work
to develop action programs to teach Mr. Anderson to be responsive to
his wife and children and Mrs. Anderson to be assertive in relation to
her husband and children.

Figure 16

*Levels of Helper Initiative Behaviors in
Phase III of Helping*

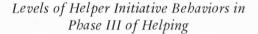
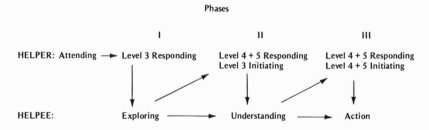

In summary, the helper has a helping technology for involving the
helpee in the exploration, understanding and action necessary for

behavior change or gain. Again, the feedback from the action behavior stimulates further exploration, more accurate understanding and more effective action. (See Figure 17.) With these skills of exploration, understanding and action available to him, the helpee can now engage in a life-long learning process.

Figure 17

Helper Behaviors in
Phases of Helping

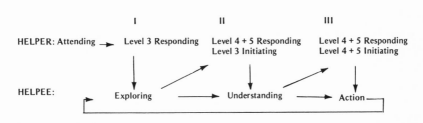

Group Applications of a
Helping Technology

Considering the proposition that the core of functioning (health) or dysfunctioning (pathology) is inherently interpersonal, group processes are uniquely disposed toward facilitating the interpersonal development of its helpees (Carkhuff, 1971b). In the group context, each group member has the opportunity to try out new kinds of behaviors directly with other members. In this regard, if the leader is effective in eliciting the development of the group participants, then the group has the potential contribution of multiple helpers available to cope with any one member's problems.

The point is that the same dimensions hold for group helping that hold for the individual, with the addition of the living demonstration of interpersonal behavior. Individually and as a group exploration precedes understanding and understanding precedes action. While the helper has multiple helpees to attend to, individually and in interaction with each other, the same helping behaviors make the effective phases of helping possible: attending; responding interchangeably; responding additively; initiating.

With regard to attending behaviors, then, the helper should set the context for maximum facilitation of group processes. Most obviously, the group must be positioned for maximum exposure to the leader and its members with no obstacles such as tables to prevent them from attending to each other. The leader must present himself in such a way as to communicate his potential contribution to all of the group members. He must posture himself to attend to the group in general and each member individually as he expresses himself behaviorally or verbally. He must maintain constant eye contact with all of the members, using visual cues in observing their behavior as well as communicating his interest.

In responding to the helpees, individually or collectively, the helper must be attuned to the subtle behavioral and verbal nuances as expressed, both within and between individuals. This means that the helper must respond not only to the feeling and meaning as expressed by an individual helpee but also to the feeling and meaning of expressions by other helpees in reaction to the individual. One way to insure effective group movement is to provide minimal training in interpersonal skills for each of its members. In this manner, the leader may set up and enforce a rule by which each member must respond interchangeably to another member before going on to initiate his own expression. This insures maximum understanding of each member by the other. In addition, it develops a model by which group members like the Andersons may conduct their own families and other relationships.

In addition, and most important, it lays the base for movement to additive levels of understanding for the entire group. By responding interchangeably to other group members, each member insures the prospect of learning to make additive responses not only to other people involved intimately in his life but also to himself. With this base of understanding, the group leader may respond additively not only to individuals within the group but to the group as a whole. For example, at a point where the individual members of the group such as the Andersons are unable to mobilize their efforts to function more fully, an effective leader might respond as follows: "What I really hear you saying is that it is pretty scary for you to live your lives at the level of initiative that I am demonstrating with you." Such an additive response points to the life (growth) and death (deterioration) implications of continuing to function as they have been doing in the past. More importantly, it emphasizes the need to do something about their deficit behaviors.

The definition of deficit behaviors is synonymous with the definition of the problem and leads directly to the definition of the goal. The goal is simply the inverse of the problem. Where there are deficits, the goal becomes developing assets. The definition of the goal serves to introduce the initiative phase of helping. In the group context, the entire group may be utilized in defining the problem and setting the goal. The use of interchangeable responsiveness serves to insure some basic level of group understanding of the problem. In addition, the individual members of the group may be utilized to expand alternative courses of action. Most significantly, with regard to both individual and group problems, the various group members may contribute to the development of value criteria and vote on the rank-ordering and weighting of the items involved. Finally, the group members may explore and weigh the facilitative and retarding effects of the various alternative courses of action upon the achievement of the value criteria involved. Again, the group problem-solving processes become a model for effective problem-solving in families like the Anderson family, as well as aiding other relationships outside of the group.

It may be concluded that group processes are a preferred mode of treatment. Effective group helping programs can accomplish everything that can be done in individual helping relations in addition to those interpersonal phenomena which are unique to group processes. Group helping processes offer a number of unique benefits and relatively few limitations to both helper and helpee (Carkhuff, 1971b). Most importantly, not only the helper but also the helpees have the opportunity to utilize their resources in such a way as to get a maximum return in human benefits for a minimum investment of time and energy.

In this context, the most effective modality for group helping processes involves the systematic training of group members. That is to say, it is most efficient and most effective to train the helpees in all of the dimensions in which we trained the helpers. It is most helpful to equip helpees like the Andersons with all of the behaviors which they need to explore, understand and act for themselves. Similarly, it is most helpful to equip the helpees with the helping behaviors involved in facilitating the exploration, understanding and action on the part of others. This means that helpees like the Andersons can be—indeed, have been (Carkhuff, 1971c, 1971d; Carkhuff and Banks, 1970; Carkhuff and Berenson, 1972; Carkhuff and Bierman, 1970; Pierce and Drasgow, 1969; Vitalo, 1971)—trained in groups to attend, respond interchangeably, respond additively and initiate effectively with each other.

It may be concluded that group training is the preferred mode of treatment. Group training systematically transforms the helpee into a helper—which is, after all, what helping is all about.

References

Carkhuff, R.R. *Helping and Human Relations. Vol. I. Selection and Training.* New York: Holt, Rinehart and Winston, 1969a.

Carkhuff, R.R. *Helping and Human Relations. Vol. II. Practice and Research.* New York: Holt, Rinehart and Winston, 1969b.

Carkhuff, R.R. *The Development of Human Resources: Education, Psychology and Social Change.* New York: Holt, Rinehart and Winston, 1971a.

Carkhuff, R.R. Toward a Comprehensive Model for Effective Group Helping Processes. In *Group Guidance and Counseling in the Schools.* New York: Appleton-Century-Crofts, 1971b.

Carkhuff, R.R. Training as a Preferred Mode of Group Treatment. In *Group Counseling: A Developmental Approach.* Boston: Allyn and Bacon, 1971c.

Carkhuff, R.R. Group Training as a Preferred Mode of Treatment. In *The Development of Human Resources.* New York: Holt, Rinehart and Winston, 1971d.

Carkhuff, R.R. *The Art of Helping.* Amherst, Massachusetts: Box 222, Human Resource Development Press, 1972a.

Carkhuff, R.R. *The Art of Problem-Solving.* Amherst, Massachusetts: Box 222, Human Resource Development Press, 1972b.

Carkhuff, R.R. *The Art of Training.* Amherst, Massachusetts: Box 222, Human Resource Development Press, 1972c.

Carkhuff, R.R. and G. Banks. Training as a Preferred Model of Facilitating Relations Between Races and Generations. *Journal of Counseling Psychology,* 1970, *17,* 413-418.

Carkhuff, R.R. and B.G. Berenson. The Utilization of Black Functional Professionals in Reconstituting Troubled Families. *Journal of Clinical Psychology,* 1972, *28,* 92-93.

Carkhuff, R.R. and R. Bierman. Training as a Preferred Mode of Treatment of Parents of Emotionally Disturbed Children. *Journal of Counseling Psychology,* 1970, *17,* 157-161.

Pierce, R.M. and J. Drasgow. Teaching Facilitative Interpersonal Functioning to Psychiatric Inpatients. *Journal of Counseling Psychology,* 1969, *16,* 295-298.

Vitalo, R. Teaching Improved Interpersonal Functioning as a Preferred Mode of Treatment. *Journal of Clinical Psychology,* 1971, *27,* 166-170.

8.
Groups for the Educationally Distraught

Milton Schwebel

Introduction

Groups are powerful. They kill. They erode self-respect, stifle intelligence and cripple decision-making competency. Sometimes they do these evil things by conscious, deliberate plan, and sometimes unknowingly.

Groups are a powerful force for good. They build self-respect. They facilitate the development of intelligence, and nourish the vitality and initiative of people. And for those who are already the victims of harmful group experiences, good groups restore self-respect. They free intelligence and release the capacity to order one's own life.

Every group leader would claim to want the group to serve good rather than evil purposes. But how to do that effectively is the problem.

The Group as a Setting for the Distraught

The children who need help most have been badly scarred by their "education." Many have learned that they are members of an unwanted group. Their experience has been marked by repeated failure, and the classroom is associated with frustration and meaninglessness. Adults and the adult world are not to be trusted, not this world that has left them with the twin destroyers of life: helplessness and hopelessness. That's what they feel even if they cope with those feelings by aggressive and belligerent behavior.

They need the kind of group experience that counters those feelings. That cannot happen from talk alone; it cannot, in fact, come from talk. Youth who have learned to distrust can benefit from a group only when that group is distinctly different in respect to trust from others they have known. They will understandably doubt the credibility of the counselor, his purposes, intentions, procedures, promises; and if he shows them any sign of being different from others they have known, they will test him by challenges even more extreme than their typical defensive measures. Unbeknownst to the naive counselor, this exaggerated behavior is evidence that the group experience has begun to penetrate protective armor.

1. **The first principle in making a group helpful to its members is to build trust.**

1.1. The counselor is absolutely honest about the objectives of the group. The purposes are perfectly clear from the behavior of the counselor, so that there is no doubt that the group operates to serve their interests, not the counselor's nor the institution's. The most *crucial* quality of the counselor in respect to trust is to be believable. There is no training for that, no skill to learn. Either the counselor really is there to serve the students or not. Either he's there for them, or he's there for other reasons: to prove himself; to defuse the school's troublemakers; to silence the vocal demands of dissatisfied parents and community groups; to collect data for a dissertation; to be "the expert."

1.2. The counselor protects the integrity of the group from external pressures. Administrators want results in the form of behavioral changes suited to their peace-keeping function; parents and some teachers will want those, and performance changes as well. The counselor's behavior can easily be influenced by those expectations, the consequence of which would be his own pressuring of the group, forcing it into directions that its members do not wish to go at all or at least at this time. Behavioral and performance modifications may be very much in order, but they become the focus of the group only as they spring from the concerns and interests of the group. That they will is almost invariable, and the difference in their origin as an agenda item is far more than a technicality in counseling, far more than a ritual or some misplaced deference to "democracy." It is the difference between asserting some power over one's own life or, being powerless, needing goals and topics dictated (or subtly introduced) by authorities. It is the difference between helplessness in managing one's life, and the experience of setting priorities for oneself. It is the difference between perpetuating the conditions that give rise to hopelessness or exercising the powers that give rise to hope.

1.3. The counselor protects the group and encourages the group to protect itself from attacks of hatred and self-hatred. The case has been well made that past as well as present groups low on the hierarchy of approval and status have tended to internalize the values of the dominant group. Chronic and deep-seated frustration under conditions of oppression and repression have led them to direct their aggression against themselves; hence, crime against themselves (their own group) rather than against those responsible for maintaining their undesirable life situation. Behavior of this kind is not by any means limited to minority groups; low-achieving middle class suburbanites who are bitter with themselves will redirect their bitterness to others in their own situations. Essentially, this is the phenomenon of self-hatred, and it is destructive whether turned against oneself or against others in the group.

The counselor establishes trust in himself when he builds security within the group against *ad hominem* attacks and when he builds an atmosphere of cooperation and support rather than competition and self-serving behavior. The counselor does this directly by speaking up accordingly, giving positive reinforcement to the collective actions and negative to the competitive. He does this also indirectly by helping the group focus on those of its interests that are constructive and that could yield short- and long-term benefits. Constructive foci are those that *build up,* build potency and hope, rather than *put down.*

Is this role of the counselor somewhat paternalistic? Does it mean that he subtly shifts the group from what interests them to what interests him? No. He maintains his genuineness about this, as about all other matters, by pointing up the meaning of hostility to the functioning of the group and to the interests of its members and by contrasting that use of group time and energy to a constructive attack on their self-defined concerns.

In the final analysis what really matters is their collective success in coping with their concerns. By now our thesis is probably clear on this point: For almost all conceivable problems of children and youth for which the group setting is appropriate, trust is the *sine qua non.* Trust is not sufficient in and of itself but necessary to an exceptionally high degree.

When a counselor experiences more than the normal difficulties in the functioning of the group, when he sees indifference, attrition, lack of cohesiveness, he had better do that most difficult of jobs, namely, determine whether his behavior, attitudes and values really warrant trust. The counselor should not complain that he is expected to be a saint, for he is not.

2. **The second principle: The counselor's technical expertise is in helping the group develop potency in coping with their self-defined problems.**

2.1. Progress in a counseling group requires structure, order and system, which the counselor helps the group develop for itself. This does not mean an obsessive orderliness whereby people speak in turns, or the speakers address each other's comments serially. In some scenes in Chekhov's *Three Sisters* the characters don't even seem to be talking to each other or discussing the same topic. They are reflecting aloud, each about her own memories and experience of life, which is structure enough for any group that aspires to be productive.

2.2. Productivity, from the point of view of immediate criteria, means participation by group members in an exchange of concerns with other people. It means the realization of shared concerns and the mutual experience of the trials and tribulations of life. Productivity means clarifying *expressed* problems through the sometimes painful frankness of group members; it means then redefining them into *manageable* problems. For example, a youth expresses his disinterest in a course and his refusal to do any work because of the teacher's obvious prejudice against him. Others might confirm his experience of the teacher's attitude but then castigate him for using her prejudice as an excuse for avoiding work and injuring himself. Or they might deny the accuracy of his appraisal of the teacher, attributing her behavior as due to his provocations or attributing his withdrawal from the work of the class as a way of rationalizing anticipated failure. "Because of her I didn't work and that's the reason I didn't pass."

Productivity requires structure, and the counselor helps the group impose it. Note that structure is not content; it is a form of operation that permits the group to direct its attention at content. If the group is speaking out against the school system, the principal and the teacher, structure means a form of operation that enables the group to carry on the discussion to some level of closure such as the release of pent-up anger after which they choose to turn to other matters, perhaps some matter more amenable to their control; or closure represents a new level of understanding about the community and the schools; or closure leads to a course of action chosen by the group or by individuals.

2.3. Structure enables individuals already overburdened with frustration and helplessness to acquire a sense of power, of carrying through a process to a useful conclusion. *What* topic they discuss and *what* level of closure they reach is the group's to determine; that they *do* work as a group, that they *move* and achieve closure is the counselor's ultimate responsibility. "Ultimate" is the modifier to mean that the counselor should take no action whatsoever if the group is managing its locomotion, a characteristic of group development that itself marks great progress: but if the group flounders, and the feelings of helplessness and hopelessness will only become further confounded, he or she must take action. The form of it varies with the style of the counselor. One sample: "Look, we're getting nowhere. Everyone's going off in a different direction and you're only getting angry. Yet a little while ago you were all wanting to *do* something about XYZ."

Structure is order, and order, one must hastily add, should not be construed as rigidity. All of the most human and creative processes involve order and structure: painting a picture, writing a poem, composing music, performing in the arts and making love (i.e., having sexual experience). There would be nothing antagonistic between form and substance, providing form is not used deliberately to suppress some particular substance. Either one by itself in the group is likely to lead to the failure of the group. Excessive form will wring all the life out of it, while content without form produces extensive verbiage, inflamed feelings and terrible frustration.

2.4. The technical expertise of a competent counselor is that of a counselor, not that of a psychiatrist, psychotherapist, neurologist, social worker, physiotherapist, nor any other specialist. That limitation to which each specialist in every field is subject must be recognized to avoid the blunders often made by counselors who do not comprehend the need for a defined professional framework. The counselor works with individuals who may need and who in fact may be getting the services of one or more of the others, but his role (and his competency) is of a qualitatively different kind. Surely there are overlapping skills (e.g., the interview) and overlapping objectives (e.g., the welfare of the individual), but the specific objectives and the professional methods are quite different.

2.5. The technical expertise may be characterized as that of a problem-solver who by his behavior and leadership of the group helps develop the attitudes and methods of problem-solving. In the best sense of the word the group counselor is a teacher, when teaching is equated with providing the circumstances wherein learning means changing.

The problem-solver uses any and all strategies and tactics to achieve the goal of a group of people experiencing human feeling and working to make their lives more effective. They use conversation, discussion, role-play, drama, interviews, spoken private thoughts, nonsense syllables or numbers to convey feelings, pantomime, guests, field trips, picnics, sculpture, painting, music, athletics, observation of others (e.g., younger children). The aims are clear and consistent, the stratagems are a matter of preference and interest of the members. By about age 11, children are able to use logical thought sufficiently well for these purposes and are able to appreciate the experience of other people. Whether the counselor is more or less directive or whether his "teaching" involves more or less conditioning (all counselors, like all psychotherapists and analysts, have used conditioning consciously or not—Pavlov was Freud's contemporary, and both antedated Skinner— the controversy today is about the degree of its use) is not crucial except that his goal be to help achieve potency and hope. Strategies that work counter to that (e.g., primary dependence on conditioning) are in my view undesirable and should be used only in individual cases when other procedures are unworkable.

3. **The third principle: The counselor understands the conditions of life of the people with whom he works.**
   3.1. Counseling deals with the substance of life even when the counseling itself must be highly circumscribed. Counseling aimed at occupational choice and planning or more simply at placement cannot be separated from the rest of life and the circumstances in which people live. This is obvious when one considers urban youth; it is equally true for others, even if it is not so obvious.
   3.2. The term "conditions of life" is all-inclusive. It includes the psychological attributes of the individual, but not to the exclusion of other aspects. It conscientiously avoids "psychologizing" people, reducing to one variable all the forces that lead them to become what they are and what they are becoming, just because the impact of these

forces end up in the psyche, among other terminal conditions.

3.3. With such knowledge the counselor's chances of relating to others is greatly enhanced. He learns to avoid practices and language usage that are acceptable to his group, but not to the groups with which he works. He learns the culturally different connotations of the word "boy." He understands that uncontrolled behavior in one group can be as destructive as rigidly controlled behavior in another. He appreciates that the first-name familiarity which means friendliness in one cultural group is anathema to another because of long historical association of such usage with subservience.

3.4. His understanding is more than normative. He learns about the conditions of life of the poverty class, working class, middle class, etc., about the conditions and the culture of each of the ethnic, racial and religious groups therein, especially those with whom he has some contact. However, he also learns about what makes their conditions of life so different as to range from upper-class wealth, power, influence, education, low mortality to lowest-class poverty, powerlessness, low education and high mortality. This knowledge is not academic because the social, economic and psychological factors that created the condition that gave rise to the problems of the youth or adults in our group are still operative.

Here, as an example, is the theoretical framework used by the "radical psychiatry" group of workers to understand those who come to them for help. Applying the ideas of this group to counselors working with groups, one starting point is that the profession is engaged in political activity in the broadest sense. The profession, counselors individually or collectively, has a position about remedying the inequality of minority and underprivileged groups. This is political in the sense that taking such a stand implies obtaining some of the benefits for the underprivileged from others who are overprivileged. The only other alternative position, one that many "behavioral scientists" fall back on, is that they are neutral. However, anyone who claims neutrality about inequality is in fact helping to sustain the status quo. The same may be said for neutrality about racism, male domination of women and the like.

The non-neutral counselor is actively opposed to oppression of any sort. He understands that alienation stems in part from the mystification of oppression. By attributing the lowly status of people *to their own deficiencies* rather than to social inequalities, their anger and rage are directed *against themselves* rather than against the society. The consequence is that they see themselves as inferior, as different from others. So long as the counselor shares in the mystifying behavior, he reinforces the alienation of the members of the group and helps perpetuate their oppressed conditions. That means maintaining the problems of our students precisely as they are. Counselors will do that if they perpetuate mystification by the continued use of the IQ and its equivalents, by the continued stereotypes about racial and ethnic differences, by ignorance of the fact our society does not have enough jobs to go around even if every citizen were "optimally" educated. Even if we are the most perfect group counselors and even if all our students make the most rapid strides imaginable, we cannot by virtue of those successes create the millions of missing jobs.

To counteract alienation, according to the point of view under consideration, our group members need to be demystified—to learn that they and the racial, ethnic and low social class groups they are identified with have been blamed for what they did not cause. Many youth today know it; others discover it in the group. When they discover it, their anger is no longer directed against themselves or their group.

Anger appropriately channelled is not sufficient; it is not unlike the sound of a fallen tree in a deserted forest. Oppression plus awareness equals anger, and that is only the first step, important as it is, in the process of change. Liberation itself requires awareness plus contact. Individuals must participate with others in moving against oppression, and it is that association with others in a group that provides the best setting for liberation. The person has the "permission" and the protection of the leader and the group to free oneself from his or her oppression (both on the internal and external planes).

3.5. The counselor puts it all together. He has the background understanding about the people he serves and their historical and contemporary conditions of life. He knows the specifics related to the work of the counselor in the educational and vocational domains. He puts it all together in working with groups.

- By what he does and says the group discovers it is there for the benefit of the members, not of the counselor or the school. (Counselor: "Don't ask me what you should talk about.")

- By what he says, but especially by what he does, the group learns it can trust him to help them

    (a) protect themselves against onslaughts from outside groups. (Counselor to Principal: "I can't help them by telling them not to smoke in the toilet.")

    (b) develop ways of looking at their own problems in constructive ways. (Counselor: "You say you don't know how you disturb a class. Let's try it here. You be the teacher, you the . . . "

- By his behavior the group learns to practice openness and genuineness. The counselor is human and acknowledges that by not knowing all the answers, by admitting to errors in working with the group and by seeking their help in planning and in process. (Counselor: "Look, I said a few things about five minutes ago and since then no one's been very interested—hardly said anything. What's happened? What did I do to you?")

- Understanding that many in his group feel little gain from their school experience, and expect little from the group, he tries to disabuse them by sharpening the focus on their defined goals and keeping them moving toward them. (Counselor: "You said you wanted to decide by today what you wanted to study next term, and here you are arguing about . . . ")

- Knowing the importance of hope and positive expectation to improve performance in school, he conveys this through all of the vicissitudes of the group and its individual members, keeping clearly before them:

    (a) the evidences of any successful change;

    (b) the value to them personally, individually, of such change;

    (c) the resources available within the school and the community, but especially within the group and within themselves to help make the changes;

    (d) the ease with which we humans rationalize our not carrying out jobs that help ourselves, preferring in groups to talk about "deeper" forces rather than concentrating on problems of self-discipline, and of overcoming the expectations of failure, and the sense of futility.

- Appreciating the experience of oppression and the rage when one discovers the use of mystification as a way of blaming the oppressed instead of the oppressor, the counselor is not frightened by the rage. On the other hand, he does not nourish it; rather he seeks to direct the energy into action: forming a new school organization; sharpening skill to be better able to succeed; calling on a human rights commission; joining action groups; developing scholastic interests related to studies on injustice and the struggles to fight it. (Counselor: "Sure you're angry and you hate. That's OK; it is even healthy, especially if it gets you to do something constructive to change things.")

- By recognizing that we counselors also suffer the consequences of oppression and mystification, and of alienation, we are better able to attune ourselves to the experiences of our students. (Counselor to self: "I was looking to be loved instead of listening to them.")

- Recognizing that working to help one person is difficult enough, we appreciate the fact that working to help eight or ten is extremely demanding. It should be undertaken by professionals, that is, people who take the responsibility very seriously, and who mean to work at harnessing this powerful force to serve the interests of people.

- Understanding that potency and hope come from action and not just talk, the counselor welcomes and is not frightened by individual or group action, whether such action is directed toward their own immediate educational problems or whether they go beyond to problems in the school, at home or in the community.

- The counselor is human. He sees humor in life and enjoys it. He strives for mastery but can reckon with his weaknesses and failures. He gets satisfaction from work; but, being quite human, enjoys the end of a day's activities.

Suggested Readings

Ernst, Ken. *Games Students Play.* Millbrae, California: Celestial Arts, 1972.

Fader, Daniel. *The Naked Children.* New York: Macmillan, 1971. (How ghetto children experience school, teachers, life.)

Gartner, Alan, Mary Kohler and Frank Riessman. *Children Teach Children.* New York: Harper & Row, 1971. (Major report on one of our untapped resources.)

Greer, Colin. *The Great School Legend.* New York: Basic Books, 1972. (Did the schools raise up *any* groups, past or present?)

"Groups." *International Encyclopedia of the Social Sciences* Vol. 6. New York: Macmillan and the Free Press, 1968, 259-293. (Five theoretical papers on group behavior, formation structure and performance; see also three papers on Leadership in Vol. 9.)

Lifton, Walter. *Working with Groups.* New York: Wiley, 1966. (An extremely useful handbook for the practitioner.)

Radical Therapist. September 1971. (Entire issue on Radical Psychiatry.)

Sager, Clifford, T.L. Brayboy and B.R. Waxenberg. *Black Ghetto Family in Therapy.* New York: Grove Press, 1970.

Sarason, Seymour. *Culture of the School and Problems of Change.* Boston: Allyn and Bacon, 1971. (How to be for change while sabotaging it.)

Schwebel, Andrew I. and D. Cherlin. Effects of Social and Physical Distance in Teacher-Pupil Relationships. *Journal of Educational Psychology.* (In Press.)

Schwebel, Robert. Youth—A View from Berkeley 1. White Youth. In Daniel Adelson. *Man as the Measure: The Crossroads.* New York: Behavioral Publications, 1972.

Sherif, Muzafer. *In Common Predicament: Social Psychology of Intergroup Conflict and Cooperation.* Boston: Houghton Mifflin, 1966. (Brilliant and relevant studies on resolving group conflicts.)

Smith, William. Youth—A View from Berkeley 2. Black Youth in Adelson, *op. cit.*

9.
Should We Continue to Deradicalize Children Through the Use of Counseling Groups?

Doris Jefferies

The use of counseling groups to deradicalize children is an unobtrusive movement that deserves close observation. The deradicalization process might best be understood by first reflecting on some conceptualizations of the term "radical" with applications to human behavior. A person who adopts a radical philosophy does so with reference to an existing organizational system. When he perceives that organization as not functioning effectively to service the good of all the people under its influence, when he perceives that organization to be upholding the status quo to the advantage of a privileged group, when he perceives that organization oppressing another group in order to maintain the status quo, he attempts to dissolve that organization in favor of another—"by any means necessary."

Because the radical person takes a position that obviously threatens the established order, he becomes the target to be changed toward a more socially conforming position. Thus, the program to bring radical behavior under the control of the "power elite" through oppressive acts constitutes the process of deradicalization.

The Status Quo

According to the educational philosophy of Robert M. Hutchins (1962), each society must have some system that attempts to adapt the young to their social and political environment. In any society the schools tend to reinforce the dominant societal values (Gross, Wronski and Hanson, 1962). The "successful" five-year-old, upon entering school in a democratic society, learns quickly that he may speak only when he is given permission to do so by the representative of social order. Further, when he does speak, he must use the socially approved

113

words, subdued intonations and the approved sexual mannerisms in order to continue to increase his success ratio. He acquiesces to the status quo.

The "unsuccessful" five-year-old speaks without the permission of the authority, often in excited tones, and perhaps with unapproved mannerisms. The success ratio of the latter decreases because of his difficulty in conforming to the system. He has rejected the rules governing classroom participation, and he actively seeks to change them. Such a child is a potential threat to the maintenance of the status quo. He becomes the subject of mental and/or physical punishment in an attempt to check his maladaptive behavior. The deradicalization process is set into motion. He is brought to the attention of school authority figures to face sentencing for his actions. His sentence might be paddling, a scolding, suspension from school, or—*counseling*.

The Oppressive Counselor

The elementary school counselor, in his developmental stages, experienced the same deradicalization process, if he did not initially acquiesce. Had he not made essential concessions, he would not have been permitted to advance to a high level within the formal educational institution. The most important strategy for survival in the schools is docility and conformity (Silberman, 1970). Being "nice," non-threatening and empathic to the school system's needs helped him get to the position where he is today.

Stubbins (1970) concludes—after a review of sociological research—that counselors, like other professionals, find themselves in a caste system through their membership in the educational bureaucracy. As a result, they too become status seekers, at the expense of their clients.

> Furthermore, the manner in which supervisors and administrators are selected tends to ensure the conservation of existing policies . . . Potential recruits are identified by their capacity to fit smoothly into the existing structure. As they gradually pass successive tests of fraternal loyalty and solidarity, they become firmly identified as reliable members of "the club."

Elementary school counselors may join the ranks of oppressors of children through their own strict adherence to the rules, job security needs and/or to help children learn conforming behaviors so that they, too, can attain the rewards of the culture. An explanation of the counselor's entrapment is offered by E.J. Doley (1971), who states: "I suspect that our main reasons for perpetuating practices which we believe to be erroneous are based on the fact that we too were trained in programs which reinforced conservatism."

Deradicalization Through Groups

Even that which appears to be a radical move in counseling, from one-to-one counseling to group counseling, is subject to being used as a tool to restrict and recondition behavior. The goal to help children "adjust" remains the same. Through the facilitative skills of the counselor, groups of children are *gently* led into adjusting to a system that does not respond to their needs. It is a one-way adjustment process.

> Wherever [therapy] functions as an agent of the system, encouraging conformity, helping people "adjust" to the realities of exploitation, antiquated roles, and a dehumanizing ethic, therapy is an instrument of oppression (Agel, 1971).

Thus, group counseling serves as a potent vehicle for the counselor to use a knowledge of peer group pressure to help large numbers of children conform and maintain the status quo.

It is important to deradicalize people while they are in the developmental stages of childhood and incarcerated in the schools. If they escape the process, they may grow up to push toward real change in the established institutions of society.

An Example

Eric is an eight-year-old black male who is one of several targets for deradicalization in a third grade classroom. He is a member of a class where the teacher is academically ill-prepared for the job, appears to have little understanding of children, and is basically dull and boring in the few lessons she does present during the course of the day. It is a room where one little boy sprawled backwards across his desk and placidly said, "There's nothing to do in here." Only four little girls seemed to attend to the lesson and repeat back the "right" answers. Most of the children were daydreaming.

Eric and four of his friends refused to accept "business as usual" and were actively plotting ways to seek radical changes in the system. They silently tore "star" papers off the wall, sent notes to the teacher which made her cry, made attempts to organize the silent majority, hid the reading books, walked out of the class and wandered through the halls.

Their activities, usually led by Eric, had frequently brought them to the attention of the authorities. They had been beaten by the teacher, school counselor, principal and their respective parents. They had been placed in solitary confinement and tested by the school psychologist. One child had even been drugged with tranquilizers in an attempt to inactivate him. Physical punishment had been rendered ineffective because it served to stimulate the boys to fight back. A new approach needed to be used in order to curtail their maladaptive behavior since, under the law of compulsory education, they must attend school. Group counseling was introduced. Of course, it was the children who were designated as the ones who must be helped to "adjust" through counseling rather than the operators of the system adjusting to the children. The required behavioral change was unilateral.

Typically, the counselor, well-intentioned, untrained and inexperienced in running groups, has read the literature and research in the field on establishing groups with children (in Dinkmeyer, 1968; Mahler, 1969; Dimick and Huff, 1970; Ohlsen, 1970) and proceeds. The counselor selects not only the children who show deviant behavior but also model children (Bandura, 1965) who can demonstrate appropriate behaviors that are in support of the values of the school. The radical children are surrounded by warm, friendly children and an adult who seems trustworthy and concerned about them as human beings in a non-threatening atmosphere. The dynamics for change are powerful. The counselor does not punish socially inappropriate behaviors but reinforces the appropriate ones as they occur in the group. The children learn quickly to cherish their time spent with the group. The contrast between the freedom to explore feelings in a non-threatening counseling situation against the rigidity of the classroom is a welcomed relief. A reason to fight against the system no longer exists. The system has provided a place for the radically inclined child to "blow off steam" through verbalizing his feelings so that it becomes unnecessary to do so in the classroom. Munson (1970) asserts, "Boys especially are interested in group counseling, seeming to enjoy the opportunity to pool their experiences and to vent some of the pent-up feelings of aggression they have not been able to express in the classroom." *The catharsis becomes the end rather than a means for resolving issues of oppression.*

Furthermore, the privilege to attend group counseling meetings is used to reinforce acceptance of the status quo. Teachers who have felt intimidated by the radical child will refuse the child permission to attend the meetings until his behavior has improved. The counselor, attempting to maintain good relationships with the faculty, is hard put to override the teacher's decision. The child must conform in order to rejoin the counseling group.

The counseling group is not the place for the exploration of free flowing feelings and behavioral changes initiated by the individual that it is esoterically described to be. As Jackson (1970) insists, "In 'progressive' prisons, as in most classrooms, the inhabitants are allowed certain freedoms, but there are real limits. In both institutions, the inmates might be allowed to plan a Christmas party, but in neither place are they allowed to plan a 'break.' " The radical children cannot design their own process for change and educational growth unless it is approved by the counselor who is a representative of the status quo. The children look to their friend, the counselor, to continue facilitating them in their plans. The elementary school counselor is caught in a double bind. He wants to be true to the children and to the system at times when the two may be mutually exclusive. Usually, the counselor submits to the side of the institution.

> I believe it is impossible to assess properly the sad state of school counseling without taking into account the organizational bind in which the counselor is caught . . . His professional integrity [is] wholly in the hands of the school principal. For instance, if he should fail to secure a positive recommendation from his superior, it is unlikely that he could get another school appointment (Stubbins, p. 613).

Consequently, the children are forced to join the silent majority who accept "things as they are" through the gently, empathic, non-threatening environment nurtured in the group counseling setting. Eric and the other third grade boys mentioned previously will undoubtedly have to make the adjustments to an unjust environment. If they identify the root of the problem, which would require the removal of the teacher, they would be facilitated by the counselor to explore other alternatives. The "other alternatives" would inevitably also require the oppression of the group of children so that they, too, can fit smoothly into the mainstream of institutionalized education.

Research

Research by Myrick and Kelley (1971) demonstrates the systematic deradicalization process through group counseling with young children. The Ss included a seven-year-old black male who was repeating first grade. He was described as restless, well-liked, inattentive, athletic and involved in frequent fights. A six-year-old white male was included and described as creative, above average academically and hyperactive. The third member was a six-year-old black female who was cooperative, careless in math and an attention-seeker. Through systematic observation and anecdotal evidence during group counseling, positive outcomes were reported. It appears as though the "therapeutic loading" of the group facilitated the children in conforming to an uncompromising system. Other researchers (Mann, 1969; Hinds and Rochlke, 1970; Lodato, Sokoloff and Schwartz, 1964) have found group counseling useful in helping children to "adjust" their behaviors to the needs of the school. Perhaps it is the system that needs to be referred for group counseling. The assumption must be abandoned that the children are necessarily in need of change because they are vulnerable and the safest to change.

Conclusion

The elementary school counselor cannot afford to unwittingly allow group counseling to take the place of the paddle. The role of disciplinarian belongs to the policeman. It is not the job of the counselor to protect the institution from children who seek to change educational inadequacies.

According to Stubbins, "The best trained counselors are the ones most acutely aware of their impotence in their relations with administrators and of their entrapment in instructional values that they do not share. Increasingly, they feel that they must be heard in those places where significant decisions are being made that affect their capacity to counsel." We cannot afford to innocently perpetuate a sick society by deradicalizing children for conformity through the process of group counseling. The luxury of innocence can serve to threaten a democracy and promote fascism. Let the buyer beware.

References

Agel, J. *The Radical Therapist.* New York: Ballantine Books, 1971, xxi.

Bandura, A. Influence of Models' Reinforcement Contingencies on the Acquisition of Imitative Responses. *Journal of Personality and Social Psychology,* 1965, *1,* 589-595.

Dimick, K.M. and V.E. Huff. *Child Counseling.* New York: Wm. C. Brown Company, 1970.

Dinkmeyer, D.C. *Guidance and Counseling in the Elementary School.* New York: Holt, Rinehart and Winston, 1968.

Doley, E.J. Counselor Education as a Reinforcer of Conservatism. *Counselor Education and Supervision,* Summer 1971, *10,* 4, 357.

Gross, C., S. Wronski and J. Hanson. *School and Society.* Boston: D.C. Heath and Company, 1962, 21.

Hinds, W.C. and H.J. Rochlke. A Learning Theory Approach to Group Counseling with Elementary School Children. *Journal of Counseling Psychology,* 1970, *17,* 1, 49-55.

Hutchins, R.M. Education and the Eternal Verities. In C. Gross *et al.* (Eds.) *School and Society.* Boston: D.C. Heath and Company, 1962, 438.

Jackson, P.W. Quoted in C.E. Silberman. *Crisis in the Classroom.* New York: Vintage Books, 1970, 146.

Lodato, F., M. Sokoloff and L. Schwartz. Group Counseling as a Method of Modifying Attitude in Slow Learners. *School Counselor,* 1964, *12,* 27-29.

Mahler, C.A. *Group Counseling in the Schools.* Boston: Houghton Mifflin Company, 1969.

Mann, P. Modifying the Behavior of Negro Educable Mentally Retarded Boys Through Group Counseling Procedures. *Journal of Negro Education,* 1969, *38,* 2, 135-141.

Munson, H.L. *Elementary School Guidance.* Boston: Allyn and Bacon, 1970, 300.

Myrick, R. and F.D. Kelley. Group Counseling with Primary School-Age Children. *Journal of School Psychology,* 1971, *9,* 2, 137-143.

Ohlsen, M.M. *Group Counseling.* New York: Holt, Rinehart and Winston, 1970.

Silberman, C.E. *Crisis in the Classroom.* New York: Vintage Books, 1970, 152.

Stubbins, J. The Politics of Counseling. *The Personnel and Guidance Journal,* 1970, *48,* 8, 613 and 618.

Group Counseling with Children:
An Annotated Bibliography*

Selected articles and research are briefly outlined in order to assist those interested in working with children in groups to be aware of possible resources. Various theories and practices are represented in the sample.

*Compiled by Doris Jefferies with help of graduate assistant Kathy Schiaffino.

Dimick, K.M. and V.E. Huff. *Child Counseling.* New York: Wm. C. Brown Company Publishers, 1970, 145-163.

The authors present a general overview in Chapter 8, "Group Counseling with Children," of the philosophy and practices recommended by other writers in the field for working with youngsters. Five different leadership models (laissez-faire, authoritarian, democratic, group-centered, leaderless) are briefly introduced. This suggests that a leader may function effectively in any of the models at given points in time and should not feel bound to any particular theory.

Dinkmeyer, D.C. Developmental Group Counseling. *Elementary School Guidance and Counseling, 4,* April 1970, 267-272.

Developmental group counseling is viewed as an integral part of the educational process. The student is encouraged in a group of his peers to work through his feelings, attitudes, values and problems to help him deal more effectively with his developmental tasks. The emphasis in the group is not on pathology or misbehavior but on normal developmental concerns. Dinkmeyer briefly suggests rationale, goals for group counseling, outlines of developmental tasks and techniques toward the organization of developmental groups. The selection process is the key to building the most therapeutic group.

Dinkmeyer, D.C. (Ed.) Group Counseling. In *Guidance and Counseling in the Elementary School: Readings in Theory and Practice.* New York: Holt, Rinehart and Winston, 1968, 271-306.

Several authors contribute ideas on counseling children in groups. Dreikurs and Sonstegard (278-287) offer an Adlerian rationale. Children, as social beings, can work toward improving their relationships best through groups. The democratic group offers equality to all the children. Ohlsen (288-294) offers suggestions on adapting group counseling methods for children. An example of how sociodrama facilitates communication in the group highlights the principle. More "rules of the game" are presented by Combs, Cohn, Gibian and Sniffen (295-302) in applying techniques to the groups. The principles of group counseling with children are summarized by Boy, Isaksen and Pine (302-306).

Ginott, H.G. Group Therapy with Children. In G.M. Gazda (Ed.) *Basic Approaches to Group Psychotherapy and Group Counseling.* Springfield: Charles C. Thomas, 1968.

A psychoanalytic approach to working with a group of children in a clinical setting is presented. Selection of members, aims of group therapy, relationships, catharsis, insight, reality testing, sublimation, physical setting, therapeutic encounters and openings, permissiveness and limits, physical fighting, the therapist, the children and group activities are topics that receive much discussion. Knowledge of diagnostic labeling is necessary for following many of the illustrations, although for the most part many of the authors' thoughts cross all theoretical positions.

Hansen, J., F. Niland and L. Zani. Model Reinforcement in Group Counseling with Elementary School Children. *Personnel and Guidance Journal, 47,* April 1969, 743.

This study investigated the effectiveness of model reinforcement and reinforcement group counseling with elementary school children using sociometric status. It was hypothesized that models in group counseling serve to strengthen learning about social behavior. Children of low sociometric status (N = 54) were divided into three counseling groups. Group One included "sociometric stars" as models. Group Two contained all low sociometric students. Group Three, a control, met for an activity period. The findings indicated that low sociometric students in the model reinforcement groups made significantly more gain in social acceptance than the other two groups. A two month follow-up showed retention of the gains. Modeling is shown to be a potent reinforcer for behavioral changes in counseling groups with children.

Hinds, W.C. and H.J. Rochlke. A Learning Theory Approach to Group Counseling with Elementary School Children. *Journal of Counseling Psychology, 17,* January 1970, 49.

The study was designed for the purpose of investigating (1) the application of a learning approach to counseling with small groups of children and (2) the effects of such procedures on subsequent classroom behaviors. The sample (N = 40) included upper elementary school children referred by teachers for problem behaviors which interfered with classroom learning. Experimental and control groups were established. The study was divided into three phases: pre-counseling, counseling and post-counseling. Positive reinforcement of adaptive behaviors became the focus for shaping the experimental Ss behavior. The children did "adapt" and there was significant transfer to the classroom.

Jensen, G. Small Group Counseling for Under-Achieving Primary School Children. In H.I. Driver (Ed.) *Counseling and Learning Through Small-Group Discussion.* Madison: Monona Publications, 1958, 286-290.

Underachievers are defined as those who have the intelligence to progress satisfactorily in school but are lagging behind. A special project was developed to cope with the problem. The group counseling project had two purposes: (1) to discover the classroom and family social relationships that might be blocking achievement and (2) to enable students to acquire insight and understanding of such relationships so that they could determine areas to be changed and re-direct their energies. The children included in the group and the methodology are described in detail. The results showed that eight out of the ten showed improvement. The project represents an early effort to promote and attempt to demonstrate the efficacy of group counseling with children.

Mahler, C.A. *Group Counseling in the Schools.* Boston: Houghton-Mifflin Company, 1969.

The elementary school counselor can use this book as a basic guide offering theory based on Erik Erikson's developmental identity-seeking paradigm and Adlerian psychology. Practical steps for forming groups, illustrations of the process, and leadership skills are thoroughly discussed. The group counseling process is divided into four stages of development, which include (1) the involvement stage, (2) the transition stage, (3) the working stage and (4) the ending stage. Although most of the examples are of adolescent groups, they are easily applicable to children. The basic principles cross all school age groups.

Mayer, G.R., T.M. Rohen and A.D. Whitley. Group Counseling with Children: A Cognitive-Behavioral Approach. *Journal of Counseling Psychology, 16,* 1969, 142-149.

Social learning theory and dissonance theory are coupled to formulate an approach for counseling children in groups. The approach suggests that the probability of an attitudinal and/or behavioral change occurring is enhanced when a child actually observes a model or models doing something that is contrary to the child's opinion or previous behavior. Counselors are encouraged to promote dissonant-enhancing situations in the group to provide opportunities for the children to observe contradictory items of information. Conditions conducive to dissonance that produce behavioral changes and a large quantity of research are cited in support of the approach.

Muro, J.J. *The Counselor's Work in the Elementary School.* Scranton: International Textbook Company, 1970, 145-163.

Group counseling is defined as "A group procedure where the emphasis is on personal exploration rather than on the provision and discussion of guidance material." It is cautioned that group counseling is not simply applying individual counseling to children assembled in a group; nor should it be employed simply because it is economical. The selection process for group membership, the use of play media, and considerations toward group counseling for parents and teachers are offered. An illustration from an actual group counseling session with sixth graders demonstrates the process.

Nelson, R. and M. Callas. Groups and Accountability. *Elementary School Guidance and Counseling, 4,* May 1970, 291-294.

Criticisms related to group counseling in school settings are presented with a restatement of the rationale for group procedures. The criticisms are based on current sensitivity groups. It is suggested that brainwashing may occur; brainpicking, where children might reveal confidential material to the group; and loss of uniqueness on the part of the individual child. However, theoretically, counseling groups do afford opportunities for socializing experiences among peers in a somewhat controlled and democratic environment.

Ohlsen, M.M. *Group Counseling.* New York: Holt, Rinehart and Winston, 1970, 224-239.

Highly practical suggestions are made to the counselor interested in establishing counseling groups with children. Explanation of the purposes of groups to the teachers and children to encourage cooperation is essential prior to the formulation of groups. Ohlsen endorses the use of play materials in group work to facilitate verbalizing in children. He stresses that the children profit most from group counseling when they are committed to talk about something rather than to ramble on about a multitude of topics. The younger children require more structure generally than the older children. Specific techniques are offered to the counselor for establishing a facilitative relationship with small groups of children.

Sonstegard, M.A. Mechanisms and Practical Techniques in Group Counseling in the Elementary School. In J. Muro and S. Freeman (Eds.) *Readings in Group Counseling.* Scranton: International Textbook Co., 1968.

A rationale for counseling children in groups is presented par excellence in this chapter.

The impact of a democratic philosophy and Adlerian psychology provide the foundation for the techniques and cases used for illustration. Group counseling is seen as a product of the democratic evolution. Children have a better chance to achieve equal status in a democratic group that contains their peers than to have to yield to adult control. However, Sonstegard stresses that children's groups must have structure to prevent the group from becoming "confused and chaotic." He presents the case of Jeff as an individual in a group to clarify the integration of philosophy and techniques.

Stormer, G. and J.H. Kirby. Adlerian Group Counseling in the Elementary School: Report of a Program. *Journal of Individual Psychology, 25,* 2, 1969, 155-163.

The purpose of the paper is to describe an elementary school group counseling program based on Adlerian psychology. The counselor's function in the group includes: (a) build relationships based on mutual trust, (b) gather information, (c) generate hypotheses concerning the purpose of student behavior, (d) test the hypotheses, (e) help students understand the motives and purposes of their behaviors, (f) make recommendations for more desirable behavior. It was observed that very young children were less able or willing to talk and had shorter attention spans. Role-playing, stories of self-understanding and unstructured play helped to maintain their interest. Teachers and parents also participated in the behavior change program.

Tosi, D., C. Swanson and P. McLean. Group Counseling with Nonverbalizing Elementary School Children. *Elementary School Guidance and Counseling, 4,* March 1970, 260-266.

The potency of social reinforcers (praise, smiles) to increase verbal and active participatory behaviors was demonstrated in the study. The nonverbalizing children randomly selected for group counseling met once a week for four weeks. A topic from a sixth grade series dealing with emotional growth was used to generate verbal exchanges in the group counseling condition. Excerpts of counseling sessions demonstrate the use of "good," "uh uhm" and "tell me more" to reinforce students' verbal responses. The findings of the study strongly suggest, though not statistically significant, that the experimental treatment contributed to the observed changes in unsolicited verbal responses. The researchers conclude, "The approach allows more economical use of the counselor's time, at least in terms of ease of adoption and apparent success in a relatively short period of time."

Yunker, J. Essential Organizational Components of Group Counseling in the Primary Grades. *Elementary School Guidance and Counseling, 4,* March 1970, 173.

Nine factors should be considered before group counseling should be introduced in the school. They are: (1) mutuality of problems, (2) compatibility of members, (3) group size, (4) age range, (5) sex composition, (6) length of group sessions, (7) duration of the group as a unit, (8) physical settings for group meetings and (9) qualifications of the group leader. It is suggested that considerations of these factors assist the counselor's development of organizational leadership abilities for younger children in counseling groups.

10.
Analysis of Research in Group Procedures

G.M. Gazda and
Roger W. Peters

This analysis is divided into two basic parts. In the first part the *group counseling research* since 1938 will be described on the basis of the following nine criteria: (1) purpose (nature of the study), (2) type of group, (3) group size, (4) control (design), (5) treatment and process, (6) instruments (i.e., evaluation devices), (7) test statistics employed, (8) experimental design and (9) outcomes. Included in this description or analysis will be 198 studies. This reporting updates two earlier reports (Gazda, 1971; Gazda and Larsen, 1968) and makes the review current as of spring, 1972. Although the review is not exhaustive because of limitations in locating some studies, it was intended to be exhaustive of *group counseling research* rather than just representative, and, as such, includes dissertation studies as well as studies reported in a great variety of professional journals. Only those studies which used group or multiple counseling in the titles or otherwise in the research report were analyzed.

The second part includes an analysis and critique of the group counseling research with recommendations for future research and a brief summary of and recommendations for the group psycho-therapy and human relations (laboratory) training research, which permits a comparison of the status of research in group counseling, group therapy and human relations (laboratory) training. The counseling segment specifies a series of general recommendations for future group research.

Nature of the Study

Approximately 62 percent of the studies were outcome; 20 percent were comparison; 13 percent were process; 5 percent were miscellaneous, such as a combination of process and outcome. Based on the studies analyzed up to 1970 (Gazda, 1971), there was a slight decrease (4 percent) in the number of outcome studies and in the number of process studies (2 percent). The increase was in the number of miscellaneous studies.

Type of Group

Three-fourths of the studies surveyed were reports of treatment groups obtained from educational settings. The largest percentage of the Ss were from high school, junior high school and kindergarten and elementary school, 23 percent, 10 percent and 10 percent respectively. These figures represent a slight increase in the kindergarten and elementary school age group since the 1967-70 period (Gazda, 1971).

The college and university Ss totaled 33 percent—27 percent undergraduate and 6 percent graduate students. These percentages are consistent with those compiled between 1938-70 (Gazda, 1971).

The remaining studies consisted of reports on group counseling with adults (5 percent), parents (4 percent), mental patients (3 percent), inmates (3 percent), disadvantaged (3 percent) and a miscellaneous category of 6 percent.

Group Size

Group size refers to the Ns reported in each study, not the size of the counseling groups. The range included a process study with an N of three to an outcome study with 266 experimental Ss; 936 was the largest total sample (experimentals and controls). The average experimental or treatment group was 38, which represented an increase of 19 over the 1938-70 report (Gazda, 1971). The treatment sample size, therefore, has increased significantly over the 1970-72 period.

Controls

Control groups were used in 77 percent of the outcome studies analyzed. This represents a slight decrease of 3 percent from 1970 (Gazda, 1971), but is not of sufficient magnitude to cause concern. Nevertheless, approximately 30 percent of the research (including process studies where controls were not always essential) does not report controls and therefore must be viewed as descriptive/process.

Treatment

The "typical" treatment can be described as consisting of 13 sessions of one hour each week for a period of 12 weeks. The decrease of three in the number of sessions and four in the number of weeks over which the treatment was conducted since the 1970 report (Gazda, 1971) appears to be the result of the greater use of marathons and behavior modification approaches. This trend bears watching, especially in regard to the effectiveness of these rather recent innovations to group counseling.

Instruments

By "instruments" we are referring to the measures employed for evaluating process and outcome variables. Since almost all of the studies analyzed reported the use of multiple instruments, we have reported the frequency of use rather than the percentage.

The relative standings of the instruments remained about the same as for the period 1938-70 (Gazda, 1971); grade-point-average (GPA) decreased about 4 percent but was still used 41 times. Ratings by judges, supervisors, teachers, etc., decreased about 6 percent, but was still used 37 times. Self-report techniques, other than those used on standardized tests, remained at approximately the same proportion of the total (23 times) as did the use of researcher-devised questionnaires, at 24. The use of achievement and ability tests on 16 occasions signals a significant increase from the 1938-70 figures where they were negligible. Interviews were down slightly in usage. They were used 13 times.

The remaining instruments consisted of Bills IAV (10), Q sorts (9), TAT (9), the Tennessee Self Concept Test (8), Semantic Differential (4) and the Personality Orientation Inventory (4). A sample of some other instruments used included the Hill Interaction Matrix, sociometric ratings (seemingly decreasing in popularity), Rokeach Dogmatism Scale, videotape ratings, measures of study habits, sentence completion and the California Personality Inventory. The relatively significant increase in the use of the Tennessee Self Concept test signifies about the only major shift over the 1938-70 data. The Bills IAV decreased in use about 50 percent over the same period.

The majority of process studies reported the use of some form of interaction analysis (based on researcher-devised instruments and the Hill Interaction Matrix), leadership scales, peer ratings, role-taking, nonverbal classifications and similar instruments.

Test Statistics

As in the reporting of the instruments, we found multiple test statistics used. Thus, rather than report the results only in percentages, which would be slightly misleading, we shall report the total number of times a given test statistic was employed. Over-all there were approximately 35 different test statistics employed.

The t-test was used 61 times and the analysis of variance was used 60 times. These figures indicate a very significant shift in the increasing popularity of analysis of variance and the decreasing popularity of the t-test in the two-year period from 1970-72 (Gazda, 1971). Some form of correlation was used 28 times or approximately 14 percent of the total. Some form of descriptive statistics was used 22 times but decreased significantly in the two-year period from about 15 percent of the total to 10 percent. Chi square (used 22 times) also showed a similar decrease during the same two-year period. An analysis of covariance was used 18 times and remained in the same relative position for the two-year period. The use of factor analysis three times suggests a slight trend toward the employment of this statistical treatment procedure.

Experimental Designs

The research designs employed for categorization of the group counseling research described herein were those of Campbell and Stanley (1963). Space does not allow us to describe these designs; therefore we shall simply report the frequency of the use. The various designs are classified under three major categories: pre-experimental designs, true experimental designs and quasi-experimental and other designs, including process.

Discussion—Experimental Designs

Approximately 73 percent of the *outcome* studies were classified as True Experimental Designs, which indicates that at least some form of control group was utilized. About 63 percent of the *total* studies reported were in the category of True Experimental Designs. The process studies and unclassifiable categories make up the bulk of the additional designs, representing 14 and 9 percent, respectively.

Two significant findings cannot be obtained from Table 1. But a comparison of the data from 1938-70 (Gazda, 1971) with that from

Table 1

Experimental Designs

	True-Experimental Designs				Quasi-Experimental Designs		
	Pretest-Posttest Control Group Design	Solomon Four-Group Design	Posttest-Only Control Group Design	Equivalent Materials Design	Non-Equivalent Control Group Design	Separate Sample Pretest-Posttest (No Control) Design	Unclassifiable
N = 119	119	0	5	1	6	3	18

	Pre-Experimental Designs				Other Designs		
	One-Shot Case Study	One-Group Pretest-Posttest Design	Static Group Comparison	Descriptive One Group Pretest Posttest Study	Descriptive Simple Survey	Process	
N = 5	5	11	2	3	8	27	

Total N = 198

1970-72 revealed that outcome studies were classified, as to design, approximately the same as for the period 1938-70. At the same time there was a significant increase in the number of process studies from 15 to 27 or an increase from about 10 percent of the total to 14 percent. But more significant is the rate of increase. There were only 15 studies of process from 1938-70 and there were 12 additional studies from 1970-72.

Criteria and Outcomes

The studies analyzed from 1938-70 (Gazda, 1971) revealed that about one-half were able to show significant gains in the predicted direction. This fact is, however, misleading since most of these studies involved the use of multiple measures and in many instances only one of several indices showed significant change. Often these indices were self-reports of self-concept improvement and the like. On the more positive side, those studies evaluating GPA increases and/or other achievement increases showed about 50 percent success rates.

A very noticeable difference between the 1938-70 period and the 1970-72 period is the greater proportion of studies which showed significant changes in the predicted direction on the variables evaluated. Almost 70 percent of the studies in this two-year period versus 50 percent prior to 1970 showed significant results. This condition may indicate that group counselors are doing a more effective job of counseling, that the journal editors are accepting fewer studies that do not report significant results, or a number of other possible explanations. The 1970-72 breakdown for the various types of studies showed 19 of 24 outcome studies, 8 of 11 process studies and 9 of 10 comparison studies reporting significant results. The remainder were unclassifiable.

Summary: Group Counseling, Group Psychotherapy and Human Relations (Laboratory) Training

Table 2 includes a summary of group counseling, group psychotherapy and human relations (laboratory) training groups. The group counseling summary is based primarily on the analysis of the 198 studies from the 1938-72 period, with some recommendations from others who have also addressed themselves to this topic.

The group psychotherapy summary and recommendations represent the work of Bednar and Lawlis (1971); whereas, human relations training research summarizes the review by Gibb (1971).

A special type of human relations training, *a la* R.R. Carkhuff, is not included here. However, his research is extensive and he and his associates are making a great impact on the helping professions. See the "Suggested Readings" for references to some of his major works.

Recommendations

The following recommendations are based on the analysis of the three content areas summarized in Table 2. The recommendations are derived from mutual agreement in each of the content areas.

1. There is a need for greater consistency across studies in terms of operational definitions of terms and an attempt to integrate the results into a unifying body of knowledge.

2. Attempts should be made to replicate studies which have made important contributions.

3. Greater usage of videotape recorders and similar equipment will aid in process studies of individuals within the framework of a group.

4. There is a need to develop and state a rationale which explains why a given treatment should produce the predicted changes.

5. The inclusion of a wider range of clients for group treatment will increase generalizability of results.

6. Greater attempts should be made to investigate the efficacy of precounseling or pretherapy training.

7. The composition of groups for greatest effectiveness should be studied intensively.

8. Experimental designs should incorporate controls for the Hawthorne effect.

9. Experimental treatment should be increased in duration, so that the likelihood of significant results is increased.

10. There is a need to assess objectively the leader's level of competency to provide evidence of the effectiveness of the model which he employs and also to permit the use of designs which simultaneously use two or more leaders.

(Continued Following Table 2, on Page 140.)

Table 2

Summary and Recommendations for Research in Group Counseling,
Group Psychotherapy and Human Relations (Laboratory) Training

Group Counseling
Nature of the Study/Purpose

Less than 5 percent were involved in the simultaneous study of process and outcome variables. Yet it is becoming increasingly important to relate group process variables to outcome measures and we recommend this type of group counseling research.

The vast majority of the studies represent attempts to use group counseling in a remedial or rehabilitative way. It may prove more effective if used preventatively and/or with a growth-producing goal (Gazda, 1971).

Type of Group

The slight increase in the number of research studies of group counseling in the early school grades suggests that it is likely to be used in a more preventative and less remedial fashion. We encourage the trend.

The fact that three-fourths of all the research studies reviewed originated in educational settings suggests that the leaders are likely to be educators. Their

Group Psychotherapy*
Nature of the Study/Purpose

Only a few of the studies investigated differential treatment effects accompanying variations in group therapy procedures. Essentially, the studies included investigations that identified (1) the treatment effects of group therapy, (2) the kind of behavior changes that are attributable to group therapy, (3) the types of clients and problems that are amenable to treatment by group therapy, (4) personality traits of therapists who have a positive influence on group procedures, (5) antecedent conditions to client improvement and (6) group interaction patterns that appear to benefit those involved.

Type of Group

The data may be summarized as follows: (1) group therapy produces good results when it is used to supplement other treatment methods; (2) group ther-

*This summary is based on a critical review by Bednar and Lawlis (1971).

Human Relations Training*
Nature of the Study/Purpose

"When considered from the viewpoint of the frequent mention in the general psychological literature of the lack of research on human relations training, the quantity and quality of available research is surprisingly high. When compared with the standards of research in the psychological laboratory and with the desirability of definitive statements about the effects of training, the methodological impurities of the studies loom large, and the results are disappointingly equivocal (Gibb, p. 842)."

Too much of the research has a "bits and pieces" quality, seems opportunistically empirical and lacks an integrating or programmatic directionality. Innovation and change in training methodology is largely clinical and intuitive in genesis. New methods go untested and research has little influence upon the evolution of methods and theories of training.

*This summary is based on 106 studies reviewed by J.R. Gibb (1971).

Group Counseling (cont'd)

training, the setting and the population all limit the type of group counseling and the group goals. We recommend that educators do more group counseling in the community apart from the educational or school setting and thus vary the population and group goals.

The majority of groups are described as being composed homogeneously. There is increasing evidence (Gazda, 1971) that groups should be balanced so that there is the opportunity for each member to learn more healthy behavior from at least one other group member in addition to the counselor.

We concur with Anderson (1969) that "Group counseling research reflects little interest in client selection or client preparation as major independent variables.... Client selection, complex as it is, must be studied in relation to both process and outcome variables.... Research is needed which will help to predict how a given client will respond under a given set of conditions and with a particular combination of group members, including the leader [p. 212]."

Group Size
The average size of the treatment sample increased from 29 to 38 in the

Group Psychotherapy (cont'd)

apy seems to have less effectiveness with psychotic clients; conversely, it seems to have more effectiveness with nonpsychotic clients; and (3) individual therapy is more effective with grossly psychotic clients and less effective with nonpsychotic clients.

More severe thought disorders and marked interpersonal withdrawal do not appear to be influenced readily by group therapy. Group therapy, however, contributes to improved self-adjustment.

Current data, in contrast to the group dynamic literature, suggest that leaderless groups with psychiatric clients are probably more potentially dangerous than professionally led groups. Group therapists play an important role in keeping the group focused on its therapeutic tasks and minimizing the accompanying anxiety. Therapists should be reluctant to sponsor leaderless groups with psychiatric clients, although there are probably conditions under which periodic absences can be beneficial.

The most basic factor for inclusion in group therapy seems to be a nonpsychotic disorder.

The bulk of the literature suggests

Human Relations Training (cont'd)

Type of Group
Creative Growth Groups: These activities are most controversial and have scant empirical findings reported.

Marathon Groups: Although the method has generated modifications in many human relations training programs and some research is in progress, there is as yet little evaluation research available.

Emergent Groups: There is evidence that training in groups without leaders produces changes in the behavior of group members.

Authenticity Groups: There is little available published research on training in these groups.

Sensitivity Training Groups: Eighty-nine out of 106 studies reviewed were performed on sensitivity training groups.

Programmed Groups: There is no clear evidence as yet to indicate differential effects of programmed and nonprogrammed groups.

Microexperience Groups: There is as yet no research evaluating outcomes.

Inquiry Groups: It is difficult to

Group Counseling (cont'd)

1970-72 period. This represents a significant positive trend which should allow for the use of more powerful research statistics and also yield more valid and reliable results.

Controls

Only 77 percent of the outcome studies used some type of control group and of these only a very small number included the use of placebo or Hawthorne effect control measures. We recommend that all outcome studies employ some form of control procedure and that they also control for the Hawthorne effect.

Treatment

The typical treatment of one hour per week for approximately 12 to 13 weeks is much too short to expect significant behavioral changes from group counseling.

More research using marathon-type approaches, contrasted to the more traditional approaches, spread out over several weeks, is recommended.

The majority of studies do not define carefully the procedures used (process), beyond mentioning the theoretical position of the counselor, nor is there any objective data reported regarding the level of functioning of the counselor. Since

Group Psychotherapy (cont'd)

that the brighter, more capable nonpsychotic clients tend to be more responsive to group therapy than are other types of clients.

There is research that indicates that about one-third of the clients beginning group therapy drop out, unimproved, within the first 12 meetings.

Research addressing the problems of group composition covers content areas of: group homogeneity and heterogeneity, premorbid history, current adjustment, emotional and intellectual resources and group compatibility.

Goldstein, Heller and Sechrest (1966) present data which suggest that there are identifiable behavioral and emotional prerequisites for effective involvement in group therapy, ranging on a dimension of severity of disturbance, intellectual and emotional resources and group compatibility.

Clinicians should capitalize on behavioral assets by placing clients in groups so that sufficient group resources are available to facilitate (1) warm, responsive interactions between some group members, (2) sufficient compatibility to increase personal attractions, (3) suffi-

Human Relations Training (cont'd)

determine from the reports in the literature what was actually done in the training sessions.

Embedded Groups: Evidence on the effectiveness of these programs in changing organizational practices is lacking.

Research results suggest that composing the training group of members of the same administrative unit or work team is effective. It is believed by some to be more effective than heterogeneously composed training groups.

Participants with more self-disclosing trainers more often entered into relationships with other group members. Members of groups that had trainers who were less self-disclosing tended to enter into relationship with the trainer.

Size

(No analysis given)

Control

(No analysis given)

Treatment and Process

Total time in group, ranges from a minimum of 12 hours to a maximum of 150 hours. There is a consensus among experienced trainers that continuous

Group Counseling (cont'd)

there is increasing evidence of the importance of the counselor's level of functioning on the growth of the counselees (Carkhuff, 1969a, b; Carkhuff and Berenson, 1967; Truax and Carkhuff, 1967) some objective index of this should be given so that one can determine to what extent the results were influenced by the counselor or the technique or methods that he used (see also Criteria and Outcome).

Instruments

The choice of instruments used for evaluating change vary considerably from the rather well-defined criterion of grade point average (GPA) to the somewhat ill-defined criteria obtained from self-reports and questionnaires. We recommend the use of criterion variables that can be defined in behavioral terms for each counselee.

The frequent use of GPAs and achievement test criteria reflect the inconsistency between the high expectations for change and the limited input in terms of type and duration of treatment. More realistic goals should be set, and instruments designed to measure the specific goals of the treatment should be developed. Thoresen (1969) recommends, "focusing more attention on specific

Group Psychotherapy (cont'd)

client courage to discuss the unpleasant and (4) sufficiently adequate adjustment to provide models for more effective ways of coping with stress.

To provide solutions for the problem of achieving desired group therapy activity, many researchers select a group of individuals to be involved in group therapy and submit them to various levels of pretherapy treatment conditions. All data suggest that the initial therapeutic sessions are of prime importance.

Pretherapy training is a relatively new concept. Its therapeutic potency is yet to be clearly established. Yet data suggest that clients prepared systematically for group therapy engage themselves in discussion of intermember relationships in the group much more quickly than did clients not so prepared.

Data indicate that pretherapy training that clarifies client role expectations and provides models of desirable therapeutic behavior has a positive effect on both the therapeutic process and the eventual therapeutic improvement.

Size

(No analysis given)

Human Relations Training (cont'd)

time, within indeterminable limits, is more powerful than time spent in short sessions spread out over long periods of time. It is clear that when the studies are arrayed simply in terms of amount of time in group, that greater differences are obtained from groups of longer duration than from short-term groups.

Several studies suggest that short-term experiences may not bring changes to a critical point. When changes become integrated into new behavioral systems that are congruent with new attitudinal substrata in the person, the changes may actually increase over time.

Most human relations training, as now practiced, is too short in duration to be of optimal enduring effect. How long training should be, and what temporal patterns of "booster shots" are optimal for long-range effects, are critical questions for future investigations.

Instruments

Measurement is a persistent problem. The more reliable measures are often of trivial outcomes. Reliable measures are often not validated against acceptable indices of mental health, personal growth or personal effectiveness in a natural setting.

Group Counseling (cont'd)

problem-relevant changes in the behaviors of individual subjects rather than on less related mean score changes on psychometric devices [p. 278]."

The frequent use of multiple measures for evaluating outcome criteria suggest a "shot gun" approach to measuring change rather than a design which focuses on well-defined criterion variables.

Test Statistics

The progressive and increasing use of multivariate analyses reflects the increasing sophistication of the group counseling researcher in line with the recommendation of the "Cohn Report" (1967).

New and more sophisticated statistical methods must be developed for use in process and process-outcome studies. Bednar and Lawlis (1971) suggest that matrix algebra and non-linear mathematics be "adopted to better characterize group process."

Experimental Design

The significant recent trend of the increased number of process studies should provide needed information to allow for the eventual combining of process-outcome research designs.

Group Psychotherapy (cont'd)

Control
(No analysis given)

Treatment and Process

Mean improvement among treated subjects is masked because of a cancellation effect between the clients who have improved and others who have deteriorated. The significant difference in variabilities between treatment and control groups has been used as a basis for inferring the potential value and harm of therapeutic treatments.

Ss involved in group therapy programs tended to show more change and variability in interpersonal behavior while Ss receiving individual therapy tended to show more change and variability in perceptual spheres.

Most of the investigations have studied group therapy in the generic form and left untouched the more complex problems of specific treatment factors and antecedent conditions contributing to client improvement or deterioration.

It is hoped that research will advance to the stage of testing group member processes instead of treating the group as a unit. Group therapy may offer

Human Relations Training (cont'd)

Researchers report an increasing resistance to multiple measurements in the training setting.

Test Statistics
(No analysis given)

Experimental Design

Barriers to training research have to do with design problems. Training is almost always done under field conditions in which the researcher is an unwelcome intruder. In most cases the researcher knowingly settles for the best of poor design alternatives or outcome measures that were permitted by such factors as expense, training conditions, participant resistance and imprecise instruments.

Researchers have been unable to find or construct adequate "control" or "comparison" groups. Matching groups that are equally "ready," and then delay the training of one set of groups so that they will serve as controls for the training groups, brings into play some indeterminable effects of the delay.

Major weakness of current training-research designs is their lack of "representativeness." Researchers often take great care in getting a random sample of

Group Counseling (cont'd)

The fact that almost three-fourths of the *outcome studies* were classified as "True Experimental Designs" is somewhat encouraging. This means that there was some type of statistical measure or control group employed. Nevertheless, if we study all of the group counseling literature, we would find what Bednar and Lawlis (1971) found for group therapy, that most is not experimental but rather descriptive of the therapist's/counselor's experience or recommendations.

Criteria and Outcomes

The effectiveness of group counseling has not yet been demonstrated unequivocally; nevertheless, there seems to be a sudden surge of studies, at least in the last two years, reporting greater statistically significant findings in the predicted direction.

Most researchers still do not indicate the rationale for the predicted outcomes with specific clientele, nor do they study the differential effects of treatment procedures on different counselees (see also Anderson, 1969). We recommend that future studies include these elements.

Few studies are replications and few apply identical treatment procedures in different settings with different clientele

Group Psychotherapy (cont'd)

more degrees of freedom for a person to find the therapeutic personality than does individual therapy.

Instruments

The data on adjustment suggest that group therapy can contribute to improving observable behavior patterns, at least in a hospital setting.

Studies can be criticized for psychological testing with such instruments as the MMPI or Rorschach during actual treatment. As a result of this testing, outcome effects could be attributed to the psychological testing or attention effect instead of to the therapeutic treatment.

Many studies have used observation techniques similar to Bales' Interaction Categories or Hill's Interaction Matrix as a quantitative method for describing overt behavior. Preformed behavioral rating systems run the risk of being invalid because the behavioral categories may be inappropriate.

Some researchers have used subjective criteria to measure both process variables and therapeutic outcome. Most of these measures included the individual's own assessment of his personal

Human Relations Training (cont'd)

only one trainer or one organization, thus limiting the generalizations of their results.

Criteria and Outcomes

Research outcomes indicate that changes do occur in sensitivity, feeling management, directionality of motivations, attitudes toward self, attitudes toward others and interdependence. Because these effects are closely related to hoped-for therapeutic outcome, the evidence is strong that intensive group training experiences have therapeutic effects.

The evidence indicates that the following conditions for learning occur with group growth, feedback, behavior visibility, member-member interaction, feeling expression and perceptual diversity.

Group Counseling (cont'd)

as recommended by Anderson (1969), nor do many use multivariate approaches comparing a variety of treatment procedures with similar counselees in similar settings as recommended by Cohn (1967).

A very limited number of studies include short-term or long-term follow up evaluations. More research is needed to compare immediate and long-term group counseling effects (see also Anderson, 1969).

Group Psychotherapy (cont'd)

happiness, his observations of his behavior in the group and the perceived growth resulting from group therapy. It is difficult to accept that a client's feelings of satisfaction with himself or with group therapy can be considered either a major goal of the procedure or evidence of its success.

No study was reviewed in which different stages of group therapy were related to physiological evidence, such as heart rate or galvanic skin response.

Test Statistics

With the availability of computers, more application of multivariate statistical analyses can be utilized. Matrix algebra and nonlinear mathematics may also be adopted to better characterize group processes.

Experimental Design

Most of the studies employed the pre-posttest method in conjunction with no-therapy control groups.

The major criticism of designs using repeated measures is the effect on the instruments and/or reliability deterioration. Even with the most reliable instruments the test-retest reliabilities are about

(continued in third column)

.90. With as many as four administrations these reliabilities would be reduced to .73.

Criteria and Outcomes

Appropriate evaluation procedures should be initiated to provide the therapist with feedback about his general effectiveness, the type of client with whom he is most and least successful and the composition of groups with whom he is most and least successful.

Follow-up treatment contacts on an increasing intermittent schedule would probably help arrest the rate of relapse after treatment is terminated.

(Continued From Page 132.)

11. Follow-up measurements of the treatment groups should be made at varying intervals after the termination of the treatment to provide evidence of the delayed and/or lasting effects of treatment.

12. Attempts should be made to incorporate behavioral outcomes as indices of change.

13. More sophisticated statistical analyses should be employed, such as: (a) multivariate analysis (Cohn, 1967), (b) nonlinear mathematics and matrix algebra, which permits analysis of group members (Bednar and Lawlis, 1971) and (c) the Time-Series Design (Campbell and Stanley, 1963) which allows the S to be his own control and avoids matching errors at the risk of lowered instrument reliabilities (Bednar and Lawlis, 1971).

In a few areas there was apparent disagreement in the recommendations. First, in group therapy as contrasted to human relations training groups, Bednar and Lawlis (1971) indicated that leaderless groups with psychiatric patients are probably more potentially dangerous than professionally led groups. Second, human relations trainers are reluctant to use multiple measures (Gibb, 1971). And third, human relations trainers prefer to work with relatively homogeneously composed administrative units of work teams (Gibb, 1971), as contrasted to general preference for heterogeneously composed psychotherapy and counseling groups (Peters, 1972).

References

Anderson, A.R. Group Counseling. *Review of Educational Research*, 1969, *39*, 2, 209-226.

Bednar, R.L. and G.F. Lawlis. Empirical Research in Group Psychotherapy. In A. Bergin and S. Garfield (Eds.) *Handbook of Psychotherapy and Behavior Change: An Empirical Analysis.* New York: Wiley, 1971, 812-839.

Campbell, D.T. and J.C. Stanley. Experimental and Quasi-Experimental Designs for Research. In N.L. Gage (Ed.) *Handbook of Research in Teaching.* Chicago: Rand McNally, 1963, 171-246.

Carkhuff, R.R. *Helping and Human Relations: A Primer for Lay and Professional Helpers.* Vol. 1. *Selection and Training.* New York: Holt, Rinehart and Winston, 1969a.

Carkhuff, R.R. *Helping and Human Relations: A Primer for Lay and Professional Helpers.* Vol. 2. *Practice and Research.* New York: Holt, Rinehart and Winston, 1969b.

Carkhuff, R.R. and B.G. Berenson. *Beyond Counseling and Therapy.* New York: Holt, Rinehart and Winston, 1967.

Cohn, B. (Ed.) *Guidelines for Future Research on Group Counseling in the Public School Setting.* Washington, D.C.: American Personnel and Guidance Association, 1967.

Gazda, G.M. *Group Counseling: A Developmental Approach.* Boston: Allyn and Bacon, 1971.

Gazda, G.M. and M.J. Larsen. A Comprehensive Appraisal of Group and Multiple Counseling Research. *Journal of Research and Development in Education,* 1968, *1*, 2, 57-132.

Gibb, J.R. The Effects of Human Relations Training. In A. Bergin and S. Garfield (Eds.) *Handbook of Psychotherapy and Behavior Change: An Empirical Analysis.* New York: Wiley, 1971, 839-863.

Goldstein, A.P., K. Heller and L.B. Sechrest. *Psychotherapy and Psychology of Behavior Change.* New York: Wiley, 1966.

Peters, R.W. The Facilitation of Change in Group Counseling by Group Composition. Unpublished doctoral dissertation, University of Georgia, 1972.

Thoresen, C.E. Relevance and Research in Counseling. *Review of Educational Research,* 1969, *39*, 2, 263-281.

Truax, C.B. and R.R. Carkhuff. *Toward Effective Counseling and Psychotherapy: Training and Practice.* Chicago: Aldine, 1967.

Suggested Readings

Anderson, A.R. Group Counseling. *Review of Educational Research*, 1969, *39*, 2, 209-226.

Bednar, R.L. and G.F. Lawlis. Empirical Research in Group Psychotherapy. In A. Bergin and S. Garfield (Eds.) *Handbook of Psychotherapy and Behavior Change: An Empirical Analysis.* New York, Wiley, 1971, 812-838.

Campbell, J. and M.D. Dunnette. Effectiveness of T Group Experiences in Managerial Training and Development. *Psychological Bulletin,* 1968, *79*, 73-104.

Carkhuff, R.R. *Helping and Human Relations: A Primer for Lay and Professional Helpers.* Vol. 1. *Selection and Training.* New York: Holt, Rinehart and Winston, 1969a.

Carkhuff, R.R. *Helping and Human Relations: A Primer for Lay and Professional Helpers.* Vol. 2. *Practice and Research.* New York: Holt, Rinehart and Winston, 1969b.

Carkhuff, R.R. *The Development of Human Resources: Education, Psychology and Social Action.* New York: Holt, Rinehart and Winston, 1971.

Carkhuff, R.R. and B.G. Berenson. *Beyond Counseling and Therapy.* New York: Holt, Rinehart and Winston, 1967.

Cohn, B. (Ed.) *Guidelines for Future Research on Group Counseling in the Public School Setting.* Washington, D.C.: American Personnel and Guidance Association, 1967.

Gazda, G.M. *Group Counseling: A Developmental Approach.* Boston: Allyn and Bacon, 1971.

Gazda, G.M. and M.J. Larsen. A Comprehensive Appraisal of Group and Multiple Counseling Research. *Journal of Research and Development in Education,* 1968, *1,* 2, 57-132.

Gibb, J.R. The Effects of Human Relations Training. In A. Bergin and S. Garfield (Eds.) *Handbook of Psychotherapy and Behavior Change: An Empirical Analysis.* New York: Wiley, 1971, 839-863.

Goldstein, A.P., K. Heller and L.B. Sechrest. *Psychotherapy and Psychology of Behavior Change.* New York: Wiley, 1966.

Kagan, N. Group Procedures. *Review of Educational Research,* 1966, *36,* 274-287.

McGrath, J.C. and I. Altman. *Small Group Research.* New York: Holt, Rinehart and Winston, 1966.

Truax, C.B. and R.R. Carkhuff. *Toward Effective Counseling and Psychotherapy: Training and Practice.* Chicago: Aldine, 1967.

Whiteley, J. (Ed.) *Research in Counseling: Evaluation and Refocus.* Columbus, Ohio: Merrill, 1967.

11.
What People Fear About Group Work:
An Analysis of 36 Selected Critical Articles

Wayne Rowe and
Bob B. Winborn

The growth of the "group movement" has been dramatic, appears to be accelerating and has touched in some way a large and increasing portion of our society. Many have participated directly in one or more group experiences organized by group leaders and trainers in business, industry, education and government. Others have been members of groups established by psychologists and psychiatrists engaged in private practice or have attended group institutes such as those sponsored by Esalen Institute or National Training Laboratories.

Aside from those who have had a direct exposure to some type of group process activity, literally millions of people have been able to experience vicariously group sessions through various forms of the mass media. Motion pictures such as *Bob and Carol and Ted and Alice* and *Made for Each Other* have given a countless number of Americans at least a superficial, though slanted, understanding of what occurs during and after a group experience. Books such as *Joy* (Schutz, 1967), *Please Touch* (Howard, 1970) and *What to Do Till the Messiah Comes* (Gunther, 1971) introduced thousands to the group world. Various types of group sessions or encounters have been videotaped and then aired on commercial television. The "group movement" also became popularized by reports and feature stories carried in newspapers, periodicals and other publications designed to reach a mass audience. In addition, as group process activities spread over the nation, they became controversial—and many citizens became aware of the phenomenon by way of local debates over the merits and potential dangers of group work.

The rapid growth of group work, the lack of appropriate safeguards to protect the consumers of group experiences, and the development of several new and unorthodox group procedures, such as sensory awareness sessions and nude marathons, has caused a number of laymen as well as members of the helping professions to become alarmed and apprehensive over the nature and practice of many forms of group work and the possible negative results that could accrue for the individual and society. Criticisms such as the following have appeared in popular and professional journals.

> ". . . much of sensitivity training is devoted to challenging and discrediting the Judaic-Christian value-system of any who may participate in a T-Group (Skousen, 1970)."

> "Let us bring some semblance of balance into the basic anti-intellectualism of group work by first making it very clear that this is no business for well-intentioned amateurs (Beymer, 1970)."

> "I have never seen any solid evidence regarding the efficacy of the group experiences (Jessell, 1969)."

> "Sensitivity training, as we have known it, is just another stage in the cycle of social failure (Carkhuff, 1971b)."

Criticisms such as these are a potentially valuable resource for those who are attempting to develop or upgrade ethical codes and standards for group leaders, trainers and facilitators. We believe that a necessary first step in the development of safeguards to protect the consumers of group work is to analyze the nature and frequency of the concerns, reservations, objections and/or fears that have been expressed in the popular and professional literature. The remainder of this chapter describes the results of such an analysis.

Method

Our first objective was to search the popular and professional literature for recent articles which focused on some criticism of group work. We have used *group work* as a generic term to include all forms of group experiences, such as encounter groups, T-Groups, personal growth groups, marathons and other similar ventures. Since group work has been heavily publicized by the mass media, we were interested in identifying the types and frequency of the fears and/or objections of group work being reported to the general public in popular magazines along with those appearing in professional journals. Books were not included in our search, which was generally limited to articles that were published between 1967 and May of 1972, a period of time when the "group movement" has been most active and controversial.

Fifty articles critical of group work were located and carefully read. In addition, the bibliography of each article was inspected to provide a cross-referenced check of the literature. At this point, 36 articles, judged to be representative of the critical literature, were selected for the analysis. Twenty-four appeared in professional journals and 12 were published in popular publications. From these articles the fears or objections to group work were tabulated and the concerns rank-ordered.

Results

The type and frequency of the objections and fears of group work are reported in Table 1. The types of objections/fears are rank-ordered on the basis of the total number of times they were reported in both the professional and popular literature. One exception to the rank order should be noted. The type of objections/fears labeled "Concerns about leader competence" and "Lack of standards for leader credentials" are closely associated, and therefore were listed together to indicate the frequency of this type of concern.

The primary reservation related to group work reported in both the professional and popular articles selected for this analysis is a lack of confidence in the people who lead groups. There is common agreement that leader competence is imperative, yet there is no assurance that all, or many, group leaders possess the necessary minimal skills. Closely related is the commonly voiced concern over the lack of standards for leadership training. At issue here is the optimum balance of formal academic training and learning obtained as a result of participation in group experiences. At the present time it is not only that adequate performance criteria have not been developed, but that the general guidelines in evidence clearly are not adequate. In short, the critics of group work are apprehensive about the lack of controls over who can become group leaders.

Table 1

The Type and Frequency of Fears and
Objections to Group Work Reported in
Selected Professional and Popular Journals

Type	Journals Prof. (N=24)	Pop. (N=12)	TOTAL (N=36)
Concerns about leader competence	12	7	19
Lack of standards for leader credentials	8	3	11
Possibility of psychological damage	8	6	14
Concern about substantiating research	11	3	14
Post-group adjustment problems	6	5	11
Doubt about generalization of learning	4	4	8
Lack of ethical standards	7	0	7
Lack of screening procedures	4	3	7
Lack of explicit procedures or goals	7	0	7
Danger of commercial abuses	5	1	6
Overemphasis on experiential goals	4	1	5
Use of involuntary subjects	4	0	4
Anti-intellectual emphasis	4	0	4
Danger of use with co-workers	1	3	4
Problems of confidentiality	3	0	3
Undermines home and family	0	3	3
Subjects learn to fake feelings	3	0	3
Lack of legal restraints and licensing	2	1	3
Use as an indiscriminant treatment	0	2	2
Based on inadequate theory	2	0	2
May help individual and harm organization	1	1	2
Undermines morality	0	2	2
Diminishes individual responsibility	0	2	2
May be addictive (T-Group bums)	0	2	2
May be damaging to young	0	2	2
Attempts to change individual and society	0	2	2
High dependency on leader	2	0	2

Type	Prof. (N=24)	Journals Pop. (N=12)	TOTAL (N=36)
Commitment of leader to organization, not group	1	0	1
Emphasis on diagnosis	1	0	1
Similarity to drug experiences	1	0	1
Techniques are gimmicks	1	0	1
Promotes emotional conformity	1	0	1
Coercion to join groups	1	0	1
Undermines personal beliefs and values	0	1	1
Emphasis on self and not others	0	1	1
Questions absolute knowledge	0	1	1
Is part of a conspiracy	0	1	1

The possibility of psychological damage to group participants and concern about the lack of substantiating research were the next most frequently reported objections to group procedures. As can be seen in Table 1, the latter reservation is advanced more often in professional journals and, in fact, is headed only by concerns about leader competence. The anti-intellectual emphasis which surrounds some approaches to group work, when mentioned, was pointed out as an obstacle in addition to the real and complex problems encountered in group process and outcome research.

What happens to an individual after he leaves a group? Post-group adjustment problems represented another frequently reported aspect of group work that appeared in both popular and professional journals. Most often, the critics mentioned that no follow-up of group participants was provided to assist with problems precipitated by a group experience. Other critics were disturbed about these people who have "re-entry" difficulties. Such people apparently become distressed when they return from a group experience to find that their environments have not changed and their newly learned behavior is not viewed as being appropriate.

It is interesting to note those types of objections/fears reported in professional journals which were not given in popular magazines. For example, those critics who published in professional journals were disturbed by the: (1) "lack of ethical standards" for group work, (2) "lack of explicit procedures or goals" for many types of groups, (3) "use of involuntary subjects," (4) "anti-intellectual emphasis" within the group movement and (5) "problems and confidentiality." To a large extent, these criticisms are focused on technical, theoretical and procedural aspects of group work of interest to members of the helping professions—but not to the general public.

The fears/objections which appeared in popular articles but not in those of a professional nature were related, for the most part, to the presumed effects of groups on the individual and society. For example, groups were seen to: (1) "undermine home and family," (2) be used as "an indiscriminant treatment," (3) "undermine morality," (4) "diminish individual responsibility," (5) hold the possibility of being "addictive" or producing "T-Group bums," (6) perhaps be "damaging to the young" and (7) "attempt to change the individual and society."

Discussion

Suppose that a consumer advocate should undertake to inquire into the practices and outcomes of group work? Could group work withstand a Nader-type investigation? On the basis of the representative articles included in this survey, such an investigator might conclude that several types of fears/objections have no legitimate basis, while other charges would indeed seem justified.

Objections such as claims that groups are part of a political conspiracy, cause participants to question absolute knowledge, destroy individual responsibility, or undermine the home and family are not frequently raised. In fact the periodicals which expressed this type of fear are all limited-circulation, non-professional magazines of special interest groups. It is noteworthy, then, that the criticisms levied in the mass circulation press and those found in professional journals are often rather similar. And these more frequently reported critical concerns would be difficult, certainly, to dismiss.

For instance, there is too much truth to the potential charge that there is almost no form of consumer protection in the group work industry. Licensing requirements, ethical standards and leader-training criteria are at best ineffectual and often non-existent. Well-meaning amateurs and the ever-present entrepreneur are all too visible, yet tend to blend in with their more professional brethren. How can the public be expected to determine who is a *competent* group leader when the profession is on record as being concerned about incompetence, though unable to specify the dimensions of a minimal level of competence? And how could we defend those instances in which the participant is induced to join a group without a clear, advance understanding of the goals of such an activity and the procedures that would be employed to attain those goals?

Imagine the consternation that would result if the public demanded to know what proof exists that group work offers any tangible benefits, aside from self-reports of being found "pleasurable." How strong is the evidence that the value received is appropriate in relation to the cost that is required? The counseling profession, as shown in Table 1, is concerned with the dearth of supporting outcome research. But consider the fertile field for a consumer advocate in the many studies which have shown lack of, or even negative, treatment results. Besides the acknowledged concerns regarding post-group adjustment, or re-entry problems, what about the serious doubts expressed about the generalization of learning in group situations to an individual's real-life environment? In the face of such an attack, it seems safe to predict that group work practitioners would be under severe pressure to embrace the anti-intellectual stance already present in the group movement. Yet this very position constitutes a serious barrier to research which is necessary to supply the data that must eventually support the group movement.

So far, no consumer advocate or commission has launched a campaign to investigate the practice of group work. How long will the counseling profession continue to be so fortunate? In the face of mounting criticism from within and without the profession, it would certainly appear that direct and immediate steps should be taken toward eliminating the legitimate sources of criticism.

The nature of the criticisms discussed in this analysis suggests that two measures should be taken by professional organizations and personnel to protect those who participate in group activities. First of all, a vigorous research program should be initiated to investigate such aspects of group work as: the types of training programs which will produce competent group leaders, the psychological effects of group work, the post-group adjustment problems generated by groups and the extent to which learning obtained from group experiences will generalize to real-life environment.

Research, however, takes time. Even if a major effort were undertaken tomorrow, it would probably take several years to obtain conclusive evidence concerning the effects of groups upon the lives of participants. Therefore, it seems imperative that rigorous ethical and legal controls over the practice of group work be instituted as quickly as possible. Such controls should have sufficient "teeth" so that professionals and non-professionals alike would respect them. In addition, they should be widely publicized so that the general public would be aware of their rights as they participate in various forms of group work. If such ethical codes and legal restrictions were available and were enforced, there should be much less of a basis for the criticisms raised about the lack of confidentiality in groups, the use of involuntary subjects, commercial abuses, the lack of appropriate screening procedures and the absence of explicit procedures and goals for group work.

The measures suggested above for eliminating the legitimate sources of criticism involve a trade-off. By adopting a more strict position for controlling those who are permitted to practice group work, some people who could benefit from this type of treatment may fail to receive it. On the other hand, those who would be subjected to the possibility of negative learning experiences would be protected. Until researchers can provide the evidence on which to build a solid scientific foundation for group work, we see the profession as being ethically bound to protect the consumer by implementing a strong system of ethical and legal controls.

References

American College Personnel Association. The Use of Group Experiences in Higher Education. Proposed position paper presented at the American Personnel and Guidance Association Convention, Chicago, March 1972. (Mimeo.)

Argyris, C. On the Future of Laboratory Education. *Journal of Applied Behavioral Science*, 1967, *3*, 153-183.

Bass, B.M. The Anarchist Movement and the T Group: Some Possible Lessons for Organizational Development. *Journal of Applied Behavioral Science*, 1967, *3*, 211-227.

Bates, M. The Fine Art of Groupmanship, or Surviving in Group Interaction. *Personnel and Guidance Journal*, 1968, *47*, 381-384.

Betz, R.L. The Marathon: Myths and Concerns. *Michigan Personnel and Guidance Journal*, 1971, *3*, 12-14.

Beymer, L. Confrontation Groups: Hula hoops? *Counselor Education and Supervision*, 1970, *9*, 75-86.

Birnbaum, M. Sense About Sensitivity Training. *Saturday Review*, November 15, 1969, *52*, 82-83, 96-98.

Blum, S. Group Therapy: A Special Report. *Redbook Magazine*, March 1970, *103*, 156-159, 163-166.

Boring, F.H. Ethical Perspective on Growth Groups. *APA Monitor*, May 1972, 3, 11.

Calame, B.E. The Truth Hurts: Some Companies See More Harm Than Good in Sensitivity Training. *Wall Street Journal*, July 14, 1969, 1, 11.

Campbell, J.P. and M.D. Dunnette. Effectiveness of T-Group Experiences in Managerial Training and Development. *Psychological Bulletin*, 1968, *70*, 73-104.

Carkhuff, R.R. The Sensitivity Fraud. *Journal of Clinical Psychology*, 1971a, *27*, 158-159.

Carkhuff, R.R. *The Development of Human Resources: Education, Psychology and Social Change*. New York: Holt, Rinehart and Winston, 1971b.

Cashdan, S. Sensitivity Groups—Problems and Promise. *Professional Psychology*, 1970, *1*, 217-224.

Dieckmann, E. Sensitivity Training—Exposed and Opposed. *American Mercury*, 1968, *104*, 7-12.

Dreyfus, E.A. and E. Kremenliev. Innovative Group Techniques: Handle with Care. *Personnel and Guidance Journal*, 1970, *49*, 279-283.

Easton, R.H., R.J. Carr and J.M. Whiteley. Issues in the Encounter Group Movement. *The Counseling Psychologist*, 1972, *3*, 89-120.

Eddy, W.B. and B. Lubin. Laboratory Training and Encounter Groups. *Personnel and Guidance Journal*, 1971, *49*, 625-635.

Gazda, G.M., J.A. Duncan and P.J. Sisson. Professional Issues in Group Work. *Personnel and Guidance Journal*, 1971, *49*, 637-643.

Goodstein, L.D. Some Issues Involved in Intensive Group Experiences. *The Counseling Psychologist*, 1970, *2*, 50-55.

Green, P.R. Sensitivity Training: Fulfillment or Freak-out? *Catholic World*, April 1970, 18-21.

Gunther, B. *What to Do Till the Messiah Comes*. New York: Collier Books, 1971.

House, R.J. T-Group Education and Leadership Effectiveness: A Review of the Empiric Literature and a Critical Evaluation. *Personnel Psychology*, 1967, *20*, 1-32.

Howard, J. *Please Touch: A Guided Tour of the Human Potential Movement*. New York: McGraw-Hill, 1970.

Human Potential: The Revolution in Feeling. *Time*, November 9, 1970, 54-58.

Jessell, J.G. The Group: Millennium or Mickey Mouse. Unpublished paper delivered at American Personnel and Guidance Association Convention, Las Vegas, Nevada, March 1969. (Mimeo.)

Kagan, N. Issues in Encounter. *The Counseling Psychologist*, 1970, *2*, 43-50.

Keen, S. Sing the Body Electric. *Psychology Today*, 1970, *4*, 56-58, 88.

Krafft, L.J. and L.W. Howe. Guidelines for Sensitivity Training in Your School. *Phi Delta Kappan*, 1971, *53*, 179-180.

Lakin, M. Some Ethical Issues in Sensitivity Training. *American Psychologist*, 1969, *24*, 923-928.

Lakin, M. Group Sensitivity Training and Encounter: Uses and Abuses of a Method. *The Counseling Psychologist*, 1970, *2*, 66-70.

Mercer, M. Sensitivity Training: What Happens When it Goes Wrong—When it Goes Right? *Glamour*, February 1970, *165*, 184-186.

Odiorne, G.S. The Trouble With Sensitivity Training. In R.T. Golembiewski and A. Blumberg (Eds.) *Sensitivity Training and the Laboratory Approach*. Itasca, Ill.: F.E. Peacock, 1970.

Rakstis, T.J. Sensitivity Training: Fad, Fraud, or New Frontier. *Today's Health*, January 1970, *48*, 20-25, 86-87.

Saylor, R. Notes on Sensitivity Training: An Editor's Personal Reaction. *Nation's Schools*, November 1970, *86*, 57-60.

Schutz, W.C. *Joy*. New York: Grove Press, 1967.

Shostrom, E.L. Group Therapy: Let the Buyer Beware. *Psychology Today*, 1969, *2*, 37-40.

Skousen, W.C. Chief, Watch Out for Those T-Group Promoters! *Law and Order*, November 1970.

The Group: Joy on Thursday. *Newsweek*, May 12, 1969, 104-108.

Thomas, D. T-Grouping: The White-Collar Hippie Movement. *Phi Delta Kappan*, 1968, *49*, 458-460.

12.
Applying Group Counseling Techniques to Future Social Problem-Solving

Walter M. Lifton

Approaches to group counseling are reflective of what is happening within a society. Moreover, a look at future social problem-solving needs will provide insight into the evolving group counseling techniques and approaches that will be useful in the helping professions.

Survey of Past Movements

Although there is evidence of group therapeutic approaches being used in Europe before they became popular in the United States, the early history of therapeutic groups in the U.S.A. started from the assumption that an inspirational lecture or mass dissemination of information was both an economical and therapeutically appropriate way to use groups. It also tended to be focused on man's productivity as a worker in society. This was a direct reflection of our Protestant-Puritan heritage with its emphasis on the importance of good work, and on the Calvinist value of work as a means of achieving salvation.

In the days of the 1930s and 40s—years of depression and stress—a person's survival was intimately linked to his ability to earn a living. Occupation, job, career could almost be used synonomously with self-concept, for man was judged by what he could produce and what he could earn. Children worried about what they wanted to be when they grew up. Clearly, helping people become self-actualized could be done very realistically through the vehicle of focusing on their need to resolve the "self-concept equals job" equation. It was during this period when the most popular term applied to groups designed to help others was "group guidance."

In the not-too-distant past, when groups to help people were not yet in style, advocates of group techniques obtained acceptance only when they showed the economy of working with several clients at once, or when they worked with people who were deviant enough that society was prepared to accept any approach that promised success. Much of the pressure for working with groups of patients developed during World War II, when the neuropsychiatric casualty rate exceeded the available personnel to provide therapy.

It is not possible to pinpoint exactly when group approaches became popular, but two influences are clearly apparent. As behavioral scientists became more effective in helping people secure a more satisfying life, and as attention turned from an earlier preoccupation with pathology to ways in which normal people could improve their lives, there arose in the U.S.A. those whose focus was on increasing the effectiveness of groups working together to accomplish a task.

In retrospect, it appears clear that the development of groups designed to help people live more gratifying lives, or what Maslow termed "engage in self-actualization," depended on a society that was affluent enough that the more basic needs had been met; and people could, therefore, afford to turn their attention to less pressing needs.

Working in this type of social setting, Kurt Lewin discovered that a "feedback" or report about how they behaved or functioned enabled the members of a group to refine their relationships with each other and to move more rapidly toward achieving the desired group goals.

In the early 1940s a strong movement developed in the field of psychology which had its roots in helping people solve problems based on discussions of the "here and now" instead of the past and which focused on the uniqueness of each man's view of life and reality. This phenomenological approach was given tremendous impetus by the work of Carl Rogers, who developed an approach for helping people which appeared equally useful with normally anxious people as it was with more seriously disturbed individuals. Although supporters of different points of view argued about the relative merits of the approaches, those techniques used with less disturbed people tended to be called group counseling instead of group therapy.

The 1950s, the period after the war, reflected society's preoccupation with the effect of authoritarian dictatorships on society. It is not surprising, therefore, that the group counseling techniques of this period showed a major concern with insuring that any helping process not foster dependency nor permit leader control over directions or goals of the group. This emphasis on a materialistic, pragmatic, effective group with its leadership developed within democratic limits really defines the place where National Training Laboratories began.

We are currently coming to the close of a different cycle. It occurs during an era when general prosperity makes economic survival easy for some parts of our society. It is also a period of over-production; goods are in surplus. It is also a period characterized by genocide, hydrogen bombs and a quest for immediate satisfactions in a world in which there might be no tomorrow. Of equal importance, it is a period where the have-nots in an affluent society have become aware of the concept of power. Power to the People: black power, teacher power, and yes, even student power. It is *not* a Puritan period of delayed gratification. It is a return, for some, to the simple life of the commune, to the soil and to hand crafts which have one important characteristic. Making concrete objects provides immediate evidence of your capability, since you can touch, smell or feel the product and know it is real. McLuhan has documented well how technology has forced people to turn from the plastic to what seems more primitive and real.

The Present Situation

Those of us who claim to be in the helping professions find ourselves being called on to assist in many new and alien situations. Sometimes techniques and approaches that are helpful in carefully controlled therapeutic settings do not work in the emotion ridden group confrontations that are part of our current daily life.

Many social agencies, much to their chagrin, are discovering that their perception of their clients' needs and the perceptions of the clients themselves are worlds apart, and that there exists a gap in communication. Clients express their resentment at the dependency status implied when they are not given a share in planning. Being independent implies freedom of choice.

We need to evaluate how we feel about our personal involvement in the social issues of the day. There may be times when we need to question whether our role is to assist people to adjust to their environment or to change it. It may be helpful to remember that aggression seems to be inversely proportional to the amount of participation.

If we feel social concern, we need to ask what steps we can take to prevent explosive situations instead of trying to heal deep wounds after a battle has occurred.

The ability of the group leader to function in a wide variety of groups depends on the breadth of his social awareness, his willingness to take risks, and his ability to cope with hostility and anger. He will need to become familiar with the techniques of social activists. He then will be able to understand what is going on instead of reacting to the threats involved. To cope with social action, the leader will need to recognize his own ties to the power structure and the ways in which these ties limit his ability to help groups to explore goals which may change the status quo.

Having faced repeated confrontations, I have discovered that there are times when the typical accepting, non-judgmental role used in counseling may contribute to the worsening of conditions rather than improvement. In retrospect, I now believe groups, like people, go through stages of development toward maturity.

For the individual seeking his own identity, the process of testing reality to see where he ends and others begin is very important. The child who arm-wrestles with his father, and feels his father is "letting him win," gets very angry because he cannot be sure that if the contest was real how much additional strength he really would need to win. Encounter and confrontation taken in this setting are a necessary part of self-definition. The therapeutic stance of being accepting does not always provide the hard crust needed to sharpen one's teeth. In fact, for some people, a permissive stance suggests a "put down," an ill-concealed attempt to cover your belief in their weakness.

I am suggesting that in many situations the height of being therapeutic is to be secure enough to permit yourself to be used in the way the client needs to use you at that moment to work through his problem. Some groups at the adolescent stage of development, where they have ambivalent dependency-independency needs, may at times seek limits to preserve security or to test their strength. At other times they may seek freedom to find their own way. The question is the stance of the helping person who recognizes what the work of the group is and how he can facilitate it by his behavior.

The leader or facilitator's ability to perceive the needs of the group basically depends on his empathic talent. But empathy cannot exist where the leader himself is involved in the problem too. At this point identification or sympathy is the more likely response, but it is not a helpful one.

Liberals rarely understand why their sympathetic claim of being identified with the black quest for power causes anger. They do not see that in their identification efforts they are repudiating the needs of the blacks to be their "own man" and valued for their difference.

For white people working as leaders with minority groups—black, brown, or just plain different—the ability of group members to provide feelings of guilt puts the white or "different" person in a double bind. If he truly feels personally guilty, he needs to do something to atone. Unless the group has reached the level of maturity where all can accept the fact that each person needs help in some area, the immature group will experience the pleasure of victory over a foe, but in the process they will have reduced the individual in their eyes to the point where they cannot use him as a model of strength or as someone against whom they can test themselves.

I have also learned that

- A non-threatening approach that leaves the initiative in the hands of the clients can prove effective in an outreach program. Sharing with people ways in which they can use you to help themselves, *when it can be believed*, results in warm acceptance and the development of the client's willingness to accept responsibility.

- When security is threatened, even liberal groups act in a reactionary manner.

- When advisory groups are formed, their purpose and scope of action must be sharply defined, or they must test the limits to discover reality. This applies equally well for student groups as it does for community action groups.

- Society as a whole is changing faster than many of its institutions, and confrontation appears to be the only device that currently produces enough motivation to force institutions to be willing to face the anxiety concomitant with change.

- The closer people are located to those they need to serve, the more effective they can be, not only in providing service but also in producing changes within the system. The more itinerant the worker, the less he is identified with an institution.

- Group leaders in educational settings have at least three tasks they need to consider:
    1. Helping students learn to accept responsibility along with freedom, while helping them learn how to apply pressure to society to force it to face problems needing solution—whether it be war, ecology, or the role of education in a changing society.
    2. Helping school people face the threat of change and helping them change their conception of their helping role from that of "telling" to "open dialogue." Assisting them to consider risk-taking so they can discover that students accept responsibility and grow with it. Help is also needed so that they can learn to test the limits of their own situation. It is necessary to replace the common cop-out of "they won't let you" with "I plan to help the Board see what we need to do and why it will improve our effectiveness."
    3. Serving as a mediator so that communication does not break down before we learn how to grow up, while both groups are learning to handle their own agendas.

Summary

Group techniques and philosophies are a reflection of the changing needs of society. Group leaders need to remember that they, as every person, have adopted beliefs about the nature of man and the way his behavior is determined. These beliefs seen in an individual's religion or ethical value system are found present in the helping relationship, as in other areas of a person's life. It is important for a person to know himself and what he believes in, because only then can he select approaches which are most congruent with his beliefs.

Tools and techniques used to facilitate human growth are essentially neuter in their character. It is only when they are applied for a specific purpose or to achieve a defined goal that tools become a part of a philosophy or psychological system. Using groups as a vehicle to help others is here to stay. Let us be sure group technology is seen as the vehicle and not as the goal sought by society.

References

Klein, A.F. Social Work Through Group Process. Albany, New York: School of Social Welfare, SUNY, 1970.

Lifton, W.M. *Groups: Facilitating Individual Growth and Societal Change.* New York: John Wiley, 1972.

13.
Readiness for Membership in a Counseling Group

Merle M. Ohlsen

Group counseling is designed to help reasonably healthy persons to discuss openly the problems which worry and upset them, to explore alternative actions, to select an alternative, to develop the self-confidence, the will and the skills required to implement the desired new behaviors, and to take action. As the therapeutic potency of the group develops, clients learn to help others as well as to accept help. Several clients are helped simultaneously (rather than treating one at a time in front of the group)—each recognizing when another's problem is also his own. Clients also learn to accept individual differences and each other's unique solutions to similar problems. Increasingly, those who do group counseling in elementary schools are learning to teach clients' parents and teachers to help the children learn to cope with developmental tasks as they mature.

Those who do group counseling should realize that there are a number of other effective group procedures too. Though they are designed for different purposes, satisfy different needs, and require different leader facilitative skills, certain common conditions must be satisfied if they are to be effective. For each, the leader must be able to describe the treatment process and its potential benefits for prospective members, in order to help each decide on the basis of precise information whether or not *he wishes to participate*; and, if he chooses to participate, what he will be expected to do to be helped and to help his fellow members. The leader also must have confidence in the treatment and his own professional competencies; realize who profits most from each technique, with whom, under what conditions; be permitted to select only those with whom he feels comfortable and feels can be helped by the treatment which he is qualified to offer; and recognize the limitations of each technique which he offers to prospective members.

Therapeutic Forces

Competent leaders also recognize, understand and know how to manage with the help of participants both the therapeutic and anti-therapeutic forces which exist within groups. These forces are reviewed here because they provide the basic rationale for the approach used by the author to introduce group counseling, to screen clients and to organize counseling groups. Perhaps a brief description of these forces also will help the reader capture some of the feelings experienced by the author's group counseling clients and to understand why they are so highly motivated to help develop and to maintain a therapeutic climate for their group (Ohlsen, 1970):

Commitment. Those who profit most from group counseling recognize and accept the need for assistance and are committed to talk about their problems, to solve them and to change their behavior when they are accepted for group counseling.

Expectations. Clients profit most from a counseling group when they understand what is expected before they decide whether to join. When prospective clients realize what is expected of them in order to increase the chances for the success of the group, and what decisions they can make, they tend to take more responsibility for helping to create a therapeutic climate, for functioning as the counselor's aides in the treatment process and for enforcing the limits they defined.

Responsibility. Increased responsibility for themselves and the therapeutic process increases clients' chances for growth within the counseling group. Meaningful involvement and participation in making decisions that affect them encourage most persons to accept responsibility and discourage them from becoming reactive and hostile. Argyris (1970) also notes that with increasing responsibility clients experience increasing satisfaction with solutions. "It is their responsibility to choose whether they will learn from the situation and, if so, how, and how much. . . No matter what is learned substantively, it should be learned in such a way that it is accomplished by feelings of psychological success and confidence in self and others, and in the group."

Acceptance. Genuine acceptance by his fellow clients enhances self-esteem and encourages a client to change his behavior. When a client discovers that he has been accepted for treatment in a group with other persons who expect to profit from group counseling, who really try to understand and to accept him, and who reach beyond mere talk to uncover the problems that bother him, they convey to him that they have confidence in his ability to solve his problems.

Attractiveness. "The more attractive a group is to its members, the greater is the influence that the group can exert on its members (Cartwright, 1951)." Cartwright reported that a group's attractiveness is determined by the importance of its perceived goals, the extent to which it meets its members' needs, whether its members are liked and whether it includes prestige members. Whenever a counselor selects clients for a group, he must always ask himself whether he believes that they can be helped best within his counseling group. For his first counseling groups this is even more critical—especially when he is first to use the treatment method within his work setting. However, his relationships with his clients and his ability to help them in groups will always affect the attractiveness of his counseling groups within which he is one of the prestige figures.

Belonging. Both those who are to be changed and those who influence change must sense a strong feeling of belonging in the same groups (Cartwright, 1951). As the feeling of belongingness increases, clients become more ego-involved in the interaction, participate more meaningfully, and increase their commitment for change.

Security. When clients come to feel reasonably secure within their counseling group, they can be themselves, discuss the problems that bother them, accept others' frank reactions to them and express their own genuine feelings toward others. The safer a client feels in the group, the easier it is for him to be open and transparent. Although he realizes that at times the experience will be painful, he is willing to tolerate the pain within this safe environment to reap the potential benefits. "It should be clear, therefore, that it is a gross oversimplification to think of open and closed individuals. What is more likely is that individuals are more or less closed or open, both in degree and in time. The more an individual seeks processes of competence acquisition, the more open he may be said to be. The more an individual resists these processes, the more closed he may be said to be. The point to be emphasized is the hypothesis that the more open an individual can be, the more he can learn from competence acquisition activities; the more closed, the more he may need therapy, at least as the initial step toward competence acquisition (Argyris, 1970)."

Tension. Clients' growth in counseling usually involves some tension. There must be enough tension and dissatisfaction to motivate change but not so much that it interferes with a person's use of his resources in achieving change. With reference to the tension, the author disagrees with those counselors who encourage their clients to purge themselves of disturbing feelings. Catharsis provides temporary relief but often decreases a client's motivation to continue to work for new desired behaviors. Rather than to settle for mere relief, a counselor should help clients implement new desired behaviors as they discuss their problems (and thus experience satisfaction with their new ways of behaving as they experience relief from catharsis).

Group Norms. When a client understands and accepts the necessary conditions for a therapeutic group, he is reluctant to ignore his group's norms, because he wants to be helped and he does not want to be perceived as a deviant within his counseling group. Argyris (1970) also notes that members facilitate a sense of trust when they exhibit respect for other members' ideas and feelings.

Introducing Group Counseling

Whenever a school counselor introduces a new guidance service, he should describe the treatment process and its potential benefits for students, parents and teachers. His presentation should include a description of what occurs typically in a counseling group, what members can expect from each other (especially with reference to keeping confidences and how they learn to help each other), the persons for whom it is designed and how they are helped. Members of the audience also should be encouraged to ask questions and/or to react to the idea, including expressing their doubts about it. After he has made such a presentation to the faculty, usually some teachers will invite him into their classes to tell students about group counseling. When he talks to students, he also should tell them how members are selected and why, and what they must do to join a group. Before concluding such a presentation, the counselor should distribute slips of paper to everyone, on which each indicates privately the extent of his interest in joining a group: no—no interest; maybe—possibly some interest; and yes—definitely interested, contact me for the next group. Students should also realize that even volunteering is not sufficient— that each client must convince himself and the counselor that he is committed to talk openly about those topics which worry and upset him and to change his behavior in order. Furthermore, every client should realize that this procedure is used to increase the chances for helping those who participate in group counseling.

The Intake Interview

The intake interview is designed (1) to help review and clarify what may be expected from a client and what he may expect from others; (2) to explore what worries and upsets him; (3) to give him an opportunity to practice discussing his problems; (4) to determine precisely how he would like to change his behavior; (5) to develop criteria that he may use to appraise his own growth toward his goals during counseling; (6) to help him assess his willingness to discuss his problems openly in the group and to make a commitment to change his behavior and to encourage others to change their behavior; and (7) to help the counselor become acquainted with each prospective client.

For example, the author recently began such an intake interview with a fifth-grader as follows:

"You remember when I visited your classroom and talked about group counseling. Perhaps you also will remember that I said that I conduct these interviews to give you a chance to ask any further questions which you may have about group counseling and to convince yourself and me that you really want to join such a group, that you will tell us what worries and upsets you, and that after we decide how you really want to change your behavior that you will really change it, and that you will encourage the other kids to change their behavior too. Though some things that worry and upset you may make you very unhappy when you talk about them, and maybe you will even cry, you will talk about them because you expect to get help in the counseling group. I will listen to you, guess how you really feel, help you tell it, help you figure out how you want to change your behavior, practice doing it and teach you how to help other kids to change their behavior. Though I want very much to help everyone who comes to me for counseling, I admit to my counseling groups only those who can do the things we have talked about, because that increases their chances for getting help in a counseling group. Tell me about you. Begin with something that is worrying or upsetting you right now."

Until they have tried it (or observed another demonstrate it) and discovered that their prospective clients do not perceive them as gatekeepers, some counselors have difficulty accepting the intake interview and the idea of screening clients for groups. Perhaps they do not realize the extent to which a competent counselor can convey his genuine desire to help a prospective client and at the same time want to include in the group only those who are ready to profit from group counseling and to encourage fellow clients to face their problems and change their behavior. The concern for helping those included is stronger than the need to try to help everyone—whether or not they really want assistance and can profit from it.

Selection of Client

Though some counselors are reluctant to screen clients for counseling, most agree that a counselor must be permitted to accept for group counseling only those whom he believes that he can help with the other clients selected for his group. After the author has completed his intake interviews, he asks himself these questions as he reviews his interview notes (or for group practicum student staffs, each prospect with his supervisor and practicum partner): "Who are the best prospects? What makes them the best prospects for my group? Who needs whom? For each considered favorably is there someone with whom he can relate or needs to learn to relate? Who requires a model? Who can fulfill this role for him?"

What may be gleaned from the literature to help counselors make these decisions? Allport (1960) concluded that the ability to become ego-involved is essential for any group member. Ryan (1958) reported that the ability to become meaningfully involved in a treatment group is related to a member's ability to empathize with others, to form relationships with others, to delay gratification of one's own needs and to derive satisfaction from helping others gratify their needs. Lindt (1958) reported that a patient is most apt to profit from a therapeutic group experience when he is able to make the necessary emotional investment in others to help them. Powdermacher and Frank (1953) found that patients' feelings of affiliation facilitated therapeutic interaction. Beck (1958), Ewing and Gilbert (1967), Johnson (1963) and Rickard (1965) concluded that those who volunteer and exhibit high motivation for treatment are the best bets. Speilberger, Weitz and Denny (1962) also found that those who profited most had better attendance records than those who profited least. Perhaps their conclusion merely suggests that the clients who were helped most exhibited most commitment and motivation to change.

Once the author decides who will be placed with whom, he contacts every prospective client—telling those selected when they will meet and telling those not assigned to a group when another group will be begun in which they will be placed. Usually those not selected do not need to be contacted because they decided at the close of the intake interview not to participate, and if they indicated that they wanted to join a counseling group later, they have already initiated plans to get themselves ready for the next group.

When clients are prepared in this manner for group counseling, are encouraged to accept responsibility for getting themselves ready for group counseling, are encouraged to participate in the process of defining specific behavioral goals and criteria to assess their own progress during counseling and are helped to understand why clients are selected with such care, these experiences seem to increase their commitment to participate therapeutically and to implement new behaviors. Most also seem to understand what is expected of them, to accept responsibility for their own growth and for helping others try new desired behaviors, and to develop and maintain therapeutic norms. Those selected also seem to feel that they have earned their way into their group, that they belong, that their group is a safe place in which they can talk openly and that therefore they are more certain that they will be helped.

References

Allport, G.W. *Personality and Social Encounter.* Boston: Beacon Press, 1960.

Argyris, C. Conditions for Competence Acquisition and Therapy. In R. Golembiewski and A. Blumberg (Eds.) *Sensitivity Training and the Laboratory Approach.* Itasca, Illinois: F.E. Peacock, Inc., 1970, 220-245.

Beck, D.F. The Dynamics of Group Therapy, as Seen by a Sociologist. Part II: Some Puzzling Questions on Leadership, Contextual Relations, and Outcomes. *Sociometry,* 1958, *21,* 180-197.

Cartwright, D. Achieving Change in People: Some Applications of Group Dynamics Theory. *Human Relations,* 1951, *4,* 381-392.

Ewing, T.N. and W.M. Gilbert. Control Studies of the Effects of Counseling on Scholastic Achievement of Students of Superior Ability. *Journal of Counseling Psychology,* 1967, *14,* 235-239.

Johnson, J.A. *Group Therapy: A Practical Approach.* New York: McGraw Hill, Inc., 1963.

Lindt, H. The Nature of Treatment Interactions of Patients in Groups. *International Journal of Group Psychotherapy,* 1958, *8,* 55-69.

Ohlsen, M.M. *Group Counseling.* New York: Holt, Rinehart and Winston, 1970.

Powdermacher, F.B. and J.D. Frank. *Group Psychotherapy.* Cambridge: Harvard University Press, 1953.

Rickard, H.C. Tailored Criteria of Change Psychotherapy. *Journal of General Psychology,* 1965, *72,* 63-68.

Ryan, W. Capacity for Mutual Dependencies and Involvement in Group Psychotherapy. *Dissertation Abstracts,* 1958, *19,* 1119.

Speilberger, C.O., H. Weitz and J.P. Denny. Group Counseling and Academic Performance of Anxious College Freshmen. *Journal of Counseling Psychology,* 1962, *9,* 195-204.

14.
Effective Group Counseling
Process Interventions

Wayne W. Dyer and
John Vriend

Group counseling as a format for helping participants to become more productive and capable human beings is the appropriate *group* experience which, optimistically, will gain broad adoption at all junctures of the entire educational network, elementary through university graduate school, and also in less formally structured educational settings. Currently there is meager agreement, if any, on the focus that group counseling ought to take, nor on precisely what activities are acceptable for counseling groups and which should be considered taboo. For purposes of clarification, the authors view group counseling in the school setting as a social and psychological helping activity which has as its over-all objective the changing of behavior which is in any way destructive to the individuals participating in the experience and the acquisition of new behavior of a self-enhancing nature.

What behaviors are deemed negative—as being self-defeating? Without cataloguing a thousand narrow specifics, it can be said that self-destructive behaviors are those which work against an individual's maximum self-acceptance, against adequate coping with or mastery of a person's environment, both social and inanimate, against being in charge of himself, his emotions, his world. Even the absence of those behaviors which most of us learn and make our own at this or that developmental stage can be construed as being self-destructive. The counseling group is seen as the safe learning laboratory in which members are committed to working on the elimination of their self-defeating behaviors, to working on their self-development formulated in highly specific, attainable ways, to working in conjunction with and reciprocation toward others likewise committed, to testing alternate ways of behaving and devising new courses of action, to exploring one's self and one's world, analyzing and assessing both in order to establish realistic counseling goals which can be achieved during the stated tenure of the group.

The concepts of group counselor functioning are not universally agreed upon within the counseling profession. Those who have assumed responsibility for training "facilitators" in the encounter group movement have established a posture on the issue of group leader role which is to a great extent antithetical to the responsibilities of the group counselor in the school setting. Encounter group facilitators tend to see themselves as player-coaches, as leaders who are deeply involved in the group process in much the same way as the other participants are; they see themselves as members who happen to have "logged" a great many more hours of group inhabitation and who are willing to share what they have learned; but they still are, nevertheless, very interested, for the sake of their own growth, in becoming engaged in the group happenings "on a personal level." They don't see themselves as experts, nor do they covet the responsibility implied in such a mantle for possible adverse consequences resulting from any group activity.

In contradistinction, the group counselor is the responsible professional, and the more expertness he can ethically deliver, the better off his counselees are. Nor can an adult who serves youth, which would be the case in most school situations, presume that he is in any way the peer of the group counselees. That he is paid under an occupational title (be it counselor, teacher, or whatever) additionally precludes the possibility as a matter of role identity. Nor is he a friend. Rather, he is a professional, supposedly trained and certified, a person hired to provide educational and helping services.

The group counselor's role is dominated by one all-embracing characteristic which distinguishes him from a group member: he does not permit himself to use the group or anyone in it to serve his own needs. His focus is always on the "other," or all of the "others" in the group taken together, and ought hardly ever to be on himself. He embraces, thinks and communicates in the second person singular voice, "you"; he seeks to snuff out the pronoun, "I"; and he only reluctantly backs into using the pronoun, "we." He attempts to serve each of the group members as effectively as possible. He therefore seeks to acquire those behaviors and competencies which will enable him to provide service and he seeks to extinguish in himself those behaviors which tend to stand in the way of effective service to each individual in the group.

William C. Schutz, in describing intervention guidelines for the encounter group leader, writes: " . . . if I wasn't sure whether or not to intervene in a group, to consult my stomach. If it felt relaxed, do it; if it was tight, don't."* We believe a far more detailed analysis of the process of group leader intervention is needed in group counseling work. The *stomach as a consultant* is simply not adequate as a guide for those who are attempting to make a difference in the lives of young people. *The notion of group counseling as an amorphous activity in which one does what comes naturally is precisely why it is conducted so ineffectively by so many practitioners.*

Anyone who has ever served as a group counselor or who has contemplated that role has dealt with the conflict of knowing exactly *when* and *how* to intervene in the group action. Over and beyond any preplanning for alternate courses of action for individuals in the group or the group as a whole done for an upcoming counseling session, the proficient group counselor has ideas about what kinds of interventions he expects to make in the course of a given meeting, where those interventions will take the individuals in the group, his reasons for making them, and when particular ones will be needed. It should be noted that an intervention does not necessarily imply that the group counselor must be the one doing the intervening. That an intervention is called for should be recognized immediately by the leader. However, as the tenure of the group unfolds, the leader learns to encourage group members to become aware of the need for interventions, and to actually channel interventions through them whenever possible, since many, perhaps even most, on-cue interventions are more readily accepted when capably delivered by peers, especially if other peers chime in and reinforce the meaning and intent of a member's helping attempts. The group counselor can serve as a model to the group members, and actually teach them leadership intervention behaviors. Early in the life of the group the group members will observe the counselor making interventions at key points in the counseling sessions. A truly capable leader helps the pressure for actually making these

*Schutz, William C. *Here Comes Everybody.* New York: Harper and Row, 1971, 245.

interventions shift from the counselor to the group members, but he retains the responsibility for ensuring that the intervention does in fact occur.

Significant, on-target "counseling" interventions, whether made by the counselor of the group or by its members, help to keep members working on their goals and gives everyone a sense of directionality. Counselees need reinforcement of their progress and interventions which chip away at impediments to that progress provide support for group counseling as a productively meaningful process. This helps members to feel better about the struggle they are going through on their way to self-enlargement and makes them more willing to work at replacing self-defeating behaviors and less willing to avoid such work. No work, no pay off.

What are some constantly recurring situations and times in counseling groups when an appropriate intervention is *almost always* called for? Any competent group counselor who has led groups for many clock hours and who seriously entertains the foregoing question can begin to take a look at his own "break-ins," examine his counselor behavior patterns, and arrive at those propitious moments when an intervention usually seemed to be effective, even characterizing the nature of those interventions which were repeatedly productive. Reduced to their most communicable common denominators, these could be transmitted to others.

In essence, this is what we have done. The short list we offer here was compiled after carefully examining hundreds of counseling tapes, many hours of co-counseling diverse groups and distilling the results of our thinking. We observed that these specific interventions were almost always effective in promoting or in laying the groundwork for the promotion of behavior change on the part of group participants.

Ten Occasions for Group Intervention

The group counselor can productively take responsibility for initiating or causing an intervention when:

1. A group member speaks for everyone.

The use of phrases such as "This is how we feel" or "The group is bogged down" or "We think we ought to . . ." is quite common in counseling groups. A group member may feel much more comfortable by stating the "we" or the "group" and assuming that everyone present feels the same, or even use the collective noun or pronoun as a ploy to muster support for a position or point of view, playing "gang up" games. This is an appropriate time for the leader to assess if everyone is in agreement. Permitting the "we" syndrome to run rampant in a group can become quite self-defeating for each group member. It encourages a sense of "groupiness," an appeal to the group to engage in consensus rather than individual thinking. If it is successful often enough, group members learn to stifle themselves and only deal with group-approved material which, almost without exception in groups where consensus thinking becomes the norm, turns out to be shallow and bland. Moreover, it inhibits individual members from challenging each other for fear of upsetting the collective spirit of unanimity or equanimity.

Appropriate interventions include: "You mentioned *we* several times. Are you speaking for each person in the group? Is there anyone who doesn't agree with the position stated?" If the counselor is aware of contrary positions due to previously exposed data or non-verbal clues, it is effective to indicate these and ask the person associated with the data or the clues how his or her thinking differs. For the leader to go directly to another member ("Carl, is Maynard speaking for you?"), preferably a strong, clear thinker, is an effective way of derailing a wrongly scheduled "we" express train. The anti-we intervention encourages members to think for themselves, to remember that *group counseling has individual rather than group goals,* and it sets a tone in the group which permits openness by allowing each member to make his own unique contribution and establish that his perceptions are at least a shade different from everyone else's.

But more important, it teaches a counselee to read behavioral data accurately, to *remember* the positions of others and to judge the extent to which there is agreement with his own. It teaches a counselee to *check out* where others stand. And it teaches him to think more realistically in terms of "some" or "one other person" rather than "all." Then, too, it teaches him that the "some" can only be included if there is evidence to support such inclusions. All of these lessons, if incorporated in the self-system and translated into habitual behavior outside the group, serve to make a person more effective in his dealings with others.

2. An individual speaks for another individual within the group.

It is quite common for a group member to speak for another individual in the group by saying something like: "This is what she means." Or, "She's not saying how she feels. I can explain it."

Almost without exception, if person B takes over for person A in this fashion, usually one of two inferences can be tellingly made. First, B has made the judgment about A that A is not up to the job of sending her messages effectively, that she is inadequate or incapable, an incompetent communicator, at least less adequate or capable than B; and when B "takes over," under the guise of being helpful, B is being condescending, saying non-verbally that A has failed. A second possibility, depending on the circumstances, is that person B is worried about where the interaction is leading downstream, and sensing more emotional rapids ahead, wants somehow to avoid them. For example, leading up to B's take-over, A is experiencing frustration, confusion, tension; A's delivery of her material is tentative, garbled, wandering; B suspects that A is feeling pressured to reveal something about herself and that she is trying to steer away from it. Because B thinks A won't be able to handle *dealing* with whatever "conflict" might arise, B jumps in. This kind of "commandeering" of a situation in order to "defuse" an impending altercation is frequent in counseling groups but seldom effective.

Both of these inferences can be checked out in any given situation, and ought to be. In each case what the behavioral data says about and to Person B is just as important as what it says about and to A. In the latter instance, for example, person B may have taken over because *she* is ineffective in handling conflict, frustration, self-revelation of personally difficult life-data, *even when it is happening to someone else.*

But regardless of the circumstances behind one individual speaking for another, an intervention is called for. It is an opportune time for individual members to set goals for themselves. The person who is allowing another group member to speak for him might establish the goal of speaking more clearly or not allowing someone else to speak for him, whether in the group sessions or elsewhere, particularly if he discovers that this occurs all the time in his life, with all kinds of people. In addition, the "talker" can establish the goal of eliminating the tendency to rescue a person when he is not speaking effectively. Certainly the talker needs to eliminate the tendency to make assumptions that she knows how someone else feels without checking it out. Rather than allowing counselees to speak for each other, the group leader should be promoting the desire on the part of the group members to help each person become as effective as possible in his message sending and receiving. This means being able to express one's thoughts, perceptions and self-definitions so that one is understood by everyone else in the group. Anyone short-changed in this area can work on overcoming deficiencies by practicing—by struggling to change ineffectual speech patterns and habits—rather than sitting back and allowing a more lucid group member to take charge. Once the group is aware that a member has set such a goal, others can swiftly zero in on helping the struggler to work through whatever is necessary to achieve adequate communication at the appropriate times.

Appropriate interventions for elimination of people speaking for each other include: "Did Sally state how you were feeling more clearly than you were able to?" If "yes," focus on the goal for speaking more clearly. If "no," ... "How did it feel to have someone else rescue you?" Or, to the talker, "Did you feel that Mary needed your aid at that moment?" Or, "Do you find it difficult to hold back when you think that you understand how someone else feels and that person can't express himself?" Or, "Would helping Herman to make himself understood be more effective for him than your assuming the interpreter's role?"

An offshoot of this tendency of one group member to speak for another which crops up in the early stages of most counseling groups is the "third person syndrome." Group members will talk about each other to or through a third person, often the group leader, using third person pronouns. When this arises in the group activity, it requires only a brief intervention on the part of the counselor, something like, "You're speaking to me about Mary and she's sitting right there." Later, only a nod of the head is required to help group members to speak *to*, rather than *about* or *at,* each other. The avoidance behavior inherent in the third person syndrome is typical of most beginning counseling groups, where some members have trouble handling eye contact, tend to seek leader approval, and engage in testing behaviors and skirmishes to determine who's who in the pecking order. The perceptive group counselor can assist the group to recognize that group counseling is most productive when counselees deal forthrightly with each other, rather than being evasive.

3. A group member focuses on persons, conditions or events outside the group.

Counseling groups can turn into "gripe sessions," particularly in the school setting, if the leader is unskilled or lacking in sensitivity. Griping about the principal, a teacher, a common acquaintance or parents can be enjoyable, as counselees tend to reinforce and support each other's attitudes about how the world (or persons in it) tend to conspire unfairly against them, and thus a good feeling of solidarity props them up in their apparently common struggle; but this is essentially a non-growth producing exercise for group members. Talking about people, conditions and events which are outside the counseling group tends erroneously to substantiate the notion that *they* are culpable, that the outsiders are at fault, shifting blame and responsibility outside the self.

The group counselor should be aware that this inclination on the part of the counselees occurs because it is the safe thing to do. As long as I focus on others, I don't have to deal with myself or accept any responsibility for what I do. Also, implied in the focus-on-others mien is the notion that if *they* would only change, somehow *I* would improve—false logic guaranteed to lead its user away from positive behavioral change, not closer to it.

Appropriate interventions for the group counselor include: "You keep talking about the principal as the cause of your unhappiness. Isn't it more important to be asking yourself what *you* can do to improve yourself or your happiness?" Or, "Focusing our attention on someone who isn't here keeps us from having to look at the people who are really responsible for our own shortcomings." Or, "Does complaining about the way someone else acts really mean that if only that person were more like me, I could be happier?" Or, "You keep mentioning your mother as the source of your being miserable. But what can you do to make yourself happier in this world?" Or, "Are you interested in becoming a critic or a doer?"

Any intervention should have as its central purpose bringing the group members back to themselves. Talking about *them* or *they* in the group can do nothing but reinforce a group member mentality of believing someone else is to blame. While venting gripes may be a necessary prelude to getting down to work in some groups where the frustration tolerance levels over institutional conditions are too high to ignore, the gripe session should not be construed as constituting an effective counseling practice. Long-winded complaints about others or the state of the world which no one can do anything about rarely serve the complainer in any positive way.

Interventions here ought to be designed to teach counselees that they must assume responsibility for themselves, that they must be able to handle themselves more effectively in encounters with the com-plained-about other, and that focusing on the character or behavior of the other is self-defeating avoidance behavior. They ought to learn from these interventions that group counseling deals with the present and the possibility of new behavior in future moments and not with historical events, that making one's happiness contingent upon other people changing their behavior is basically the thinking of a fool, and that griping about the behavior of others is wasteful of time and energy, a proverbial shoveling of sand against the tide.

4. Someone seeks the approval of the counselor or a group member before and after speaking.

Approval-seeking is one of the most common forms of unhealthy human behavior; and, when it is done in the counseling group, this is no exception. The group leader should become aware of such a proclivity on the part of a member and be prepared to intervene when such behavior surfaces. Some individuals look for constant non-verbal acceptance by the leader—a nod, a glance, a smile. Such persons may be intimidated by personal strength, or by significant or authority figures, or have such a poor sense of self-worth that they are always going outside of their own resources for support and self-endorsing approval. It is essential for the leader to point out approval-seeking behavior so that the individual is made aware of it and recognizes that the counseling group is an experimental laboratory for working on this behavior in safety.

Approval-seeking may take many forms. Often a group member will look directly at the leader both before and after speaking to assess if he has the leader's agreement. An appropriate intervention in this case is for the counselor to deliberately look elsewhere, scanning the faces of the other members, forcing the speaker to appeal to others and change the direction of his delivery, the leader thus taking care not to reinforce the client's neurotic need. If the behavior persists, identifying it to the individual is most appropriate, along with setting up individual goals which might include working on understanding why the need for approval exists, as well as alternate behavior to be practiced in the group.

Approval-seeking might also take the form of asking for group consensus, or for various group members to agree with a certain position. Once again it is important to point out the approval-seeking acts and to ask if the individual is interested in working on eliminating this essentially non-productive behavior. In school counseling groups, students frequently talk about feeling bad because someone (a friend, parent, teacher) doesn't agree with them about a position they have taken. Here again, approval-seeking behavior is present. The group leader can confront the student with why it is important to have others agree with him. Such interventions as these are appropriate: "Do you think that your need for Mike to agree with you is based upon a strong desire for him to like you?" Or, "You always look at Maryanne before you speak, almost as if you're asking permission." Or, "Why is it so important for other people to share the same opinion as you?"

If the leader provides a model for these kinds of interventions, the group members will begin to ask each other similarly vital questions as the group gains maturity. Interventions designed to point out approval seeking behavior in counseling groups will aid participants in improving their own self-awareness and self-concepts. In addition, it teaches counselees that they will always encounter disagreement in life, that being psychologically healthy means being able to accept one's self when others have contrary opinions, and to have a solid rationale for one's point of view which puts one in a position of not needing others to be on one's side.

5. *Someone says, "I don't want to hurt his feelings, so I won't say it."*

This is a common practice in the early stages of counseling in a group. When a leader observes this kind of sentiment in a group, he can suggest that two alternatives are responsible for such a mind-set: 1) the recipient is so fragile that he would collapse if you shared your honest perceptions about him, or 2) you're afraid to say what you think because of your own self-doubt (i.e., "someone might not like me if I don't say nice things, and I can't chance not being liked"). Either choice is inhibiting to self-growth, and therefore a leader intervention is proper. If the group member who is reluctant to share heartfelt feelings and perceptions fears the brittle composition of the potential recipient, he ought at least to be sincere enough to check out his concern with the individual, especially as such an assumption almost always turns out to be apocryphal. The perceptive group leader would be cognizant of the resistance to being candid, and of the dynamics behind the reluctance. Pointing out reasons for the fear of being forthright will contribute to destroying the barriers and will encourage group members to share perceptions and feelings which they see as a contribution to the welfare of another member.

6. A group member suggests that his problems are due to someone else.

There is some overlap with number 3, above, but this call for intervention has unique overtones. So often do counselees suggest that their problems are caused by others that the counselor needs to be aware of how to intervene when this defensive phenomenon crops up, as it inevitably will when one works with students. Adolescents particularly enjoy making others responsible for their own non-productivity. When an individual intimates that if someone else (my teacher, mother) were different, then I would be more effective, the group must be made aware of the discrepancy in this kind of self-defeating thinking. Such interventions as these get the therapeutic process started: "Who is really in charge of you?" "Why should someone else change for you?" "Can't you be what you choose to be, despite the way others are?" Or, "You assign blame to everyone or everything except to what is really responsible for your problems."

A productive group counseling program will help students to cope effectively with these kinds of questions and to examine how they can personally take charge of themselves to become more effective human beings. The authors are not suggesting a nonsympathetic counseling posture; the group, however, is an arena for effectively coming to grips with how each person can assess what he can do for himself to become all that he wishes to be, rather than providing just one more futile environment where the student assigns the responsibility for his failures to someone else, and continues to function at less than optimal levels. The group counselor must be constantly alert for the manifestation of member behaviors which imply or assign responsibility for personal effectiveness on "others" and he should search to build an arsenal of interventions geared to refute such self-crippling thinking.

7. *An individual suggests that "I've always been that way."*

When a counselee mentions that "I've always been that way," or, "That's just the way I am and I can't help it," he is engaging in self-defeating thinking of the first order. This becomes a propitious moment for the leader to intervene and help the group member to see that a person is really what his choices make him, rather than someone over whom he has little or no control. Group counselees frequently plead that they can't really help the way they are, sometimes supporting each other, Greek chorus-like, in the perniciously fatalistic idea that they have had no (and won't ever have any) control of their development and destiny.

Appropriate interventions for the group counselor include: "Do you feel that because you've always been ineffective, you are destined to remain that way?" Or, "You're suggesting that someone else is in charge of what you are and always will be, and you can't help it." Or, "Do you feel that everyone has certain areas of his life over which he has no control?" The group counselor has the responsibility for seeing that the group helps each member to deal effectively with the areas of his thinking which inhibit growth. Believing that one's past necessitates one's future is fallacious thinking which encourages people to function at lower levels than what they could attain. Learning that all of the self-defining "I'ms" (I'm shy, I'm lazy, I'm lousy in math, I'm . . . *ad infinitum*) are really choices that individuals make which allow them to keep from working at self-development is an important lesson one absorbs on the way to psychological health. The "I'ms" result in some highly circuitous thinking which in turn determines self-defeating behavior: a) I'm shy; b) I think I'll approach that attractive and likable person; c) Oh no, I can't. I just remembered that I'm shy. Thus we live out our self-fulfilling prophecies.

Interventions of the type described in this section will help group members to identify the thinking and behavior which leads to their being ineffective in specific areas of their lives. They will also learn that they are not doomed to repeat the mistakes of their past, if they will take constructive action to become different. In addition, they will soon recognize that all people have a list of self-descriptions which they conveniently bring into their consciousness when they want an excuse for not working hard at changing. The effective group leader is aware of this tendency in group members, and makes the appropriate intervention. If the interventions do not occur, it is most likely that the group will reinforce the inert, nonproductive thinking simply because it is a safe approach: everyone can remain comfortable, do nothing and stay the same.

8. An individual suggests, "I'll wait, and it will change."

This posture is one that members commonly assume in the early meetings of a counseling group. The faulty thinking goes something like this: "I want to be different. But I don't want to do anything, so I'll postpone action and things will get better." Group members are often willing to talk about their self-defeating behavior patterns. The competent group leader should be aware that talking about a problem is only the beginning step toward becoming more effective. When any group member suggests that doing something about it is impossible or very difficult, then the counselor needs to intervene in a way that will put the group member onto an action path leading to a resolution of the difficulty. All interventions of this type are designed to teach group members that inertia is not the strategy for eliminating any self-destructive behavior, and that until some striving, at least, occurs, only a piddling change can be expected.

9. Discrepant behavior appears.

A group leader intervention is essential when discrepancies occur in a member's behavior in the group. Discrepancies take many forms, but the following appear with regularity:

a) A discrepancy between what a member is currently saying and what he said earlier. (Obviously, the group counselor must be aware of what counselees say throughout the life of the group.)

b) A discrepancy between what a member is saying and what he is doing. The discrepancy between what he says he does and what he actually does is important, and a group counselor must be willing to point out any obvious gaps.

c) A discrepancy between what a member says and what he

feels. Here the counselor can intervene with a facilitating description of how the member is coming across, how he is unconvincing, how his non-verbal behaviors, the indices of his feeling states, betray and contradict the content of his utterances.

d)   A discrepancy between what a member is saying and what the counselor is feeling in reaction. The group leader may be incorrect in his assumption that his own reactive feelings point to a discrepancy, but his checking it out helps a counselee to clarify where the psychological truth lies. The intervention is appropriate, regardless, and the skilled group counselor will find that the majority of his feelings about the group members are usually "right on." Helping counselees to learn the extent to which their interpersonal actions are affect-laden, and the character of such emotional loading, is an important first step toward psychological congruence of thought and action.

e)   A discrepancy between how a member sees himself, according to his own data, and how others in the group have been seeing him, according to data they have at one time or another proffered. Again, it is important here to signify the fact that effective professionals pay hard attention, have long memories, excellent recall of specifics, and can muster forth a therapeutic feedback reference swiftly.

The interventions which identify discrepant behavior are confronting in many ways. The group leader who is professional, however, remembers that the road to trust-building in counseling groups is strewn with open, forthright confronting, rather than a warm accepting approval of everything a member says or does. It should be made clear that group members are never on trial in a hostile setting, and that anger and hostility are not in the repertoire of the effective group leader's interventionistic mind. With the identification of the discrepancies which arise in counseling groups, the group members see for themselves that here is a setting in which being plain and direct is a way of life. The name of the game is seeing and naming what constitutes the intrapersonal and interpersonal reality as a condition of counseling movement. Moreover, the path to being self-actualized or self-fulfilled is one in which an individual learns how to be direct and unabashedly candid in dealing with himself. If the group counselor provides the environment which accepts less than honesty, then he does a disservice to each counselee in the group.

10. *A member bores the group by rambling.*

Seeking approval through overtalk, or simply being unable to facilitate self-closure on a verbalization is a widespread typical behavior in counseling groups. A possible intervention would be to turn to another person and say: "Mary, repeat what Duane just said." If she is unable to do so, then a goal of Duane's to speak more succinctly is in order. If she can repeat it, perhaps a statement which approximates the following is in order: "How come it took you two sentences to say what it took Duane three minutes to say?" This intervention can be handled most tactfully by involving the other group members with helping people to avoid turning the group off with their rambling and groping. A corollary to this issue involves the overly intellectual member who is attempting to impress the group with his or her knowledge, acumen, discerning perspicacity, or stunning ratiocination. The counselor can ask other members to react to what the "intellectual rambler" has just said and to suggest that they provide the rambler with feedback about his ability to be long on obfuscation and short on present moment meaningful message sending, particularly when his real intent is clearly not communication, a meeting of minds over bloody ideas, but a desire for strokes.

Final Thoughts

This elaboration of ten occasions for group counseling process interventions, the rationale behind the need to intervene, and the explication of specific leads and counselor behaviors concludes a presentation of suggestions for more effective group counselor functioning which is by no means exhaustive. It barely scratches a bulging surface. But it does present a model of the kind of group process analytical thinking which the counseling profession can surely use more of—an antidote to "stomach consultancy" for group leader functioning.

The ten areas we have covered are general enough to be taken as an umbrella of guidelines from which a myriad of specific differential interventions can flow. But the number of umbrellas could be increased a thousandfold. What effective leader interventions are possible at the beginning of a group session which have an anchor in theory, a rationale and a predictability record to recommend them? Or at the ending of sessions? Or when and why and how should interventions occur which serve to recapitulate, to take stock, to assess and re-evaluate particular kinds of progress for this or that group member? Practically all of the tried-and-true group counseling practices are still out there waiting to be drawn together and effectively communicated to the interested professional membership. Effective counseling in groups is a complicated business, and hardy hunters, or as Robert R. Carkhuff calls them, helper-warriors, practitioners in pursuit of an ever-higher level of functioning, those dedicated to their own professional development, need help from every source they can find.

May our model multiply!

15.
Minimal Necessary Conditions in Schools for Effective Group Counseling

Clarence A. Mahler

The rapid expansion in popularity of group counseling and sensitivity groups gives rise to a grave concern on the part of many counselor trainers. This concern is in the extreme difficulties met by counselor trainers and school pupil personnel directors in establishing and expanding programs of group counseling in the public school setting. An analysis of the factors contributing to this problem and the necessary minimal conditions for effective group counseling in schools are discussed below.

What are the major obstacles that have impeded the development of comprehensive group counseling programs in the schools? The obstacles can be summarized under six areas: community resistance, administrative resistance, teacher resistance, student resistance, counselor resistance and lack of clearly developed programs.

Community Resistance

Group counseling programs, like sex education in the schools, hit close to conflicting values of parents and community leaders. The freedom of students to discuss personally relevant material is still a threat to parents, administrators, teachers—and even to students and counselors. In California, the John Birch Society has been as concerned about "sensitivity groups" as it has been about sex education.

Inherent in parent resistance, as well as teacher and administrator resistance, has been the lack of agreement that the affective side of man should have a significant place in the educational process. While some counselor trainers, this one included, blend the cognitive and affective into the group process, there is no denying that one of the main values of group counseling lies in the stress on the affective side of the person.

Administrative Resistance

The organization of public schools, both elementary and secondary, in which the development of new curricular programs resides largely in the school principal, makes the introduction and expansion of new programs, such as a group counseling program, extremely difficult. Each individual high school must select and establish new programs such as group counseling. Seldom does a school district have an organizational pattern that facilitates expanding new programs. Many large school districts seem to stay stuck in the pilot study phase of implementing new curricular or guidance programs. In contrast, the author was able to provide extensive group counselor training, over a three-year period, to over 200 State Employment Counselors throughout California.

The present widespread criticism of school leadership is not conducive to strengthening administrators to support new, creative and innovative programs in curriculum revision, let alone group counseling.

Teacher Resistance

Teacher resistance seems to stem from a lack of clear understanding that the freedom to talk about anything which concerns a group member does not mean the group leader is encouraging and condoning criticism of teachers and parents. A second area of real concern on the part of teachers has been in school settings where scheduling patterns make it necessary to take group members from a class.

Student Resistance

By and large, students in present-day elementary and secondary schools are very eager for the opportunities provided by group counseling programs. However, some resistance can be expected from two sources: when shyness makes participation very difficult and when the group counseling program is perceived by the students as being Establishment-oriented. If the counselors are seen as part of the administrative hierarchy, then participation in a group may be perceived as a more subtle way of manipulating the student toward adult-imposed values.

Counselor Resistance

Of all the resistances to initiating group counseling programs, the most prominent and widespread is counselor resistance. In one high school district, a creative superintendent tried to push counselors in three high schools into establishing a group counseling program. When he left, after four years of intensive inservice training, the counselors went back to their clerical and crisis intervention duties. It must be admitted that for many counselors trained five or more years ago very little group counseling training was then available. But even where districts have been willing to provide inservice training in group work, many counselors are reluctant to risk entering into the realm of group counseling. With many graduates of training programs being much better trained in group work and eager to institute groups, it can be expected that this area of resistance will diminish gradually.

Lack of Clearly Developed Programs

Counselor trainers and directors of pupil personnel services must accept responsibility for a decided weakness in establishing integrated guidance programs and in developing ways of getting the new programs into each school. Groups in a school setting must clearly fit the school program and have a continuity built in. Only a few program leaders have established a program of guidance efforts that show clearly where and when group counseling is indicated. The greatly improved quality of training in group work now throughout the country will lead to counselor discouragement and apathy unless pupil personnel program developers begin to establish coordinated programs.

Minimal Necessary Conditions

The resistances and difficulties of providing a group counseling program in the school setting have been stated. Let us now review the minimal necessary conditions that are needed for an effective group counseling program.

First: A Designed Program

An effective group counseling program needs both a theoretical framework and an organizational plan. Counseling, let alone group counseling, has been greatly hindered by inadequate theoretical foundations to build helping techniques and procedures. Psychoanalysis, as a dominant theory in the helping professions, has had serious limitations when applied to the mass education setting.

Translating psychoanalytic theory into therapeutic practice has always been a difficult process. Efforts to translate psychoanalytic theory to the educational setting have been even more difficult.

The slow growth of learning theory has handicapped educational practitioners in both teaching procedures and counseling procedures. Fortunately, recent developments in behavior modification have shown that procedures used in helping students can be based on theoretically sound ground. Furthermore, it has been demonstrated that theoretical assumptions can lead to specific counseling strategies for a wide array of client problems. The fear among some counselors that behavior modification efforts were based on too narrow a realm of behaviors needing change has been countered effectively by Thoresen's development of a humanistic behavioral position (Thoresen, 1970).

So, it is necessary that each district desiring to install a group counseling program specify the goals of the program. These goals must fit closely the over-all instructional goals of the school district.

For example, a district might specify the following goals for its group counseling program:

1.   To assist academic underachievers.
2.   To assist students who have ineffective social skills.
3.   To train all students in more efficient decision-making skills.
4.   To assist students with excessive fears and anxieties.
5.   To help students to explore life style and career possibilities.
6.   To reduce interpersonal hostilities in our school.

With a prepared list of goals and objectives the counselors are ready to explain their efforts to the school board, parents, administrators and teachers.

The development of goals for the total program then permits the counselor to prepare procedures for helping students, parents and teachers to identify individual needs and select experiences that aim to alleviate the problem or provide for growth in specific skills.

With the development of goals for the group counseling programs and for the individual student, attention must be given to organizational aspects within the school setting. It is clear from the list of six possible objectives for a group counseling program that a wide variety of group experiences would be indicated. The time needed to help students with various problems and concerns will vary widely. Underachievers often take more than a school year of group work for change in actual achievement, whereas other problem areas, such as poor study skills, could take a much smaller number of experiences to gain a stated goal. The school schedule needs to provide time for group counseling experiences and preferably not from regular classes. One solution, when a group counseling goal involves a total class, is to have two counselors divide the class on a once-a-week basis for a period of weeks.

The group counselor should not be allowed to define his program by size of group. With the curriculum development of many Personal Development units, such as the *Decision-Making Units* of the Palo Alto School District in California, we can expect counselors to return to even class size groups to carry out program objectives.

Second: Administrative Support

Assuming the first minimal necessary condition for establishing a strong group counseling program is met, one is faced next with the necessity of strong administrative support. Numerous administrators would need only the first condition to be carried out to insure their strong backing of a new program. However, in those schools where the principal is more of a status quo, don't-rock-the-boat type of person, it is virtually impossible for a strong group counseling program to get established. Problems, misunderstandings, misperceptions and conflict of values cannot all be resolved ahead of time. A program needs a chance to get started and a design for gaining broad acceptance as it develops. Strong administrative support is a basic necessity.

Third: Counselors Willing to Work

The final necessary condition for establishing a new program is the quality of the counselors. There is accumulating research evidence to show that training in individual counseling does not prepare one adequately to be a group counselor. In fact, in one study by Conger (1970), the findings indicated that poor group leaders left their group members worse off in academic performance than a control group not receiving any counseling. The strong group counselor, however, did influence the attainment of increased academic performance.

Without an intensive inservice training program in group work, it is not fair to insist that all counselors must do group work.

It is very important that the inservice training be a practicum type experience, with audiotape or videotape reviews of the counselors working with their own groups.

Summary

In summary, to institute a new group counseling program for a school district the following minimal necessary conditions are needed:

1. A theoretical framework and organizational design must clearly focus on change in behavior—it must enable participants and interested observers to know what is happening.
2. Strong administrative support is necessary to get innovative school programs established. Such programs cannot be mandated or authorized, however; the program can grow only with creative leadership.
3. Counselors who are willing to *risk* are needed to begin the new group counseling program. It is not possible to hide what one does in a group. Thus, it takes courage to go ahead and begin a new program. Not all *individual* counselors can be expected to become good *group* counselors.

With these necessary conditions met, a school district is ready to begin a group counseling program.

References

Conger, Virginia. *The Differential Effects of High and Low Functioning Group Counselors Upon the Academic Performance of Students in an Educational Opportunity Program.* M.A. thesis, Chico State University, California, 1970.

Mahler, Clarence A. *Group Counseling in the Schools.* Boston: Houghton Mifflin, 1969.

Thoresen, C.E. On Developing Personally Competent Individuals. Paper presented at American Psychological Association Convention, Miami Beach, 1970.

16.
Group and Individual Goals:
Their Development and Utilization

James E. Doverspike

Recently, the writer attempted to bring together some of the salient features of group guidance and group counseling to create a synthesized group approach called GUICO (Doverspike, 1971). There are seven major features of the GUICO approach.

1. Co-counselors, one male and one female
2. Medium-sized group with heterogeneous composition
3. Developmental/social and remedial problem-solving goals
4. Considerable structure and regular assignments
5. Hierarchical ordering of group events
6. Strong emphasis on role-playing
7. Continuous evaluation to chart growth

Having employed the GUICO approach a number of times and having studied feedback from colleagues who have used the approach, it appears that some clarification and extension is needed concerning the feature referring to goals. What follows is an attempt to describe the purposes, origins and types of goals; to illustrate how goals are refined; and, finally, to relate goals to planning through the processes of application and revision. Other selected sources which include somewhat different treatments of goals are: Dinkmeyer and Dreikurs (1963), Krumboltz (1966) and Ohlsen (1970).

Purpose

If handed paper and pencil and asked to list our goals, most of us probably would be hard put to come up with a list which is acceptable to us. Probably most of our goal statements would be vague, highly abstract and idealistic or childishly mundane. Also, many of us would draw a blank. We are so unfamiliar with thinking and operating in a goal-oriented frame of reference that we are momentarily stunned when asked to change. Goals are refined statements of our desires and needs. They are destination points used to guide us on our journey through this week, next month, next year and on into the future.

Origin

Most of us have goals, whether or not we are consciously aware of them. We are also aware of the future. And one way we relieve our insecurity about the future is to formulate some sort of goals. If our feelings of insecurity are intense enough, we may become overwhelmed and deny the necessity of developing goals and merely try to live from day-to-day, taking each day as it comes, proceeding one day at a time into the future.

While goals are expressions of our desires and needs, contaminating influences frequently prevent or tend to obstruct realistic goal development. For example, significant others may try to set our goals for us or a limited environmental situation may restrict the kinds and numbers of goals potentially available to us. Also, our goals are related to our uniqueness as individuals, our abilities, interests and personality characteristics. Our family, friends, social organizations and culture also affect our goals in an indirect though influential manner.

Types

Since goals are diverse and related to age, time and circumstances, it is essential that we classify them in order to better understand their nature. A continuum model may be helpful in understanding the nature of goals if we remember that polarities are seldom isolated but rather are connected by degrees of difference and shadings of meanings. In Figure 1, goals are divided into two major types based upon a time-space dimension—immediate and long-range. Characteristics of each major type are shown at the extremes of the continuum and three subclassifications are given based upon the order in which we usually proceed when developing and utilizing goals—statement, refinement and planning. Also to be noted is the major principle undergirding the processes of goal statement, refinement and planning—flexibility.

An illustration of stating a goal, altering it by attending to cognitive, realistic and specific characteristics might appear as follows:

The orginal goal statement might be, "I want to get along better

Figure 1

Goals: Statement, Refinement and Planning

affective		cognitive
idealistic	**Stating Goals**	realistic
general		specific

complex		simple
whole	**Refining Goals**	parts
opinion		facts

developmental-social		remedial problem-solving
life style	**Goals and Planning**	units of behavior
intrinsic motivation		extrinsic motivation

Long-range	Processes feature	Immediate
goal characteristics	flexibility	goal characteristics

with others." The tone of the statement is largely affective, especially the "I want" lead segment. The segment "get along better" is too general, and the word "others" implies all others, which is idealistic and also too general.

Altering the original statement first to emphasize the cognitive and realistic, we may for example, define "get along better" to mean "learn one skill" and also, "help me begin to become a friend."

Altering "others" to emphasize the specific, we may identify one person as a potential friend, for example, Bill.

The original goal statement is now in altered form and appears as "I will learn one skill that will help me begin to become a good friend of Bill." This form places emphasis upon cognitive, realistic and specific goal characteristics.

Refinement

As noted in Figure 1, the process of refining goals involves altering the goal statement so that it becomes simpler, its parts and their interrelationships become evident, and opinion-laden segments are converted to facts. The principle of flexibility characterizes the refinement process, and the featured method is "honing." Honing implies sharpening, rearranging to gain precision and rewording to attain operational form.

An illustration of goal refinement might appear as follows:

Beginning with the altered goal statement developed above, "I will learn one skill that will help me begin to become a good friend of Bill," we may first move from the complex to the simple and from whole to parts by identifying "one skill."

Assume that we identify the skill as "initiating a conversation." The emphasis may now be placed upon parts and facts. What is involved in initiating a conversation? For example, knowing at least one thing that the other person is interested in; knowing how to make an opening remark; knowing how to make a response to another person's comment or question; and knowing how to make a closing remark are important subskills related to initiating a conversation.

The altered goal statement has now been refined into related subskills or parts which are simply stated and factually oriented. "I will initiate a conversation with Bill after (1) learning to make an opening remark based upon one of Bill's interests; (2) learning to respond to his comments or questions; and (3) learning to make a closing remark."

The goal now emphasizes simplicity, related parts and facts, and is sufficiently refined to be used in planning and application.

Application

Up to this point, goals have been stated and refined; our emphasis now shifts to using goals in planning. The writer's purpose here is not to construct a detailed plan but merely to highlight some important features of the planning process.

Using refined goals as a starting point, we build a step-by-step plan which we think will lead to goal achievement:

1. List activities that might lead to achievement of the goal.
2. Order the activities into steps in a hierarchical manner according to logical sequence and estimated ease of accomplishment.
3. Reword each step in the hierarchy so that each activity is described operationally, i.e., in terms of specific behaviors that the individual is capable of accomplishing.
4. Place the steps on an estimated time schedule of completion.
5. Put step one on the plan into practice, and after a degree of success has been attained, begin step two, and so on.

Revision

Most plans do not work perfectly on first trial; therefore, revision is necessary. Once again, flexibility undergirds the process of revision. If any step of the plan is not accomplishing its purpose, discussion, examination and critique should take place in order to locate roadblocks. Possible roadblocks include:

1. Successful accomplishment of each step of the plan is not properly rewarded.
2. A particular step of the plan is not carried out appropriately.
3. A step is out of sequence and therefore too difficult or untimely.
4. Behavior required is inappropriate.
5. Behavior is not closely related to the goal.
6. Goal is inappropriately stated or has not been sufficiently refined.

Once a roadblock has been identified, revision again takes place. Then application begins anew with the individual proceeding to completion or until encountering another roadblock.

Group Goals in Problem-Solving

While it is clear how an individual's goal may be better stated and further refined, it may not be readily apparent how the same procedures are applicable to groups. When we classify counseling groups as either developmental or remedial, it is necessary to understand that goal statement and refinement procedures will differ, depending upon the group's classification.

Since development groups are heterogeneously composed and concerned with long-range goals of a developmental/social nature, it is not necessary to feature a high degree of goal statement and goal refinement. For example, an appropriate goal for a developmental group might be "to develop a number of ways to become more independent." Through discussion, the group finally arrives at, let us say, six means of achieving independence; and each group member is encouraged to employ any or all of the six depending upon how he feels they meet his needs.

A major shift of emphasis should occur when we work with remedial groups. Remedial groups are homogeneously composed and possess immediate goals of a remedial problem-solving nature. Goals in this type of group, as is the case in individual counseling, must be well stated and highly refined if successful problem-solving is to occur. Referring to the "goals and planning" subclassification of the preceding figure, we see that immediate goals are characterized by extrinsic motivation, units of behavior and remedial problem-solving.

If each individual in a remedial group is to solve his problem, we cannot employ procedures which are designed to solve the group's problem directly. By employing what the writer calls the "umbrella approach" we endeavor to have each group member solve his particular problem, thereby indirectly solving the group's problem. With younger children we actually label a modern, see-through umbrella, using masking tape. The outside arc of the umbrella is labeled with the group's goal and each of the ribs is labeled with an individual member's goal. With older children and adults we prepare large charts instead of using the umbrella itself. Before proceeding with problem-solving, then, each individual is helped to state and refine his individual goal. What follows is a brief description of using the umbrella approach in remedial group problem-solving.

The "Umbrella" Approach

Individual goals now stated and refined, we choose a volunteer from the group to serve as a model for problem-solving. We proceed through the problem-solving process with the volunteer to the point where an assignment can be made. The assignment is the first of a series of assignments that the individual will complete outside the group setting as he works toward "doing things" to achieve his goal. As the remaining group members observe and assist the volunteer in the problem-solving process, two important benefits are forthcoming. First, they "learn" how the problem-solving process works and, second, they are now in a position to "tranfer" the process to the next phase wherein each of them will be solving his own problems.

The model now completed, group members review the problem-solving process before proceeding. It is essential that the process be thoroughly understood by all group members. If necessary, the counselor restructures unclear elements of the process. Major elements of the problem-solving process include:

1. Develop alternative course of action which leads to the goal (list on large chart).
2. Weigh each alternative course of action (use plus-minus tallies).
3. Decide on the course of action to be tried out *first* (implies that others may be tried later in the event of lack of success).
4. Develop a list of assignments which puts the courses of action into effect (each member completes at least one assignment between sessions).

Remaining members of the group now go through the problem-solving process together step-by-step. For example, the counselor and group members assist any individual who is having difficulty formulating alternatives before the group proceeds to weighing, deciding, or developing assignments.

After all assignments are listed and are being carried out between sessions, the session format is altered to feature discussion and critique of assignments in order to evaluate, and, if necessary, revise courses of action which are not working to the satisfaction of group members.

Possible explanations of lack of success in carrying out a course of action may include an inappropriate alternative, mistakes in carrying out the action, unrealistic assignments, poor critiques and detrimental influences outside the group over which we have little or no control.

Finally, each group member lists his assignments, writes down critique points and charts his progress from session to session. These procedures will tend to eliminate forgetfulness and at the same time provide each group member with a concrete picture of his activities, learnings and outcomes.

Conclusion

Our awareness of and insecurity about the future requires that, throughout our lifetime, we continually develop goals and plans. Not to do so, or to do so haphazardly, results in feelings of frustration and confusion, playing it by ear, or being washed to and fro in the sea of change. Understanding the purpose, origin and types of goals sets the stage for refining and applying our behaviors in such a way as to achieve desired outcomes. Revising our behaviors enables us to overcome roadblocks and move forward toward goal achievement and the rewards which accompany it.

References

Dinkmeyer, D. and R. Dreikurs. *Encouraging Children to Learn: The Encouragement Process.* Englewood Cliffs, New Jersey: Prentice-Hall, Inc., 1963.

Doverspike, J.E. GUICO: A Synthesized Group Approach. *Personnel and Guidance Journal,* 1971, *50,* 182-187.

Krumboltz, J.D. (Ed.) *Revolution in Counseling: Implications of Behavioral Science.* Boston: Houghton Mifflin Co., 1966.

Ohlsen, M.M. *Group Counseling.* New York: Holt, Rinehart and Winston, 1970.

17.
Demystifying the Group Process: Adapting Microcounseling Procedures to Counseling in Groups

Allen E. Ivey

Can skills of effective group leadership be taught? Or is the successful group leader simply an individual with a "gift"? This chapter takes the position that group leader behavior is definable and teachable, that one need not be a charismatic *guru* to lead a group. Rather, meaningful group leadership styles can evolve as the individual examines himself and his behavior in a systematic fashion.

Typically, group leaders learn their skills through participation in groups. The process of becoming a "good" leader is generally seen as a complex and difficult task. However, brief training focused on specific skills of group leadership can be helpful in developing competent group leaders. The skills of group leadership discussed here are drawn from research and writing in microcounseling, a systematic method of imparting basic skills to counselors-in-training.

> Microcounseling is a scaled-down sample of counseling in which beginning counselors talk with volunteer "clients" during brief five-minute counseling sessions which are video-recorded. These scaled-down sessions focus on specific counseling skills or behavior. Microcounseling provides an opportunity for those who are preparing to counsel to obtain a liberal amount of practice without endangering clients. While microcounseling has other possible purposes and uses, its principal aim is to provide pre-practicum training and thus to bridge the gap between classroom theory and actual practice (Ivey *et al.*, 1968).

Microcounseling has proven effective with a wide variety of trainees ranging from school counselors (Hutchcraft, 1970), medical students (Moreland, 1971), junior high school pupils (Aldridge, 1971), to lay counselors (Haase and DiMattia, 1970; Gluckstern, 1972). In each case the specificity of the single behavioral skills taught within the microcounseling framework has demonstrated immediate and important changes in counselor behavior. These and many other applications of microcounseling are summarized in *Microcounseling: Innovations in Interviewing Training* (Ivey, 1971b).

Group leader behavior is equally amenable to systematic training as is individual counseling. Microcounseling skills training can be useful to the prospective group counselor as he enters the even more complex world of group counseling. Further, microcounseling offers a technology through which group members can learn communication and interpersonal skills via the same instructional procedures as those used to train leaders.

The Procedures of Microcounseling

It seems appropriate that the specific methods of microcounseling be summarized, with special attention paid to group counseling issues. Microcounseling when used in group counseling instruction involves a leader-in-training and four or five volunteer "group" members. The group is videotaped for short segments of time. During these segments, *single skills* of group leadership are emphasized.

The standard microcounseling paradigm consists of the following steps:

1. Videotaping of a five- to ten-minute segment of group interaction
2. Training
   a. A written manual describing the single skill being taught is presented to the trainee. Rather than try to produce an "instant" group leader, microcounseling training focuses on improving one skill at a time.
   b. Video models of an expert group leader demonstrating the skill are shown, thus giving the trainee a gauge against which to examine the quality of his own behavior.
   c. The trainee then views his own videotape comparing his performance on the skill in question against the "expert." Seeing oneself on tape within a specific context is a powerful learning experience.

      d.   A trainer-supervisor provides didactic instruction and emotional support for the trainee.

3.   A second five- to ten-minute videotaped group session

4.   Examination of the last session and/or recycling of the entire procedure as in step 2, depending on the skill level of the trainee

The time period for the training is approximately one hour, while a recycling of training adds another 30 to 45 minutes to the process.

One important variation of this basic procedure uses a group consisting of trainees in group leadership, each of whom takes a turn in demonstrating the specific skill in question. It cannot be stressed too strongly that the single skills emphasis is vital for success of microcounseling in group work. While it is tempting to try to "correct" a trainee's behavior on several dimensions, experience has revealed that improvement in one dimension before other skills are introduced is sufficient for beginning trainees. The confidence engendered by being able to do one thing well provides a solid basis for further growth in group counseling skills.

What Are the Skills of Group Leadership?

Within the microcounseling format, 12 basic skills have been identified for use with dyadic counseling instruction. They are available in written form with suggestions for developing videotaped models (Ivey, 1971b). It has been found that these same skills are useful in group counseling procedures.

For example, the first skill within the microcounseling paradigm is "attending behavior," the behaviorally defined skill of active listening. The three key aspects of attending behavior are eye contact, physical attentiveness through posture and verbal following behavior. Both the counselor and the group leader must engage in some form of attending or listening if they are to "tune in" with their clients. Thus, when working with beginning group leaders, basic instruction in simple listening skills such as eye contact, non-verbal expressiveness and staying on the topic is important. Unless one first listens, he cannot be expected to be an effective group leader. While attending skills may seem obvious, observation has revealed that many beginning counselors and group leaders have difficulty "staying-with" or listening to members of their group. They are often so concerned about what to say next that they forget the most basic skill of leadership, that of attending to what others are saying. A simple rule effective for many beginners is, when in doubt, "listen."

Another skill of the beginning counselor is the use of open versus closed questions. Too many beginning group leaders ask closed questions, thus cutting off discussion and ending in "yes-no" type interaction. Minimal encouragements (head nods, uh-huh, restatements) is another skill which helps group members realize the leader is interested in them.

But simply opening up a client to talk is not enough. A group of microcounseling skills focus on selective listening. Important among these skills are reflection of feeling (defined as selective attention to the emotional aspects of the group members' participation), paraphrasing (helping clarify verbal statements) and summarization. The group counselor interested in directing his group into areas of emotional concern and/or decision-making will want to be capable in these skill areas. Microcounseling training has revealed that counselors can learn these somewhat advanced conceptual skills of group leadership in relatively short periods of time.

Another skill important to the group leader is that of sharing one's own knowledge and experience. Some group leaders feel that they should not express themselves in a group, and restrict themselves unnecessarily to an exclusive listening role. Other leaders, of course, take the opposite path and talk too much. Through training in the skills of expression of feelings, sharing behavior and direct mutual communication, microcounseling provides counseling and group counselor trainees with the opportunity to explore sharing their ideas with a small group in a protected setting.

Clinical examination of a variety of counseling and group situations suggests that direct mutual communication may be one of the most facilitative and useful skills within the entire microcounseling paradigm. In direct mutual communication the group leader focuses on an individual or on the group interaction as he perceives and feels the situation in the "here and now." The leader shares his personal perceptions of the experience, his emotions and feelings. This skill, closely related to what encounter trainers may call personal sharing or feedback, seems especially important in helping groups express themselves openly about personal concerns. Interpretation skills are another skill examined within the microcounseling framework, but interpretation seems limited to certain types of groups more oriented toward therapy and may be of less interest to the group counselor.

One need not restrict himself to the skills suggested here. A number of other skills of counseling and/or group leadership can be identified and taught within the same microcounseling paradigm. For example, it would be possible to use these techniques to specify behaviorally the methods of the vocational group leader, a person interested in psychological education in the classroom, or any of a wide variety of specialized group techniques.

One final dimension of group leadership skills should be mentioned. A major distinction between dyadic counseling skills and group leadership lies in the area of focus (Ivey, 1971a). In traditional dyadic counseling, the counselor focuses constantly on one client, whereas the group leader may focus on one participant to the exclusion of others, a sub-group or participants, or on the total group. There is a major difference between what happens in a group, depending on the focus statements of the leader. There are some group leaders who constantly give leads relating to the total quality of group interaction ("Right now the group seems to be . . . .") and the emphasis of discussion in this type of group is on the totality of reactions. On the other hand, other group leaders focus constantly on one or two individuals and never use group focus leads; this type of group leader is doing basically individual counseling in a group situation. The effective group leader will find his own balance of individual versus group focus, but will in some way use the powerful forces of the total group to reach his aims.

Group Counselors Determine What
Will Happen in Their Groups

When a counselor focuses on a client, it may be predicted that the client will talk about himself. Similarly, when the group leader focuses on group process, it may be predicted that the group will talk about its own interaction. If the group leader focuses on an individual and his problems, the individual will be likely to respond by talking about his concerns. In effect, what the group counselor does determines what happens in his group.

If the leader engages in attending behavior, it may be anticipated that group members will continue talking so long as they are listened to (and the topic is meaningful to them). Further, it may be anticipated that the group counselor who models careful listening to others will be teaching his group members an important lesson and they may be encouraged to listen to others as well.

Similarly, it may be predicted that the group leader who reflects feelings accurately will hear emotions discussed in his group. There are counselors who wonder why their groups never talk about emotions; one of the main reasons is their inability to attend to, reinforce, or reflect feelings among their participants. The group leader is a powerful modeling agent and what he attends to and reinforces may be expected to appear again and again among the group members.

When a leader asks a closed question, he may ordinarily expect a short yes or no answer. If he asks an open question, he may expect his group to respond in a more open and lengthy fashion. Those individuals who have difficulty ending a group hour may find that even though the time has ended they are still reflecting feelings and asking open-ended questions instead of engaging in appropriate termination behavior.

It would be possible to belabor the point. Suffice it to say that group leader behavior determines what will happen in any particular group. This point has been investigated by Gluckstern in a study training parents as lay drug counselors. She used the Taxonomy of Group Leader Behavior (Ivey, 1971a) and found that changes in counselor behavior resulted in marked change in client behavior. After training, counselors used more reflections of feelings and their clients talked more about emotional issues. This may appear an obvious point, but it is one that cannot be stressed too strongly. Too many people think that group process is a mystical procedure in which the leader somehow guides the participants. While this may be true for some leaders, it is also possible to define specifically what the leader is doing, the effect his behavior is having on the group, and then to change his behavior and the behavior of those in his group. Gluckstern also found that the specificity of the microcounseling paradigm brought the parent counselors to a level of proficiency in which they were able to use these constructs for supervision of each other's counseling sessions. All this was accomplished in a 40-hour training session.

Passing Group Leader Skills on
to Group Members

Carkhuff (1971) has pointed out that the successful helper will change those "helpees" or clients with whom he works into helpers. It is no longer sufficient for a counselor to "help" people; he also has the responsibility to teach the skills he has mastered to others, thus multiplying the helping process.

In essence what is being suggested here is that if group leader skills are definable, teachable and facilitative, then it becomes incumbent on the group leader to help his group members learn the same skills so that they can help others as well as themselves. Microcounseling with its specificity of method is particularly adaptable to the teaching/learning process.

Aldridge (1971) used microcounseling with a junior high school population to see if they could learn counseling skills. He found that they could readily learn the skill of attending behavior, a skill important both in interpersonal relations and in being an effective student. Goshko (1972) has more recently adapted the microcounseling format successfully for the instruction of elementary children in behavioral skills. He found that children in the fifth grade can readily learn the skills of microcounseling in small groups and is currently examining the generalization of the skills to classroom behavior. Bitzer (1972) has developed an innovative blend of microcounseling skills and behavioral psychology in a successful parent training program in child rearing skills. Rollin (1970) provides similar data for teacher training. Thus, the evidence suggests that a wide variety of client populations can learn and profit from microtraining skills.

How would a group counselor integrate the teaching of micro-counseling skills into his group procedures? Three methods seem most appropriate. The first is in groups which can be formed for the teaching of basic skills within a human relations skills unit in a classroom or counseling group. This type of group focuses on didactic learning of skills. As a second alternative, microcounseling skills can be used as a supplement to on-going group counseling sessions. When a student learns in the group that he is not attending (or not expressing emotion, or not speaking up clearly), he can be referred to a microcounseling skills laboratory to work on the skills in which he has shown some deficiency. Having learned the skill through more systematic feedback than is usually possible in group counseling, he can then return to the group to test out his newly learned skills. Finally, the effective group leader, through modeling and "on-the-spot" instruction, can teach behavioral skills as needed.

The Dade County (Miami) School System (Collins, 1970) has successfully used microcounseling procedures to train cadres of high school students who then work as peer counselors. Zeevi (1970) has demonstrated the value of these techniques in group procedures with teen-age camp counselors and "hot-line" operators. As peer counseling becomes more popular and viable on the secondary school scene, the role of the counselor as teacher of counseling may become important.

The skills of the counselor are too important to be hidden and kept from the public. The major question is how can we translate our skills to others? One method which shows promise is microcounseling. Systematic skills training can be used by the counselor in a new role as psychological educator and teacher of human relations skills.

Summary

Microcounseling is only one route toward effective group counseling. While the value of microcounseling as a method of skills acquisition has been demonstrated and evidence exists that these skills generalize to practical work situations, there is undoubtedly more to group counseling than the application of a specific skill to a specific situation. This "something more" lies in the unique ability of each individual to define his own method for working with groups. While all group leaders use skills in some fashion, it is our belief that ultimately the individual must find his own blend and combination of skills.

Systematic methods such as microcounseling are probably most valuable in helping to get an individual started on the path to effective counseling. There are many people running groups with a deep sense of involvement and caring for those with whom they work. However, compassion without competence can lead to frightening and complicated situations in group procedures. Skills training provides one avenue through which competence can be given to the individual as he begins work with groups. Skills training can provide the individual with a reservoir from which he can draw to sustain himself and his group as they face together the process of personal growth and self-exploration.

References

Aldridge, E. The Microteaching Paradigm in the Instruction of Junior High School

Students in Attending Behavior. Unpublished dissertation, Amherst, University of Massachusetts, 1971.

Bitzer, L. *Parent Program in Behavioral Skills.* Unpublished manual, Amherst, Massachusetts, Regional Public Schools, 1972.

Carkhuff, R. *The Development of Human Resources.* New York: Holt, Rinehart and Winston, 1971.

Collins, E. Personal Communication. Miami, Dade County Public Schools, 1970.

Gluckstern, N. Development of a Community Training Program for Parent-Consultants on Drug Abuse. Paper presented at the meeting of the American Personnel and Guidance Association, Chicago, April 1972.

Goshko, R. The Microcounseling and Media Therapy Framework in the Instruction of Elementary Students in Behavioral Skills. Unpublished paper, Amherst, Massachusetts, 1972.

Haase, R. and D. DiMattia. The Application of the Microcounseling Paradigm to the Training of Support Personnel in Counseling. *Counselor Education and Supervision,* 1970, *10,* 16-22.

Hutchcraft, G. The Effects of Perceptual Modeling Techniques in the Manipulation of Counselor Trainee Interview Behavior. Unpublished dissertation, Bloomington, University of Indiana, 1970.

Ivey, A. A Predictive Taxonomy of Group Leader Behavior. Unpublished paper, Amherst, University of Massachusetts, 1971a.

Ivey, A. *Microcounseling: Innovations in Interviewing Training.* Springfield, Illinois: C.C. Thomas, 1971b.

Ivey, A., C. Normington, C. Miller, W. Morrill and R. Haase. Microcounseling and Attending Behavior: An Approach to Prepracticum Counselor Training. *Journal of Counseling Psychology, Monograph Supplement,* 1968, *15,* 1-12.

Moreland, J. Video Programmed Instruction in Elementary Psychotherapeutic and Related Clinical Skills. Unpublished dissertation, Amherst, University of Massachusetts, 1971.

Rollin, S. The Development and Testing of a Performance Curriculum in Human Relations. Unpublished dissertation, Amherst, University of Massachusetts, 1970.

Zeevi, S. Development and Evaluation of a Training Program in Human Relations. Unpublished dissertation, Amherst, University of Massachusetts, 1970.

18.
Role-Working in Group Counseling

Wayne W. Dyer and
John Vriend

In a counseling group with college graduate students, a 34-year-old black woman talks about her feelings of inadequacy because, as it turns out, she was hired by a local college to serve as a "black statue." Assigned the title of assistant dean, her major job responsibilities include guiding the cheerleading team, answering the telephone and recording minutes at weekly department meetings. She has come to feel used, only a token giving visibility to racial quota-filling, a feather-bedder rather than a vital contributor in an important position.

After she has related her concerns and frustrations, explaining how thwarted and underrated she feels, the group counselor suggests conducting a simulated departmental meeting in which she actively confronts her "colleagues" about one aspect of her job, her secretarial role of minutes-taker at the weekly meetings. She describes each member of her department, and then selects a group participant whom *she* feels could portray that person with sufficient fidelity. When all roles are assigned, she is required to talk about her previously customary conduct at the departmental business meetings which is objectionable to her and to set as a personal goal a presentation of her dissatisfaction at the next staff gathering.

The leader sets the scene, and a contrived departmental meeting gets underway. She struggles to make her position known to her ersatz colleagues, who all attempt to deal with her as she would be treated in the genuine setting. After working through the scene, in which she is successful in making her point, and evaluating her experiences with the members of the counseling group, she leaves the session determined to have an effective confrontation at the upcoming departmental meeting. She returns for the next group counseling session having implemented her plan and having insisted that she will no longer demeaningly serve as a secretary to a group in which she is designated a co-worker, unless it is done on a rotating basis. Thus she has actively begun to redefine her job status and functions: she is working at being more in command of herself in her world.

A 15-year-old boy has talked about his many brushes with disciplinary officials because he is afraid that his friends "won't like him" if he assumes a conforming posture. In the safe experimental climate of the counseling group, the boy proceeds through a variety of exercises in which he tries out simulated new behaviors with his friends. Group members assume a mixture of roles in a number of scenes realistically characteristic of the young man's life, all designed to demonstrate to this counselee that he has alternatives, and that most of the fantasies of impending events he has created for himself are based on false assumptions. As the enactment unfolds, group members take turns being his alter ego, being spokesmen for what he feels as contrasted with what he thinks and says, or doubling as more aggressive versions of a possible self. He has the opportunity to observe others acting out his role, to hear his doubles put into words and actions what he would genuinely like to get across to his friends. After working through his conflicts with the helping group members who have assumed the identities and behaviors of his real-life chums, he tries out his newly discovered alternative ways of dealing with his friends, and he learns that being what he chooses to be makes him feel better, and that his peers continue to accept him after his forceful insistence on his position.

An eight-year-old girl, obviously shy and lacking self-confidence, quietly tells her group that she doesn't know why she is a non-talker; she usually is just afraid, and that's that. She is able to tell that she really would like to be different, more like Suzy, a spontaneous talker and an easy mixer in most social situations. She is given the opportunity to act for a few minutes with other children in the group who assume the role of (1) a favorite person and (2) a person who always "scares" her and "makes" her hangbackish and tentative. She shows the group members how she characteristically behaves in situations with such people, and the group counselor assumes the role of her "real feelings," saying aloud how the girl really feels (or what she would *like* to say) each time after the girl speaks. Thus the reticent child has the opportunity to practice new and more effective behaviors, and to observe first-hand a skilled person verbalizing those inner feelings and fears which have seemed to imprison her in a mysteriously internalized shell of timidity and, at times, panic.

These actual accounts taken from the case files of the authors, and an unlimited number of group member concerns, life conditions and situations, troublesome or neurotically debilitating relationships with significant others, many of which lend themselves to therapeutic recreation in dramatized forms, are the typical stuff of focused group counseling activity. While it has been traditional in psychological and educational literature (see Corsini, 1966, as an important instance of the former and Shaftel, 1967, as a knowledgeable instance of the latter) to refer to the practice of spontaneously dramatizing situations and relationships in a person's life as role-playing, what the "playing" part of that term connotes mitigates against its significance as a vital, highly productive counseling strategy.

Actors "play" their parts for the sake of an audience, for love or money, not so that they can live their lives in a more personally rewarding way. The "play" is a work of art, created for its own sake as an enduring entity; it is not "life." When a youngster says, "I was only playing," this is understood to mean that he is defending against real intent; what he *did* is not supposed "to count." In this sense the word "play" carries with it a loading pejorative to counseling purposes.

Also, the sense in which "play" means having fun, passing time in an amusing or delightful game or make-believe activity, is hurtful to the ends being sought for a member's sake when the strategy is employed in a counseling group. In a counseling group such play is too serious to be so misnamed: it is not play at all. It is work. It is testing activity, the trying on of new (albeit, uncomfortable) behaviors. It is not a substitute for life; it is a practice ground, a precursor of life. In many cases it *is* life; what many a counselee "works on" in a dramatized episode constitutes an experience in and of itself. The action in the group is not fun and games, meaningless, unreal. Rather, it is group members working together in an assortment of role techniques using the personal real-life data of one or more of their number, recreating scenes for enactment which will result in specific self-enhancing gains to that person.

Psychodramatic procedures are an exceptionally powerful category of the armamentarium available to group counselors, and if they are to be executed tellingly, they require the manifestation of skill and expertise on the part of the group counselor and hard work on the part of everyone in the group. Labeling these procedures "role-playing" ought to be considered the product of a profession in its infancy, one struggling in hit-or-miss fashion to find its proper voice; it is time for a more mature professional stance, a consolidation of gains. We suggest a shift of emphasis, "role-playing" to "role-working." Role-working connotes a "working through" of difficult psychological material while "in a role." It is safe, because it is an experience not yet actualized in one's life in a "counting" sense—a cushioning, precursory shakedown cruise. Role-working connotes professional seriousness. It suggests a technology of dramatic methods, a well-planned and tested battery of group counseling strategies which can be set to work. Group members working in roles can help themselves to eliminate self-defeating behaviors in a psychologically therapeutic environment where co-helpers are supportively hard at work at their side.

What Is Role-Working?

Role-working in a group counseling session is a deliberately, though spontaneously, contrived helping structure in which group members receive assistance by working through old behavioral patterns and trying out previously unselected alternatives in a snug social enclave minimizing risk and maximizing involvement, feedback and openness. The group members seeking help are provided with an opportunity to check their own defenses, reactions, strengths and weaknesses in a simulated environment, and to develop insights into their own behaviors in given settings. Role-working is a total group process in which a variety of methods can be utilized for the purpose of helping individuals to observe and feel, on the spot, how they characteristically comport themselves in troublesome circumstances, and to learn fresh approaches to handling themselves in the presence of significant others in their lives which were not previously incorporated into their repertoires of behavioral alternatives.

Role-working involves the creation or recreation of dramatic episodes out of the real life (often visceral, almost tangible) data from the personal world of a particular member, which are then enacted within the counseling group. The procedure is happenstance, spontaneous, arising out of the present moment needs of a group member or members seeking greater behavioral effectiveness and freedom, understanding, three dimensional feedback, or the enriched opportunity to communicate volatile person-to-person material to other group members through demonstration (role-working is brought into being in a counseling group because of some such rationale, one which is either remedial or growth-promoting for a particular member or members). Helping the group to decide on a script, deciding which role-working techniques to employ, directing the episodes and members of the "cast," selecting or collaborating with the protagonist to select the role workers, modeling many of the role-working behaviors—all of these functions and more require a skilled and competent group counselor trained and experienced in group psychodramatic technology. In addition, the group counselor helps to establish the climate in which the role-working occurs, protecting each member of the group by assuring voluntary participation in each role and by careful monitoring of what is going on to make certain that in no case are the ego-strength limitations of group members exceeded.

Some Specific Role-Working
Principles, Structures, Techniques

While there is an extensive literature of psychodrama and enough qualified regular practitioners of this method of psychotherapy to comprise a "school" (see the Sacks chapter in this book), psychodrama is often misconstrued or ignored by counseling professionals as being inappropriate, too specialized or esoteric, for incorporation in counseling groups. Group counselors who take such a posture reject out of hand a fertile and important resource for adding to their storehouse of effective group counseling techniques. Illustratively we herewith present some specific role-working structures, principles and techniques which, while not unknown to psychodramatists accustomed to working on a stage, are adaptively suited to the purposes and milieu of counselees working together in groups.

1.0 In one-to-one counseling, role-working succeeds most productively when the counselor takes the role of the counselee and the help-seeker in turn assumes the role of the "significant other," be that person the counselee's mother, girlfriend, teacher, or whomever. The counselor can mimic his counselee's actions accurately for he has accumulated the necessary behavioral evidence, but he usually fails in portraying accurately any important figure in the counselee's life because he can know that person only through the prism of his client's distorted perceptions. By having the client work in the role of the "other," the counselor learns more poignantly how the "other" is seen by the client, something about the quality of the relationship, and what kinds of emotions arise in his client. By the counselor working in the role of his client, in turn, he is able to mirror back behaviors which his client has been manifesting in the counseling sessions, which, if judiciously selected and properly analyzed, promote therapeutic movement.

   1.1 The same principle applies in groups; if group members work as other group members, they are more successful than if they attempt to work in roles of people not present. Of course, it is not always possible to have group members working exclusively in each other's roles. Whenever it is appropriate, under such circumstances, the counselor coaches a group member in working in the role of the missing figure, helping the counselee whose life circumstances are thus being dramatized to flesh out and bring into the group the pertinent behavioral variables of the newly introduced character, to show the group members in a more tangible fashion what there is that is important for them to know for the sake of the scene that is to be worked through. Such a demonstration then allows a different member to facilitate accurate role-working when roles are later reversed. After a counselee has shown how his "others" behave, the roles can be reassigned, the new role-workers being enabled to perform more capably in their efforts to achieve the desired outcomes.

   2.0 The use of doubles allows for a variety of role-working stratagems in group counseling. If a member has difficulty in handling or expressing his feelings with another person in his life, a spouse or a sibling, for example, the leader can assume the role of his double and another group member can work in a second-double role. The protagonist sits in the center of the circle with the counselor on his left and the second-double on his right. Sitting opposite the protagonist is the significant other in his life (in role) with whom he has understanding, communicating and relating difficulties. Each time the protagonist speaks, or every second or third time, the group counselor verbalizes what the protagonist would like to say, and the second-double verbalizes how the protagonist really feels at the moment he is speaking. This extended double technique allows the counselee to actually hear the discrepancy between what he says, what he would like to say and what he is feeling. In the evaluation session following the role-working, the dynamics behind such discrepancies can be pointed to and alternate ways of behaving can be considered.

2.1 As here suggested, the number of double possibilities is endless. One double could do the work of portraying any and all negative emotions, another simultaneously portraying the positive emotions of a group counselee who is filled with ambivalence. Doubles could be assigned roles of id, ego, or superego (or child, adult, parent, in the framework of transactional analysis—see Berne, 1964). A skilled group counselor, aware of the potential in this technique, learns to apply it creatively and helps side-by-side double arrangements arise in the group for any number of given client concerns.

2.2 Doubles can be assigned productively to role-workers in roles other than that of the protagonist. A double in such a situation, for example, might be used as a pump-primer, as a collaborator in more effective role portrayal.

3.0 Allowing a group member to be a mentally but not physically involved observer of his own life problems being worked on by others is a potent role-working method. The group counselor and a group member demonstrate a more expedient and satisfying way to work through a trying social situation while the help-seeker observes. This technique permits the observing counselee to watch two people who are working in his role and that of a significant other in his life deal with each other on a higher level of effectiveness than he has experienced in his own living. Group members are prone to suggest that a protagonist behave in a certain way and he will be much better off, but the natural tendency is for a counselee to believe that such would be impossible, given the circumstances and people in his real life. After he has demonstrated how each of the "others" in his life behaves, he then observes as a skillful group counselor works in the role of the protagonist and literally adopts new and effective strategies for working with the troublesome "others." The "if I were you, I would act thus and so" approach to helping takes on a credibility when it is demonstrated that it lacks in advice-giving form.

4.0 The scenario role-working technique is described in the

opening paragraphs of this chapter. Here several or all of the group members assume roles which are given in the context of the presented problem. Perhaps a family or a classroom subgroup are involved. The group counselor stays out of the action as a role-worker, preferring to function instead as a director, perhaps now and then sliding into a double-like relationship with this or that role-worker to facilitate in pump-priming fashion more effective ways of working. The protagonist assigns the group members to the various roles as he sees fit. New behavioral alternatives are stressed by the group counselor, and those working in roles are encouraged to help the protagonist in trying out more effective methods for working in this important-to-the-counselee social setting.

5.0 In every counseling group there are certain members who, in their customary interpersonal transaction styles, more nearly resemble significant others in the lives of some participants than do certain other group members. This is to say that while Pete is 40 years younger and the wrong sex, he behaves in a fashion remarkably similar to Mary's grandmother, a person she has trouble dealing with; at least Mary sees an obvious resemblance in ways important to her. When such a connection is noted, a productive role-working structure can be instituted by having Pete work in the role of grandmother and help Mary to work out new behaviors and communication patterns.

5.1 When conflicts arise, or counseling blocks, or any of the possible logjams which tend to occur in counseling groups, whether they involve the group as a whole or develop just between a few or two of the members, role-working is fruitful in helping to surface the causes and psycho-personal dynamics of the discontent. Group members exchange member roles. The role-working script comes from the interaction of the group itself.

5.2 Even without discontent or group logjams being present, role reversals among members constitute a productive technique. Having each member work in someone else's role for a time period of 30 minutes or so provides a kind of feedback which, for some members, tends to be as meaningful as anything else they experience in the group. With this exercise, as with most of those cited, post-role-working analysis by the group becomes crucial. Elizabeth finds it hard to ignore when the entire group agrees that she was accurately portrayed by Carl, even though she herself thought that Carl's work in her role was too ridiculous to be an honest reflection of her behavior.

6.0 In addition to scenes constructed out of the real-life personal data of a group member, imaginary scripts can be improvised and worked through in the group which have high therapeutic value. Getting-into-Heaven scenes enacted at St. Peter's Gate, courtroom scenes (group member witnesses testifying for each other), wedding and funeral scenes, even scenes in which abstractions such as death, ecstasy, guilt or justice are given roles in the manner of the morality dramas of the Middle Ages, any one of these and more can be brought appropriately into the group counseling process in order to help a member work through self-defeating behavior or learn to contend more effectively with life conditions and circumstances. If such scripts are selected on the basis of their relevance and commonality to all people, wherein the significant thematic elements touch the lives of everyone in the group in some vital way, the ratio of counseling meaningfulness to more group members increases.

7.0 Finally, the simplest and most easily effected role-working technique ought not to be overlooked. Skillful group counselors "put" members into role-working behaviors by becoming a significant "other" in spur-of-the-moment show-me-don't-tell-me-fashion. This, as noted earlier, is most effective when the counselor slides into the role of another member in the group whom he has studied and can imitate with fidelity. "All right, Monica. Now I'm not me. I'm Sam. And I've been sitting here thinking that everything you've said in the last five minutes is absurd, that you're just trying to protect yourself . . . ."

Suggested Role-Working Precautions

The above delineations of some structures and techniques in role-working hardly begin to exhaust the known technology nor the possibilities. They are presented here to give the reader a flavor of how role-working can be introduced effectively into the group counseling process.

Beyond this, it is important to note that competent group counselors who employ role-working structures and techniques exercise principled cautions and controls, tried and tested operating guidelines to more effective role-working behavior in counseling groups:

1. A group needs to be prepared for the frequent or occasional introduction of role-working. The most appropriate time for this is

during its initial use. The first role-working experience in the group, therefore, should be carefully brought into being, handled supportively, with non-evaluative reactions to member efforts. (One does not *fail* or *do well* as an actor; one can only *behave* in a certain way, which may or may not induce a desired outcome, and a role-working behavior is like any other behavior in the group: grist for study and analysis productive to its originator and owner. As with all behaviors, one improves with practice.) Following its initial use, time laid aside for analysis and evaluation of the experience is important. A counseling group is an on-going entity and early-laid building blocks undergird the parts of the structure which are added subsequently. In role-working there is a teaching and learning phase through which groups must pass.

2. Effective role-working depends on cooperation, not coercion. A worker ought to assume a role willingly, even if he has not volunteered, as may be the case when he is chosen by the protagonist. Similarly, a protagonist ought to endorse the transformation of his concerns into a script or scenario to be worked through in the group. Counselees know themselves and are the authorities on their limitations, and to push them into possible areas of hypertension without their consent and considered agreement is to invite irreconcilable difficulties, perhaps even chaos, which may be more damaging to the group counseling process than any role-working gains could offset.

3. The role-working setting, the direction the "plot" will move, who the characters are and what they are trying to achieve in the scene—these ought to be made known clearly to all participants.

4. The presence of a group counselor trained in role-working is vital. What strategies he employs in the group depend on his level of professional functioning. When he is venturing onto new role-working turf, it ought to be in the presence of a more highly trained group co-counselor whose expertise is adequate to the demands of the situation.

5. A competent group counselor is the decision-maker (or final endorser) about what role-working activity takes place in the group. As such, he is clear about the goals of the activity and helps the counselee whose script is being enacted, if not all of the group members, to understand beforehand what outcomes are expected and exactly *why* the role-working is a desirable part of the here-and-now counseling process.

6. Problem areas, interpersonal relationships and social situations to be worked out in role, ought not to be, in the considered judgment of the group counselor, beyond the capabilities of the group participants.

7. Allowing discussion to occur prior to the rendition of any conjured role-working episode is particularly important in counseling groups; and in earlier role-working episodes in the life of the group, such is essential. Every group member has an equal right to understand what is going on in the group, to partake of its beneficial effects, to be allotted a dancing time on the drum. All questions which relate to the reason for role-working at this particular time in this particular instance, or to reservations of any kind, should be dealt with in a forthright and non-evasive manner by the group counselor.

8. Role-working is a spontaneous enterprise. A group counselor who evaluates the action of previous group sessions as calling for the introduction of a role-working episode for the sake of the growth of a particular member or members always does so, if he is realistic, on a tentative basis.

9. Reluctance to role-working is common, and competent group counselors see this as normal rather than as surprising. A statement such as, "I really don't think it will do any good" is typical. But even given such reluctance, the working in roles will usually be beneficial if the participants are not fearful of the process. No group member should be cajoled or forced to do role-working against his will. Group members tend to join in when they see the process as being of genuine help.

10. Avoid dull, nebulous, wandering, inconsequential scenes which serve no purpose other than to turn off group counseling members to this technique.

11. Don't kill the efficacy of the technique by role-working every concern raised by group members. Role-working techniques and structures are powerful counselor protocols inviting free and frequent usage, but not to the exclusion of other group counseling resources. If a group counselor, at any given moment in the life of the group, makes role-working the number one treatment process over other choices, he ought to have a rationale to justify his choice to himself and the group.

12. Inasmuch as a role-working episode usually grows out of the real-life data of a particular member, it is possible that some group participants neither identify with any part of the activity, with the

goals, nor are even willing to pay attention when role-working events transpire. Such a situation can be the cause of a group rift which works against what happens in the group as a therapeutic process for the service of all. Therefore, a chief counselor objective ought to be the involvement, on some level, of everyone in the group, whether in roles or post-role-working analyses and evaluations.

13. Role-working which ends when a group counseling session ends is not effective. A group needs time to evaluate what has gone on, to understand and profit from the experience. Then, too, many experiences are highly emotional and require an unwinding time, a return to homeostasis for many role-workers.

14. Post-role-working evaluation ought to determine: (a) Was the experience effective? For whom, in what ways? (b) Was this the most productive way for the group to spend its time? (c) What conditions, procedures, roles, or whatever ought to be changed in the next use of this procedure? (d) What was learned, socially, behaviorally, emotionally? By whom? In what context? (e) Why did the group decide to enter into this activity? Did it achieve what it set out to do?

Counselors Trained in Role-Working

Virtually all counselee problems, concerns and discovered objectives that materialize in counseling groups are amenable to role-working. The presence of many willing co-helpers committed to common goals who can participate in an array of episodes and roles makes the counseling group format a consummate one for this potent behavioral modification methodology.

The key to successful role-working is the training and expertise of the group counselor in psychodramatic skills and structures, in his directorship. As we have indicated, when working in roles is taken seriously and is executed effectively, the training and acumen required of the counselor are considerable. A call for the inclusion of courses in role-working, where burgeoning counselors can receive the needed varieties of experiences actually working in roles to develop the necessary expertise, ought to be heard throughout the counseling profession.

References

Berne, Eric. *Games People Play: The Psychology of Human Relationships.* New York: Grove Press, 1964.

Corsini, Raymond J. *Role-Playing in Psychotherapy: A Manual.* Chicago: Aldine, 1966.

Shaftel, Fannie R. and George Shaftel. *Role-Playing for Social Values: Decision-Making in the Social Studies.* Englewood Cliffs, N.J.: Prentice-Hall, 1967.

19.
Psychodrama: An Underutilized Resource in Group Counseling

James M. Sacks

History

In 1922 J.L. Moreno described his improvisational theater in Vienna devoted to the facilitation of spontaneity and creativity. Moreno, however, was not an impresario but a social psychiatrist. He soon developed a method for the diagnosis and measurement of group relationships which he called "sociometry" and a method of psychiatric treatment which he named "group psychotherapy." Years later he revived his interest in theatrical improvisation, combining it with group therapy in the form of "psychodrama." He founded the American Society of Group Psychotherapy and Psychodrama (1943) and the journals *Sociometry* (1937) and *Sociatry* (currently titled *Group Psychotherapy* and *Psychodrama*). He and others have written extensively on the subject, so that a thousand-item bibliography on psychodrama is now in publication (Greer and Sacks, 1972).

The Psychodrama Session

The psychodrama group meets in a small theater-like room. The therapist or director begins with a "warmup"—a limited structuring of the session to reduce anxiety, build cohesion and to prepare the members for action. In the second phase of the session, the dramatic production, a protagonist is selected who enacts relevant scenes from his life. The "auxiliary egos" who play the complementary roles may be either group members or specially trained professionals. After the dramatic scenes have reached their natural climax, a final discussion is held.

Goals

Psychodrama corresponds in its goals to analytic psychotherapy insofar as it attempts to release repressed ideas or affects. In this sense psychodrama is essentially a subtractive method aimed at the removal of pathogenic complexes through insight. Psychodrama corresponds in its goals also to educational methods insofar as it attempts to expand the behavioral repertoire by teaching. In this sense psychodrama is additive, introducing new material into the psyche from without.

Action

Psychodrama's unique contributions to psychotherapy include the use of action, temporal flexibility and role flexibility. Physical acting out usually facilitates derepression more readily than verbal interpretation. The psychodrama protagonist who waves his arms and shouts angry words at his mother is more likely to experience hitherto repressed hostile feelings toward her than the analytic patient who only hears his analyst's interpretation that he bears unconscious resentment against her. Active involvement also helps develop interpersonal skills. Role rehearsal is an essential ingredient in the gaining of social skills just as practice is required in the development of any ability. It is a truism that one learns by doing.

Time

The therapeutic mechanism of analysis relies on the revival of repressed memories of past experiences which have been producing deleterious influence in the present. In group therapy of the interpersonal school the past is essentially ignored. Current interpersonal behavior patterns within the group are observed and pointed out, but no attempt is made to explore the original cause. In psychodrama the here-and-now aspect of interpersonal psychotherapy is maintained while at the same time regression to pathogenic experience of the past is also employed. Traumatic memories of the past continue to be experienced in the unconscious as if they were still present. In psychodrama, therefore, the past is reenacted as present. The reliving of these experiences, as if they were still occurring, releases emotional catharsis more effectively than does the mere retelling of stories. Psychodrama also deals with future oriented states such as hope and fear. Aimless, indecisive or conflicted individuals may try various action possibilities just to see how they feel or a protagonist may be able to objectify the details of what he most fears by means of a psychodramatic scene.

Role

The psychodramatic protagonist has the option of changing identity or role from one person to another. Such changes introduce a myriad of psychodramatic techniques useful both in analytic psychodrama and role training. Typical variations are the following:

Monads: Scenes with One Role
1. *Soliloquy*—in which the protagonist speaks as himself.
2. *Individual role play*—in which the protagonist takes the role of another person speaking alone. He thus explores another person's view of the world.
3. *Mirror*—in which an auxiliary ego takes the protagonist's part. Here the protagonist is freed from the action entirely and is able to watch himself perform. Some protagonists who would be threatened by immediate involvement can use the mirror as a bridge to fuller participation later.
4. *Modeling*—in which an auxiliary ego demonstrates an alternative way of behaving for the benefit of the protagonist.

Dyads: Scenes with Two Roles
5. *Multiple-self*—in which the protagonist enacts ambivalence or self-confrontation by moving back and forth on the stage, alternating in role and personifying two different facets of himself.
6. *Monodrama*—in which the protagonist enacts a scene between himself and another person, again moving back and forth on the stage presenting the relationship by taking both roles.
7. *Double*—in which an auxiliary ego stations himself behind or beside the protagonist stimulating his productivity by adding occasional comments. The double may represent some latent or deeper self. The double may also move directly face-to-face with the protagonist for a scene of self-confrontation. The protagonist assumes the role of either of the two parts of himself by means of role reversal.
8. *Dialogue*—in which the protagonist as himself enacts a scene with an auxiliary ego who takes the role of another person. A life

relationship is simulated but the substitution of the auxiliary ego for the real other frees the protagonist to discover where his actions and feelings will lead when the restrictions of real relationships are removed. The presence of the auxiliary ego as a flesh-and-blood human enables the relationship to develop through back-and-forth conversation.

9. *Objective monodrama*—in which the protagonist, by taking both roles alternately, illustrates interaction between other people. He might, for example, reenact a disturbing argument between his parents which he had observed.

10. *Objective double*—in which the protagonist takes the role of another person and, moving slightly to the side also takes the role of this other person's double. He can then show both the manifest and latent levels, which he perceives in them.

11. *Role reversal*—in which a protagonist and auxiliary ego in dialogue exchange positions and see the world and themselves from the other's point of view. One advantage of role reversal in exploring a conflicted relationship is that each person finds it easier to see himself through the eyes of his opponent, knowing that his opponent is making the same momentary sacrifice of self-esteem.

12. *Patterning*—in which the protagonist adds an action dimension to the modeling situation. That is, he becomes the double of or a simultaneous copy of the one who is providing the role model.

13. *Objective dialogue*—in which the protagonist takes the role of a person other than himself, in dialogue with an auxiliary ego who is in the role of a third person. In this technique the protagonist avoids the inconvenience of the role shifting required in the objective monodrama.

14. *Multiple mirror monodrama*—in which an auxiliary ego presents two roles representing two parts of the protagonist's personality while the protagonist watches.

15. *Multiple mirror*—in which two auxiliaries illustrate various versions of the protagonist or enact their version of his inner conflicts while the protagonist watches.

16. *Mirror Dialogue Monodrama*—in which one auxiliary ego takes both parts in a dialogue between the protagonist and another person while the protagonist watches. In this way the auxiliary ego can demonstrate his perception of a protagonist's pattern of relating.

17. *Mirror dialogue*—in which two auxiliary egos demonstrate an interchange in which the protagonist is involved. This technique is

frequently used by members of a therapy group to show the protagonist how he acts with another member. The dialogue form is necessary since the protagonist's pattern may not be clear from a single act but only from a pattern of interaction.

18. *Modeling Double Monodrama*—in which an auxiliary ego enacts two parts of the personality of a person significant to the protagonist, while the protagonist watches.

19. *Modeling Dialogue Monodrama*—in which an auxiliary ego taking both roles demonstrates a dialogue between two people significant to the protagonist while the protagonist watches.

20. *Modeling Double*—in which two auxiliary egos enact two sides of the personality of someone significant to the protagonist, while the protagonist watches.

21. *Modeling Dialogue*—in which two auxiliary egos enact a dialogue between two people significant to the protagonist while the protagonist watches.

Sixty-five further variations are possible as triads, such as the *Dialogue with Double,* in which the protagonist with a double at his side engages in conversation with an auxiliary ego. The protagonist's double throws in occasional comments which strike slightly beneath the surface of the protagonist's manifest role. It is an effective form of psychological interpretation which can take advantage of the heat of the moment.

Psychodrama in an Educational Setting

The same basic laws of human psychology apply whether a person is considered as a psychotherapy patient or as a student. While therapeutic and educational goals differ, it would be surprising if there were not considerable overlap in methodology. Defenses against understanding of the world as well as defenses against understanding of self dissolve under analogous conditions. Psychodrama helps disarm the one as well as the other. Nor would it be correct to assume that the role of the educational institution must be confined to learning about the world or that insight has no place in the school. An atmosphere in which children are free to describe or enact their feelings is certainly conducive, even essential, to learning. Maximum absorption takes place with an optimal balance between intake and output. The child who is a passive sponge is both rare and deplorable.

While psychodrama can contribute to learning, its abuse can certainly frustrate that goal. Psychodrama is a tool for the use of the protagonist and never to be used as a device of psychological instruction. A probing atmosphere is anti-therapeutic in a clinical context and anti-educational in an academic context.

The Vice-President of the United States (Agnew, 1971) has recently extended this caveat into a general attack on educational psychodrama. He states: "[the time of the metamorphosis of the teacher into a learning clinician] is already here in what some would term our more progressive public schools. Perhaps you have heard of the so-called 'psychodramas' that children of all ages are forced to act out in the classroom. Listen to this account that I read recently in a newspaper: '... teachers frequently ask the pupils to act out such things as obtaining an abortion, interracial dating, smoking marijuana—and how their parents would react.' Parents find even more objectionable 'psychodramas' in which children act out an actual incident from the home, something which parents consider a clear invasion of their privacy. There have also been 'talk ins' where two or three children will go to the school counselor and answer highly personal questions, such as: 'What does your father wear when he shaves?' or 'Do you love your parents?' ... Instead of psychodrama in the classroom, let's restore conditions that permit and encourage learning. ... I would think restoration of discipline and order ought to be a first priority, even ahead of curriculum, in the schools of this country."

I trust the reader will indulge the inclusion of this comic note and be assured that psychodramatists are above any attempt to gain sympathy for our view by the all-too-easy honor of being on Spiro Agnew's evil witch list.

References

Agnew, Spiro. Address before the Illinois Agricultural Association. *Congressional Record,* November 18, 1971.

Greer, Valerie J. and James M. Sacks. *Bibliography of Psychodrama* (1972). Privately available: V.J. Greer, 505 West End Avenue, New York, New York.

Moreno, J.L. *Das Stegreiftheater.* Berlin: G. Kiepenheuer, 1923.

Moreno, J.L. *Psychodrama and the Psychopathology of Interpersonal Relations.* Psychodrama Monograph Number 16. New York: Beacon House, 1945.

Moreno, J.L. *The First Book on Group Psychotherapy.* New York: Beacon House, 1957.

20.
Game Theory, Simulations and Group Counseling

Barbara B. Varenhorst

Studying life from the standpoint of game theory, one is impressed with the realization that what is so explicit in games is extremely vague and confusing in the life game, i.e., the goals or objectives of play and the methods of achieving the goal. Whereas those of us engaged in helping roles would not desire to pre-determine the goals for individuals when it comes to living a life, much of what we do is analogous to attempting to delineate the scoring system and to teach the strategies and skills leading to a higher probability of "winning."

Game theory and the relatively recent application of this theory to social simulation appears to have unique potential as a teaching tool. When both are utilized effectively by teachers and counselors, students do seem to emerge with greater clarity as to "how to win the game." Because social simulation games and the group counseling process share many similarities, it is particularly relevant for the group counselor to be aware of simulation games and to be knowledgeable of game theory. To know of games, or to have used a simulation game, does not necessarily lead to an understanding of game theory. Both, however, are useful to the group counselor. Commercially constructed or individually designed games can be employed in group counseling to assist in the accomplishment of the goals of counseling. Game theory can be used for the basic principles for conducting groups, and one could argue that direct application of game theory to all group counseling would result in a more systematic and effective group experience. The major content of this chapter will be devoted to making explicit why this is so.

Due to the integral relationship of game theory to systems analysis and behavior theory, the writings on these subjects (see those by Ryan and by Krumboltz and Potter in this book) are relevant to a more complete understanding of the material presented here.

Games and Simulations

Games are commonly viewed as activities associated with fun, relaxation, competition and make-believe. When associated with education or human relations in terms of "playing games," an assumption is made of frivolousness or of a type of deception. Such stereotypes lead to *no-no* responses from potential game users.

However, the wide use of "game" as a metaphor for many social activities is illustrative of the similarity between the formal structure of games and reality-tested life. Games may be played casually or seriously. When constructed for serious playing, games can combine analytical thinking about problems with emotionally expressive activity.

Abt (1970) has defined a game as an activity among two or more independent decision-makers seeking to achieve their objectives in some limiting context. He defines their characteristics and attributes as those of high motivation and dramatic representations of real problems which communicate efficiently concepts and facts on many subjects. Players assume realistic roles, face problems, formulate strategies, make decisions and get fast feedback on the consequences of their actions. Games accomplish this through their formal structure of procedures, rules and role descriptions, and create motivation by employing the winning and losing aspect which leads to amusement, competition and involvement. Coleman (1968) argues that games especially facilitate learning because of their properties of focusing of attention, requirement of active rather than passive observation, the abstraction of simple elements from complex confusion of reality, and the intrinsic rewards offered for those who master the game.

Simulation, while not negatively stereotyped, suffers from vague and imprecise usage. Popularly used, a simulation is that which has the appearance of something without having its reality. In this sense any construction of a "model," whether symbolic (pictorial, verbal, mathematical) or physical might be termed simulation. Technically speaking, a simulation is a miniature model, accurately replicating the whole or some part of the whole existing in reality. A physical simulation is a model of an object. A social simulation is an operating model of a process, social system, organization or environment. The choice of the reality being modeled depends upon the purpose for which the model is constructed. Significant to the design of a simulation is that the components and variables built into the model respond in a manner comparable to that of the behavior of the real system.

While all games simulate something from the real world, not all simulations are games. Combining the unique characteristics of games and simulations, games can become the vehicle for communicating the functioning and implications of the analytical model.

A social drama evolves whereby the student is motivated to experiment actively with the consequences of various "moves" or changes in the system being simulated. The same applies to physical simulations. However, for the purpose of this topic, further use of simulation will refer to *social* simulations.

Game Components and
Game Theory

Game theory has been used to examine, explain and research sophisticated problems and ideas in mathematics, economics and the military. It is this theory that provides scientific, logical and quantitative analysis of competitive processes and hence is labeled "game" theory. Games are the structured models of these competitive processes, stripped of most incidental details. The theory encompasses probability and thus risk estimations, media of exchange, strategy and measurements of gains and losses in competitive environments.

Simulation games are based on a combination of game theory and behavior theory. The rules form the structure of the model and thereby simulate the actual motivations, constraints, rewards and consequences of behavior acting in a purposive but competitive process toward a goal.

The basic format for a social simulation game is that of a *player* or *players* acting in a *social environment*. The environment is established in two ways. One is to have each player in the game act as a portion of the social environment of each other player. Rules determine the obligations upon each role, and the players acting in this role interact with one another. An example of this is the role of Legislator in the Democracy Game. The second way is to have the rules themselves represent the environment by determining responses for actions of persons who are not present in the play of the game. An example of this type of representation is found in the Life Career Game. The rules governing job applications, school admission procedures and marriage applications represent determined responses of job employers, potential spouses and admissions officers. Many games utilize both methods of creating the social environment.

Game Rules and Group
Counseling Analysis

Superficial analysis would indicate an antithesis between games and group counseling. Rules and competition are an integral part of games. Few specified—and predetermined—rules exist in group counseling, and competition or threat of competition is avoided or controlled. However, groups do function along loose—perhaps unsystematic but fairly predictable—guidelines, sometimes based on a group theory about sequential stages or process leading to individual growth. Any social event, including group counseling, involves some levels of competition, however unsystematically it is produced or demonstrated. Students in groups compete for the attention of the leader, individual members or the group as a whole. Competition exists for the right to speak, the most impressive incident, etc. Knowing what competition exists, between whom, for what reasons is important information for the counselor conducting groups.

Simulation Game Rules

To understand the structure of a simulation game, one must study the categories of rules and their functions. Rules are the framework on which the simulation game is built. They move players around and create the experience from which learning takes place. Since groups are a "natural" as contrasted with a "contrived" simulation, game rules can serve as a conceptual and analytical guide to what happens in group counseling.

There are four basic categories of rules in simulation games: (1) Procedural Rules, (2) Behavior Constraint Rules, (3) Environmental Response Rules and (4) Rules Specifying Goals and the Means of Goal Achievement. They are all predetermined previous to play and are either read or explained to players before play commences.

The *Procedural* rules describe how the game is put into play, and the general order in which play proceeds. They must reflect the actual order of events of that which is being simulated. A subtype of procedural rules is the *mediation* rule which specifies how an impasse or conflict is resolved.

Behavior Constraint rules specify role obligations and indicate what a player must do and what he cannot do.

Environmental Response rules represent the probable response of that part of the environment that is not incorporated in the actions of the players. Presentation in this form can reduce the complexity of the game and reduce the number of player roles that would be otherwise necessary for a comprehensive model.

Rules Specifying *Goals* and the method of winning or achieving the goal in a simulation game must correspond roughly to the goals that individuals in the given role would have in real life. The goal may be a reduction of anxiety (as in the Community Disaster Game) or increased satisfaction (as in the Life Career Game).

Applying these rules to an analysis of counseling groups can be helpful and enlightening, given some flexibility in interpretation of the rules. Usually the only predetermined "rule" in counseling groups is the specified goal. However, basic group counseling principles do approximate procedural rules. Counselors do have "procedures" for "putting the group into play" and for causing movement from one stage to another. The ways in which a counselor deals with silences in the group, with dominating talkers, anger or physical acts are types of "mediation" rules and are usually established based on principles of group dynamics or past experience.

But analyzing the effect of words and statements coming from whom and in what patterns can also be significant to the way a group progresses. A counselor conscious of procedural sequencing can structure his ordering of responses and cues. He certainly should examine the effect of what he says and does on the group's behavior, as this is one aspect of group dynamics over which he has control. Utilization of systematic procedures might lead to increased relevancy of the group experience.

Viewing the actions and problems of individual group members from the standpoint of behavior constraints can be extremely productive, and may actually serve to explain impasses or confusions regarding how individuals behave in and out of groups. What behaviors does a person have? What behaviors does he think he has? What effect does the presence of differential others have on the behavior of the group member? Does a member assume a particular "role" in this group; in certain interactions with other particular persons? Is the person confused about his actual role and obligations in various social environments? What is the confusion? Is the group used to test out the validity of assumed behavior constraints, or to clarify what constraints actually exist?

Behavior constraints do exist in life. Knowing explicitly what they are increases one's freedom, because one can choose to live within them, or attempt to change them. Concrete, as opposed to vague, or assumed knowledge of such restraints increases one's alternatives for action. This seems very relevant to group counseling and should be a powerful argument for using a structured (simulated) approach to groups, both in terms of group members and the group counselor.

The behavior constraint concept is what Eric Berne has made popular in his book, *Games People Play.* Although he uses the theory of this rule to analyze and explain behavior and its relative pay-off, one should recognize that Berne has not thereby defined game theory. His theory represents only *one* aspect of game theory.

Closely related to the concept of behavior constraints is the estimation people make of the probable response of people not present in the group and environments not simulated in the group. Such estimations have a controlling effect on personal behavior, and the degree of accuracy of such estimations affects the degree of appropriate behaviors. Equally important in working with individuals is the estimation of degree of control a person feels he has over structuring his environment. Such information is vital for one using the group process to help people with their problems.

Although group members presumably have agreed to the goal of the group counseling, individuals may actually have different goals which may not even be clear to the individual. Such conflicting goals may be a hindrance to the progress of the group and may need to be identified. Even more critical is the establishment of a clear understanding as to methods of achieving goals and the recognition of evidence that a person or group has reached its goal. What do I do to reach my goal? What will I do differently when I have reached it? These are important questions to answer.

Use of Simulation Games in
Group Counseling

Structured simulation games can be a useful aid to the work of group counseling. The arguments used to justify such games as educationally sound and powerful illustrate their potential for group work. A game may be used either as the entire activity of a group, or in combination with traditional group counseling with equal positive and productive results. The author's own experience in using the Life Career Game to integrate and motivate a seventh grade group demonstrated this clearly (Varenhorst, 1968).

The essence of a game, as in group counseling, is in interaction. Both are therefore social activities. Interaction is critical. Games require interaction, and the greater the degree, the less one can withdraw. Players actively encourage the isolate or withdrawn into play and participation.

Further capabilities of games are these:

1. Games provide for experiential learning as opposed to cognitive or abstract learning via the written or spoken word. In groups, individuals are led to abstract concepts of learning primarily through a verbal exchange. Many complex behaviors and ideas cannot be taught effectively this way. Complex processes which involve simultaneous interactions are difficult to describe with spoken or printed words.

2. Games have built in motivation not dependent on the skill of a game leader or group counselor.

3. Games provide training in intuition-building, problem-solving and social behaviors. They teach facts, processes, relative costs and benefits, risks and potential rewards of alternative strategies of decision-making.

4. Games provide for tailored instruction for individual problems and capabilities. They do this by utilizing other players as fellow instructors. As peers teach one another, they individually are learning different things on different levels in the same game, according to their abilities and needs.

Use of game simulations in group counseling involves appropriate selection to meet stated group purposes. A vast array of games is now on the market for classroom use. Many of these are relevant to counseling. Several efforts have been made to compile lists of games for the purpose of selection. Such lists indicate the grade level for which a game is intended, its purpose, the time required for playing, subject, publisher and cost. Thompson's list is included in this chapter's references (Thompson, 1971).

Another approach to use of games in counseling would be to design a game to meet the needs of a particular group. Designing one's own game could be an effective learning experience regarding games, game theory and group counseling. Designing would require a careful study of the critical variables to be simulated and a formalization of the contingent behaviors impinging on the model being built. A game called SYSTEM I listed in the Thompson reference is a basic learning game. Teachers or counselors can devise materials and rules for whatever the subject matter. This would be an example of how to proceed in designing a game. However, the subject of designing games requires a chapter in itself.

Words are not always sufficient in teaching, counseling or covering verbal critiques. Experiential activity leads to increased understanding, changed attitudes and behavior. If one would come to a fuller understanding of the relationship between games, simulations and group counseling, one would play games, use them in group counseling, design them and evaluate them relative to other modes, techniques and theories of group counseling.

References

Abt, Clark C. *Serious Games*. New York: The Viking Press, 1970.

Berne, Eric. *Games People Play*. New York: Grove Press, 1964.

Coleman, James S. Social Processes and Social Simulation Games. In S. Boocook and E. Schild (Eds.) *Simulation Games in Learning*. Beverly Hills: Sage Publications, 1968, 29-53.

Dawson, Richard E. Simulation in the Social Sciences. In H. Guetzkow (Ed.) *Simulation in Social Sciences: Readings*. Englewood Cliffs: Prentice-Hall, 1962, 1-16.

Thompson, Lee E. *Educational Simulations and Games: A Compilation and Presentation*. (Mimeo.) California: Mt. Diablo Unified School District, 1971.

Varenhorst, Barbara B. Innovative Tool for Group Counseling: The Life Career Game. *The School Counselor*, May 1968, 357-363.

21.
Can Technology Help Us Toward Reliability in Influencing Human Interaction?

Norman Kagan

The most basic issue confronting mental health is reliability, not validity. Not, can counseling and psychotherapy work, but does it work consistently? Not, can we educate people who are able to help others, but can we develop methods which will increase the likelihood that *most* of our graduates will become as effective mental health workers as only a rare few now do? It is my basic premise that attempts to validate therapy derived from personality theories have failed, not because of the inadequacy of the theories, but because the average practitioner has not been educated adequately to implement the theory. This is not to deny that better theories are needed but rather to assert that there is enough truth in extant ones to ameliorate the critical mental health problems of our world if only we could translate their implications into effective action with greater consistency. Films of Carl Rogers leading an encounter group are powerful arguments in favor of the potential of dynamic psychology. Viewers can see participants learn and change visibly and can hear the participants describe what they have learned. A *few* well controlled studies (i.e., Ofman, 1964) do provide statistical data of a variety of measures (including behavior outcomes) to support the validity of traditional counseling groups. *Most* studies, however, fail to provide evidence in support of the achievement of important outcomes using traditional treatment.

General improvement in mental health, in addition to symptom removal, is the usual goal of traditional intervention. If it cannot be achieved reliably, then there appear to be only two options available to a responsible profession. One is to find ways to make these "heroic" goals more reliably attainable. The other option, currently popular, is to abandon the concept of improving the global interpersonal functioning of clients in favor of modifying only highly delimited aspects of interpersonal functioning which can be behaviorally specified and reliably treated. I prefer the former option.

Can technology help us? At the risk of appearing immodest, I should like to describe my own adventures. They seem to be relevant to the issue. During the past 10 years, my colleagues and I have spent considerable time and energy in research related to reliability in training and treatment. We have found that some of the most modern technologies—videotape playback, film simulations and physiological recording—can be powerful aids not only to help us to implement our goals consistently but also to help us to understand better the nature of the issues which confront us. With the help of technology we have devised methods which seem reliable in the attainment of traditional analytic-existential goals in mental health. The methods which ultimately evolved have been used and evaluated in dyadic, small group and in community-wide intervention.

Evolution of a Teaching Strategy

The first methodology we devised was the use of stimulated recall (Bloom, 1954) by means of videotape playback combined with an unorthodox supervisory role (Kagan, Krathwohl and Miller, 1963). Clinical "interrogator," or preferably "inquirer," are the terms which have been used to describe the role of the recall person who has been taught new ways in which to help participants maximize the learning-by-discovery potential of videotape playback. The methodology seemed potent enough to enable many students to gain important understandings of the counseling process, but unfortunately not enough understanding and for not enough of the students. Controlled evaluation failed to support the value of the method or any *one* variation in individual and in small group applications (Gustafson, 1969; Ward *et al.*, 1972; Hurley, 1967).

Years of controlled studies led us to what should have been obvious from the start—therapeutic behavior is too complex to be learned by most students through any single *type* of supervisory experience. This possibility led us to the formulation of a teaching strategy based on the principle of counselor or therapist developmental tasks. The tasks were designed so that they were specific enough that the majority of students could be expected to grasp the concept or learn the skills, yet not be so finite as to be of dubious relevance to the complex dynamic behavior of counselor or therapist as a positive influence in human interaction.

The general teaching strategy to implement the tasks has evolved as a sequential progression of lessons beginning with a didactic presentation of concepts, then to simulation exercises to interpersonal affective stress, to video and physiological feedback, to study of self-in-action, to feedback from clients and, finally, to understanding of and skill at dealing with the complex bilateral impacts which occur when two people are in relationship with one another.

No assumption is made about the trainee's knowledge of personality theory or about his previous experience. The method is being used extensively in medical schools (Jason *et al.*, 1971) and with such diverse groups as psychiatric residents and para-professional high school students. Although statistically significant differences between this model and traditional supervisory or pre-practicum models have been obtained in as few as eight to ten hours (Goldberg, 1967; Spivack, 1972), most people who have conducted programs find that 30 to 50 hours of total time is desirable. The methods have been recently "packaged" in six hours of film (Spivack and Kagan, 1972). The series is not instructor-free and assumes that a psychologically sophisticated supervisor is present and available to trainees. A manual of suggestions is given to the instructor.

The Program

In the first film, trainees are told about the purpose of the experiences and are given an overview of the teaching strategy. The instructor is encouraged to stop the film frequently to comment and to answer questions. The following is a typescript of the opening statement:

Narrator

What you are about to engage in is a series of videotape instructions, demonstrations and exercises. The purpose—the over-all general purpose—is to help you become a better listener to other people and a more effective communicator. We expect you will be better able to concentrate on what a client, patient or student is telling you and especially the feelings and covert elements of the client's

Figure 1. A person watches a stimulus film of an actor looking directly at her. The image is projected through a dark tunnel on a rear screen at a distance of approximately two feet from the viewer.

communication. You will be better able to recognize and label the impact the other person is having on you. We expect you will be able to tell the client the things you are hearing and when it is appropriate to do so the reactions they are engendering in you. These abilities (and others which we will describe more specifically as we go on in each unit) will assist you to more fully understand the dynamics of a client's life style or typical interpersonal postures, behaviors and attitudes. We expect that clients will respond positively to you, will feel that you understand them, that you are interested in them and they will be encouraged to become more deeply involved in the interview or the encounter. They will talk more freely about themselves. Over time it is expected that your clients will be better able to understand themselves, will try to change in those areas in which they are dissatisfied with their interpersonal relations and will make changes in their life style, situation and behaviors. The methods have been tried in experiments and controlled studies. There is every reason to believe that each of you will be able to learn the skills.

In summary, then, the basic purpose of the lessons you are about to engage in is to teach you to listen more closely, to become more deeply involved and to respond to another in such a way as to encourage that person to go further, to explore deeper, to cooperate and to change.

We will help you achieve these skills through a series of specific learning experiences, each of which is designed to help you achieve a certain dynamic interviewer developmental task.

Let me explain. In Unit I we will acquaint you with specific response modes of effective interviewer communication. We will discuss the logical effects of using such responses and provide you with some exercises so that you may become able to incorporate these elements of communication into your interviews and encounters.

Figure 2. While the viewer engages in the simulated interaction, a video camera records her image.

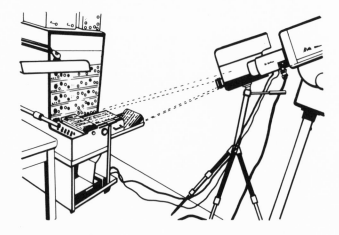

Figure 3. Simultaneously a second camera records the viewer's physiological activity. Both the viewer's image and the record of her physiological responses are transposed onto a videotape in a split-screen format. The third camera is wired directly to a monitor for use during recall.

Figure 4. After the simulation experience the viewer is joined by a staff person. The videotape of the viewer and her physiological reactions along with a sound recording of the simulation material are played back to the viewer. The viewer is encouraged to stop the playback as frequently as she is able to recall and describe her thoughts, feelings, images and any other covert processes.

Figure 5. As the staff person conducts the recall session, he is able to observe the viewer's ongoing physiological behavior on a second monitor located over the viewer's shoulder and connected to the third camera (see third figure).

In the second unit specific stimulus material will be provided to help you become more sensitive to client concerns by looking at ways in which other people may threaten you. You will be encouraged to look at different kinds of interpersonal situations in order to come to know better the kinds of stresses which are most difficult for you to deal with, to give you an opportunity to think through and become less threatened by these.

In the third unit you will be encouraged to look closely at your own interview behavior by means of stimulated recall using videotape. You will be able to examine ways in which you fail to behave the way you would like to. You will be encouraged to tune in on yourself—to look as deeply as you can and learn through self-study the specifics of your own areas of interpersonal frustration and ineffectiveness. In subsequent sessions, during Unit III, you will become better able to recognize, talk about and overcome what had been areas of stress and difficulty for you.

In the fourth unit you will be taught the inquirer role. (We will tell you more about that later, of course.) This will enable you to supervise each other in Interpersonal Process Recall (IPR) sessions or to conduct recall sessions with each other's clients. One of the most immediate outcomes of such inquirer training is that you will learn new ways to help people think about themselves. You will also find that certain kinds of assertive interviewer behavior can be very productive.

In Unit V you will be put into situations in which it will be possible to learn more about client communications—that is, to get direct feedback from clients about the effect of an interviewer on them. This will be accomplished by having you serve as inquirers for each other's clients. You will each conduct an interview. After the interview a fellow trainee will review a videotape recording of that interview with your client. Later you will review a tape like this with his client. It can be quite an experience. In the sixth unit, you will be taught how to use the ongoing interview as a vehicle not only for understanding the life style of the client you are with but how to change his relationship with you. You will be taught how to use the here-and-now, ongoing relationship as a means to enable you to understand the person you are working with and to help that person understand himself. Finally, there is a summary and theory unit.

In Unit I we have delineated four characteristics of therapeutic response—"exploratory," "affective," "listening" and "honest labeling." The student is shown vignettes in which an actress-client makes a statement and an interviewer responds to one facet (i.e., cognitive) of her statement. In the next vignette the client repeats her statement to a second interviewer who responds to a different (i.e., affective) component of her statement. Several client types and interviewer types are presented for each of the four sets of concepts. The instructor points out that the cognitive, non-exploratory, etc., response modes are those usually associated with social conversation while the other response modes are those which are frequently contained in therapeutic communication. Students practice the new response modes with a series of simulated clients on film who look directly at them and make statements varying in complexity and intensity. Students are reminded that the response modes being taught are helpful but are not used by effective interviewers as a way of responding to every client statement and that indeed it is frequently inappropriate to use them.

Unit II is far more complex and took considerably more time to develop (Kagan, Krathwohl *et al.,* 1967; Kagan and Schauble, 1969; Danish and Kagan, 1969; Archer *et al.,* 1972; Danish and Brodsky, 1970; Grossman, 1971; Gustafson, 1969). The following is a part of what students are told:

Narrator

This next unit is designed to help you further tune your "third ear." The ability to help a client know some of his more subtle messages, moods and feelings, I think, is determined by two factors. First is practice, practice at labeling feelings, especially interpersonal fears—finding words for the basic dimensions, the basic shapes, the general characteristics of gut level emotion. Second, and perhaps even more important, is the ability to overcome your own resistances to becoming involved in a psychologically intimate and meaningful way with another human being.

How can we help you achieve this? The methods we will use with you are based on examination of numerous stimulated recall protocols. We asked a simple question: "Are the resistances which people have to becoming involved or leveling with each other in interviews, generalizable? Are there interpersonal concerns or interpersonal blocks to communication, which most people seem to have?" We have found that there did indeed seem to be certain, almost universal, recurring themes . . .

Based on these observations we developed a series of simulation exercises which should help you become better able to label feelings in general and to deal with factors which might otherwise interfere with your effectiveness in human interactions. In each of the vignettes you are about to see, please forget about the surroundings you are currently in. Try to imagine that you are alone with the person on the screen . . . I ask you now to fantasize that you are alone with each of the people you will see. Pretend you have been talking with them. They are not being interviewed by you, they are not your clients, they are not your patients. Please allow the person you are watching to have an impact on you.

After each of the vignettes your instructor has chosen, you will be asked to talk about your reactions. Ask yourselves the following questions as you proceed:

What did you feel? What were your bodily reactions? When else in your life did you feel that way?

What did you think? What would you probably do? What would you really want to do?

What did you think the person was feeling about you? What made him think he could talk to you that way—that is, what did he see in you or think he saw in you which gave him the right? What did you think he or she really wanted you to do or really wanted to make you feel?

If you've never before experienced that kind of interaction, have you ever felt that someone wanted to tell you what the person you were viewing did? What does that usually do to you?

There are four ways in which these simulations are then used. First, in small groups, trainees are encouraged to share their reactions with each other. Students soon learn to increase their repertoire of descriptors for covert processes. They also learn that people react differently to the same stimulus, and that finding out "what happened" to someone may be less important than finding out what meaning it had to the person. With the help of a skillful instructor, many of the benefits of group sensitivity encounter can also accrue. A second format has trainees working in pairs where one trainee serves as "counselor" as his fellow tries to verbalize the impact a vignette had on him. A third format involves the use of simultaneous videorecording. As a student watches a vignette he is videotape recorded. A videotape playback, using a stop-start switch and the instructor as inquirer, greatly facilitates recall of the details of the impact of the vignette. Of equal benefit, students can see how they looked while watching sexual, affectionate, hostile or "guilt slinging" simulations. Where vignettes of children are used with teacher-students, for instance, the teachers are often impressed with the extent to which they do not hide their emotional reactions nearly as well as they had thought. A fourth format is currently of great research interest. The potential for important learning is limitless. A student views a vignette. He is videotape recorded. On the same videotape, also recorded, are some of his physiological responses. The stop-start playback which follows then contains the vignette, the subject's physical reactions and a visible presentation of his changes in heart rate, palmar sweat rate, respiration and shoulder muscles. During the replay the inquirer has also available to him the ongoing physiological reactivity of the student during the recall. In this way, both inquirer and student can know not only what the student's physiological reactivity *then* was, but can also determine if and when the student is actually reliving the experience in the same way during recall. As we learn more and more about physiological patterns associated with denial and suppression, it becomes increasingly possible for inquirer and student to recognize areas of "blockage" and to also know when denial or avoidance to that stimulus is being overcome. Although this format is currently being applied where facilities are available (usually with medical students) its full potential, yet to be achieved, will incorporate an on-line computer to facilitate pattern recognition.

By Unit III the student is usually ready to study himself in action. Typically he has learned some basic skills at therapeutic responding and has had practice labeling interpersonal stress and examining his own reactions to a variety of types (hopefully the full spectrum of basic types) of interpersonal stress and strain. The next step would logically be to help the student learn about what clients want and need in interpersonal encounter—why do they come for help? What are some of their more subtle messages? What do they really want from us? One might assume that an effective way of teaching the student about the nature of client concerns would be through client study—not so! We observed through the years that *all* trainees perceive infinitely more information about the nature of client concerns and client communication than they appear to have. This feigning-clinical-naivety is a universal pattern. If the student already has perceived infinitely more data than he dares use or that he knows how to use, the next logical developmental task is not the study of clients in interviews, but the study of the student himself as he tries to be of help to another. The student is videotape recorded. At the end of the interview, he is joined by an inquirer after the client has left. During the videotape playback the inquirer encourages the student to relive the experience in as much depth and detail as possible. He is encouraged to remember what he was thinking and feeling, what he thought the client was thinking and feeling, what he wanted the client to think and feel, fantasies that he was having, images that were going through his mind, and any awareness he had of his own bodily state. The inquirer is careful not to be judgmental or to convey to the student criticisms or evaluation. His task is to encourage the student to relive and verbalize covert behavior in the just completed interview. Typically, students are able to make explicit their own strategies and concerns which had interfered with their achieving their own goals in the session—what they themselves had perceived as necessary and desirable. Perhaps most important, students almost universally recognize the feigning-clinical-naivety phenomenon. They recognize ways in which they perceived subtle, often complex, messages; but, usually out of fear of involvement, pretended that they did not perceive the message at all. Invariably, new supervisors are amazed to hear students clearly verbalize awareness of very subtle phenomena which to the observer appeared to have been completely missed during the interview. As students explicate such covert phenomena, they appear more and more willing to take interpersonal risks, using data communicated by the client but which had previously been ignored or avoided.

The next developmental task is as much for the convenience of the instructor as it is for the benefit of the student. Most students need to learn that aggressive, assertive behavior is not necessarily hostile behavior. In the course of normal social interactions, one does not typically become aggressive and confronting without the hostility which ordinarily accompanies it. The inquirer role, though relatively non-judgmental is nonetheless confronting and assertive. It requires that one ask such questions as, "What were you feeling? What were you thinking? What did you want the other to think of you?" etc. The safety of videotape recording of behavior (rather than face-to-face interaction where the next moment in time is unknown), and the clearly structured cues to be used in the inquirer role, usually enables one in the inquirer role to use and become comfortable with assertive non-hostile behavior. The specific cues one uses in the inquirer role and the learning-by-discovery philosophy of the recall process are also very useful skills and attitudes for the student to have. In Unit IV, therefore, students learn and practice the inquirer role. Students then have the basic tools necessary to conduct recall sessions for each other without reliance on the instructor. From the instructor's point of view, of course, an extremely time consuming (and fatiguing!) process can now be assumed by trainees for each other.

In Unit V it is assumed that the student is ready to expand his knowledge of client wants, perceptions, aspirations, and to learn something of how clients avoid, deny, suppress or learn to grow and change. Throughout the film series students are presented with conceptualizations but the meaning and impact of such material has its limits. Trainees seem to learn more about client dynamics experientially through which the client himself becomes the trainee's instructor. A student interviews a client. At the end of the interview he asks the client to review the videotape recording with one of his colleagues. He assures the client that in order for the experience to be of value to the client and instructive to his colleague that the client recall his thoughts, feelings and moment-by-moment reactions as completely and as honestly as he possibly can. The counselor introduces his colleague to the client and then leaves the room. The colleague assumes the role of inquirer and learns from the client the moment-by-moment impact, the aspirations, the kinds of interventions which started new thought processes and those which were perceived as mundane and meaningless. Most clients are able to provide considerable feedback. Students conduct two or three such client recall sessions for each other. In this way students learn about client dynamics not from a supervisor's wise counsel or interpretations, but from an almost unimpeachable source, the consumer himself.

Among the many things about client dynamics students typically learn, one which almost always occurs is the awareness of the importance of the here-and-now interaction between counselor and client. Trainees learn that, almost no matter what the content of the interview, a large proportion of the client's emotional energy was devoted to concerns about how the client was being perceived and how the client wanted to be perceived by the counselor. This realization leads logically to the final major developmental task.

It is one thing for a student to recognize that the way in which a client interacts with him probably represents faithfully his interactions with significant other people in his life. It is one thing for the student to recognize the importance of the feelings which a client engenders in him as a clue to the client's probable impact on significant other people in his life, but it is indeed a matter of a different order for the student to bring himself to label and to act overtly in the immediacy of their occurrence with the client. Students are often frustrated because they are unable to make effective use of their ongoing here-and-now perceptions as they occur.

In Unit VI an interview is videorecorded. During the recall both interviewer and client are present. An inquirer encourages *each* one to talk about the unexpressed attitudes, intentions, feelings, thoughts, strategies and expectations he had about the other—*each participant equally.* It is not a session in which inquirer and counselor "gang up" on the client. The inquirer asks the interviewer to describe what his underlying thoughts and feelings had been—as often as he asks the client to describe *his.* These "mutual recall" sessions afford additional possibilities for learning. After one participant has stated what his underlying thoughts or expectations had been, the inquirer can ask the other participant, "At that time did you suspect he was thinking or feeling what he just stated?" If the inquirer does his job well he has helped the client and the interviewer not only to talk with each other and to listen to each other in new ways and at more levels but also has helped each confirm or refute perceptions they had had of each other. In interviews subsequent to such mutual recall sessions the client and interviewer tend to have more interactions which are prompt, open and overt, using much of the potent material in their ongoing interaction which previously had been unused.

A final unit summarizes observations my colleagues and I have made about human interaction. It is designed to provide cognitive frameworks to enable trainees better to understand the meaning of some of the experiential learning they have engaged in.

Does It Work?

The methods, then, are logical but complex. Hopefully the newly completed manual and film series will enable most competent counselors or psychologists to implement the program. Prior to the film "packaging" many studies evaluating the methods were completed. In this section, several of these are summarized.

An early version of the model was used in conjunction with a graduate practicum (Kagan, Krathwohl *et al.*, 1967; Goldberg, 1967). The IPR methods were compared with intensive "traditional" supervision. The traditional supervision was one in which a student's supervisor observed *each* of his interviews through a one-way mirror and then immediately spent an hour reviewing the session with the student, using an audiotape of the interview whenever the supervisor or the student chose to. The IPR model did not include the affect simulation films, which by then had not yet been adequately experimented with. Each treatment was limited to a total of only 10 hours over an eight-week period. Though hardly an adequate length of training to achieve competence, there were large, statistically significant differences in counseling skills as rated by independent judges between the groups in favor of the IPR treatment. A second criterion, client satisfaction, also significantly favored the experimental treatment. The findings were replicated with different sampled groups in each of three academic quarters.

Spivack and Kagan (1972) compared an IPR model which included the affect simulation films with a traditional seminar approach to a pre-practicum course. The traditional approach made use of videotape, audiotape and film demonstrations, small group discussions and lectures on theory. Significant differences in favor of the IPR model were found on interview behavior after 15 hours of training. The findings were replicated during the second half of the course.

Dendy (1971) provided a 50-hour program to undergraduate students, most of whom were sophomores. The program was conducted over a six-month period. Among his findings were significant improvement in interviewing skills, significant growth on an affective sensitivity scale, and no loss of skills during a three month no-training period. Most exciting of all, before the program was undertaken, independent judges rated the sophomores' interview skills and also rated tapes of Ph.D.-level supervising counselors employed at the university's counseling center. Both groups interviewed clients from the same client pool. Before the 50-hour program, there were large differences favoring the Ph.D.s (fortunately!) but, after training, independent judges found no significant differences between the groups on scales of empathy and other basic therapeutic communication skills.

Archer (1971) then found that these same undergraduates could, in turn, train other undergraduates so that the peer-instructed students scored significantly higher than other students who experienced an encounter group of similar duration. They also scored higher than a comparable no-treatment group, not only on measures of affective sensitivity and self-actualization, but also on scales given to roommates and other peers not in the study. When given lists of all participants, dormitory residents selected the IPR trained students as the ones they "would be willing to talk to about a personal problem," significantly more frequently than they rated either the encounter trained student or the control group member. Apparently, then, dormitory residents were able to identify the increased therapeutic skills of those peer-instructed students in the IPR group. A non-hypothesized observation is that the residents described the dorm as a better place in which to live than it previously had been. There was a complete absence of suicide attempts during the remainder of the academic year—apparently students who behaved in a depressed manner were not permitted to go unnoticed by their trained peers.

It must be pointed out, however, that the undergraduates used in both the Dendy and the Archer studies were carefully selected and all were highly motivated. Heiserman (1971) applied a 16-hour variation of the model to a population of court case-workers who did not seem to perceive their roles as requiring or including counseling skills. No significant gains were found. The learning potential of IPR is not irresistible! Nor have we yet achieved measurable success in rehabilitating alcoholics (Munoz, 1971) with IPR.

Grzegorek (1970) applied the method to the inservice teaching of 42 counselors employed in all of the state prisons of Michigan. His 50-hour program compared one model which emphasized trainee's own affect and cognition with an identical program in which reference to the trainee's own affect was avoided whenever possible and instead additional time was devoted to client (inmate) recall and examination of client dynamics. The basic question was, "Must we probe a trainee's own feelings or is it enough to help him learn response modes and about client dynamics?" Only the affect groups made significant pre-post gains in interview behavior, suggesting that trainee's exploration of his own affect is a crucial part of the IPR model.

In the summer of 1971, most of the teaching staff of the Spohn Junior High School (Hammond, Indiana) were paid to participate in an inservice workshop. Units I and II of the IPR model were included* and accounted for most of the program, which also included encounter sessions conducted by consultants. During the next 10-month school year, the typical student expulsion rate (150 to 170/year during each of the previous few years) was found to have been reduced to near zero while expulsions in the other schools within the system had not

---

*The total program was designed and administered by Edward Ignas.

changed appreciably. Teacher attendance improved as did student attendance. Expulsion rate and attendance were not themes dealt with directly during the training nor were any administrative edicts issued. Teachers simply seemed to find work a bit more satisfying and apparently were reluctant enough to "throw" people out of school to affect an important change in the lives of many children.

Schauble (1970) used IPR as an adjunct therapy with clients at a college counseling center. He found statistically significant differences on several process measures favoring the IPR clients over other clients of the same therapists who were given equivalent treatment time. Schauble's data contain interesting evidence to support the applicability of IPR to therapy but they also help us to understand the function which the technology performs. One of his therapists was rated lower than the other on a scale of therapist functioning, although each had equally excellent reputations and more than adequate training credentials. Clients of the lower functioning therapist made few, if any, gains in traditional therapy, but all of his clients gained at least somewhat when he had the aid of the technology.

The last study to be referred to is an application of IPR to use with groups. Hartson (1971) conducted groups as a counseling experience for clients and with volunteers as a sensitivity experience. IPR was used with half of the groups and significant gains in several self-reported and judge-rated dimensions were found favoring the IPR over the traditional group methods.

What Then?

If reliability is the most critical issue confronting us and if there are ways to achieve increased reliability (i.e., IPR), in what new ways can we influence the mental health of the community? One is to increase the power of the methods. This will require continued research and development. The other is to disseminate the learnings to key populations and communities. In college settings can Dendy's and Archer's findings be replicated *en masse*? Can IPR be established as a course of study for which academic credit is given? If we teach literature and art, why not intra- and interpersonal behavior? Can 1,000 students in a single large dormitory take such a course? We have already begun this massive effort, using a pyramid model. Whether the technology, theory and concepts can be implemented with really *large* numbers of people remains to be seen. Clearly, years of evaluation and experimentation lie ahead.

With the aid of technology to achieve a more reliable implementation of mental health goals, the future is bright.

References

Archer, J., Jr. Undergraduates as Paraprofessional Leaders of Interpersonal Communication Skills Training Groups Using an Integrated IPR (Interpersonal Process Recall) Videotape Feedback/Affect Simulation Training Model. Unpublished doctoral dissertation, Michigan State University, East Lansing, Michigan, 1971.

Archer, J., Jr. *et al.* A New Technology for Education, Treatment and Research in Human Interaction. *Journal of Counseling Psychology,* 1972.

Bloom, B.S. The Thought Process of Students in Discussion. In S.J. French (Ed.) *Accent on Teaching: Experiments in General Education.* New York: Harper and Brothers, 1954, 23-46.

Danish, S.J. and S.L. Brodsky. Training of Policemen in Emotional Control and Awareness. *Psychology in Action,* 1970, *25,* 368-369.

Danish, S.J. and N. Kagan. Emotional Simulation in Counseling and Psychotherapy. *Psychotherapy, Theory, Research and Practice,* 1969, *6,* 261-263.

Dendy, R.F. A Model for the Training of Undergraduate Residence Hall Assistants as Paraprofessional Counselors Using Videotape Techniques and Interpersonal Process Recall (IPR). Unpublished doctoral dissertation, Michigan State University, East Lansing, Michigan, 1971.

Goldberg, A.D. A Sequential Program for Supervision of Counselors Using the Interpersonal Process Recall Technique. Unpublished doctoral dissertation, Michigan State University, East Lansing, Michigan, 1967.

Grossman, R.W. Limb Tremor Responses to Antagonistic and Informational Communication. Unpublished doctoral dissertation, Michigan State University, East Lansing, Michigan, 1971.

Grzegorek, A. A Study of the Effects of Two Emphases in Counselor Education, Each Used in Connection With Simulation and Videotape. Unpublished doctoral dissertation, Michigan State University, East Lansing, Michigan, 1970.

Gustafson, K.L. *Simulation of Anxiety Situations and its Resultant Effect on Anxiety and Classroom Interaction of Student Teachers.* Final Report, Project No. 9-E-039, U.S. Department of Health, Education and Welfare, Office of Education, 1969.

Hartson, D.J. Videotape Replay and Interrogation in Group Work. Unpublished doctoral dissertation, University of Missouri, Columbia, Missouri, 1971.

Heiserman, M.S. The Effect of Experiential-Videotape Training Procedures Compared to Cognitive-Classroom Teaching Methods on the Interpersonal Communication Skills of Juvenile Court Caseworkers. Unpublished doctoral dissertation, Michigan State University, East Lansing, Michigan, 1971.

Hurley, S.J. Self-disclosure in Counseling Groups as Influenced by Structured Confrontation and Interpersonal Process Recall. Unpublished doctoral dissertation, Michigan State University, East Lansing, Michigan, 1967.

Jason, H. *et al.* New Approaches to Teaching Basic Interview Skills to Medical Students. *American Journal of Psychiatry,* 1971, *127,* 1404-1407.

Kagan, N. *Influencing Human Interaction* (a filmed six-hour mental health training series and accompanying 186-page instructor's manual). Instructional Media Center, Michigan State University, East Lansing, Michigan, 1971.

Kagan, N., D.R. Krathwohl and R. Miller. Stimulated Recall in Therapy Using Videotape—A Case Study. *Journal of Counseling Psychology,* 1963, *10,* 237-243.

Kagan, N., D.R. Krathwohl *et al. Studies in Human Interaction: Interpersonal Process Recall Stimulated by Videotape.* Educational Publications Services, College of Education, Michigan State University, East Lansing, Michigan, 1967.

Kagan, N. and P.G. Schauble. Affect Simulation in Interpersonal Process Recall. *Journal of Counseling Psychology,* 1969, *16,* 309-313.

Munoz, D.G. The Effects of Simulated Affect Films and Videotape Feedback in Group Psychotherapy with Alcoholics. Unpublished doctoral dissertation, Michigan State University, East Lansing, Michigan, 1971.

Ofman, W. Evaluation of a Group Counseling Procedure. *Journal of Counseling Psychology,* 1964, *11,* 152-159.

Schauble, P.G. The Acceleration of Client Progress in Counseling and Psychotherapy Through Interpersonal Process Recall (IPR). Unpublished doctoral dissertation, Michigan State University, East Lansing, Michigan, 1970.

Spivack, J.D. and N. Kagan. Laboratory to Classroom—the Practical Application of IPR in a Masters Level Pre-Practicum Counselor Education Program. *Counselor Education and Supervision,* 1972.

Ward, R.G., N. Kagan and D.R. Krathwohl. An Attempt to Measure and Facilitate Counselor Effectiveness. *Counselor Education and Supervision,* 1972, *11,* 179-186.

22.
New Trends in Traditional Technology Management in the Training of Group Counselors

Randolph B. Tarrier

Technology is upon us. The image is one of flow charts, data banks, mechanical men, waxen women, larger classes, resisting faculties, hypnotic students, sterile studies and dehumanizing methods.

But it need not be this way.

The Carnegie Commission on Higher Education predicts a technological revolution on the college campus. And this revolution will take place. The time is right. It is inevitable. The only question left to answer is whether or not we can make the correct decisions in the directions we move.

It is clear that educators must be more efficient. That we can do. We know how to be efficient. But will this efficiency preempt our responsibility to assure that each student reaches his full potential? Technology will help us become more efficient. Like the computer in business, the videotape recorder is a cheaper and faster means of reaching educational goals. The critical value decisions will be made by the educational planners, and what they decide will determine our fate—not the technology.

This chapter is about some decisions which have been made in a technological center for counselor education. It has been written not because we are the best or the only technological center but rather because some of the decisions we have made concerning the use of technology in counselor training will concern the reader; some of the methods we use, you can use.

First, the chapter describes our Laboratory and student body. Second, it attempts to convey a feeling for our evolution from simple-to-complex technology. Third, it tries to create an understanding of the newer ideas, from the simulation project, of "making things happen" to trainees.

The Laboratory

The Guidance Laboratory of the City University of New York (CUNY), designed by Arnold Buchheimer and Leo Goldman, is an example of farsighted planning. Begun in 1965 as a center for the practicum experience, both individual and group counseling, it has entered a new phase—materials development. Although this chapter speaks of counseling, the program's implications transcend this and go into all levels of education and interpersonal relationships.

The Laboratory is a central facility which serves the colleges within CUNY as a counselor practicum site and as a counseling materials development center. The facility is an elaborate electronic complex with capability for closed circuit monitoring via video and audio, 1/2-inch videotaping and studio production. Each of our 10 interview rooms is "bugged" with video camera and audio microphone, which activate as the lights are turned on. It is one of the finest counseling laboratory facilities in the world.

The Trainees

The students in this university are all part-time students, who are torn among studies, family, transportation complexities and their jobs. At the time of this writing, nearly all our students are teachers in the New York City Schools. In keeping with new State certification requirements, more and more non-teachers are entering the Programs in Guidance and Counseling. Technology will help us to absorb these trainees with different backgrounds.

The Program

In the early years of the Lab, the guiding principle was that students be assisted in examining their experiences. In order to accomplish this goal, interview rooms were outfitted with audio- and videotape recording facilities. Once the tape(s) is recorded there can be several styles of "examining" the experience. *Individual Playback:* In this style, the trainee simply plays back the tape of the interview and, using a guide, rates himself in microcounseling skills such as attending, questioning, reflection of feeling, clarification. *Supervisory Conference:* The next step in this process is to arrange a meeting with the supervisor to review individual ratings and to discuss alternative behavior. The following script is an example of an audiotape critique. The supervisor's comments are in upper case letters.

THE MONITOR ROOM. From this room up to ten interviews can be audio-recorded and up to two interviews video-recorded simultaneously. Shown on the monitor is puppet used in a knowledge module on career choice.

INTERVIEW ROOM. Scene as would be viewed in videotape assisted supervision.

INTERPERSONAL PROCESS RECALL. First, the counselor leads a counseling session which is being videotaped.

INTERPERSONAL PROCESS RECALL. Second, the supervisor conducts a recall session by playing back the videotape as the counselor views from behind the one-way mirror.

Supervisory Conference—Audiotape Assisted

Co: What would you like to talk about today? (SUPR: GOOD: YOU'RE
        ALLOWING THE CLIENT TO SET GOALS FOR THE SESSIONS.)

Cl: Well, things are better at home. My mother seems to understand my
        moods better but now I'm really worried about a friend. She is smoking
        more and more and seems to like it. What can you do with somebody who
        likes it? What can you do with somebody who likes to do something but is
        kind of afraid of it at the same time?

Co: (Tentatively) I don't think you're talking about a friend, are you? (SUPR:
        NO—YOU'RE STRICTLY PLAYING A HUNCH—NOT ENOUGH DATA
        TO MAKE THAT JUMP.)

Cl: Yes, I am. She's a good friend—I don't get it??? Oh, you thought I meant
        myself—like the girl who has a friend that's pregnant. No. You're wrong
        there (laughs).

Co: Then you really are worried about a friend who is smoking too much?
        (SUPR: BRINGING HER BACK TO FOCUS—NOT BAD.)

Note the subtle changes in the dialogue between Supervisor and
trainee when the video component is added and the conference is a
critique of a videotape.

Supervisory Conference—Videotape Assisted

Supr: Let's watch the tape. There are several places I want to stop and talk. You
         stop the tape when you want to, also.

         (starts tape)

Trainee: (Immediately) Oh god, look at how I am sitting, I'm as tense as a banjo
         string. And my hair—oh god.

Supr: (Stops tape) How do you mean tense? Were you tense? How were you
         feeling at the time?

Trainee: That's strange because I didn't know how tense I was until I see myself
         now. Maybe if I had known I could have . . . (trails off).
Supr: Let's watch some more (turns on the tape).

Trainee: (After some time.) Look at that. I never finish a sentence, do I? Am I that way here with you? I know I'm that way some of the time but I didn't think in counseling . . .

Supr: Like right now.

Trainee: Right now? . . . Oh, I didn't finish that last sentence, did I?

The supervisor goes easily from trainee's behavior on the tape to here-and-now behavior in the supervision hour itself. It is an easy transition because the total behavior of the trainee is the focus of the session. Techniques, non-verbal and verbal actions and feelings all are the determinants for successful helping relationships and they are evident in videotape playback supervision.

With the addition of body posture, facial expression, gestures and other physical manifestations of behavior the supervisory conference moves closer and closer to a critique of all the elements of the counseling session, as well as of the supervision session.

These methods are time-consuming, for they demand a 1:1 interview and playback sequence—a 40-minute interview needs 40+ minutes for review. Because of this time demand and a need for more varied alternatives to counseling, the multiple counseling critique evolved.

Multiple counseling critique. Group review is the emphasis in this technique. The entire interview tape is not needed to carry out this design. Six counselors run six groups for a finished critique tape running 51 minutes.

Taping Schedule

Start		Midpoint	End
4:00	Counselor A	4:18	4:36
4:03	Counselor B	4:21	4:39
4:06	Counselor C	4:24	4:43
4:04	Counselor D	4:27	4:45
4:42	Counselor E	4:30	4:48
4:15	Counselor F	4:33	4:51

Using a dial access system, each counseling group can be viewed six times on the complete 51-minute videotape (three-minute segments—beginning, middle and closing).

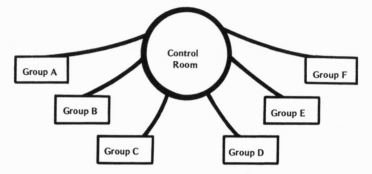

Following the videotaping, all six counselors meet with the supervisor to critique each other. Each group is presented in three three-minute segments, beginning, midpoint and closing. The group critique session seems to work especially well as each counselor can contribute from his own "set." And each group has an audio recording of the entire session for further research.

Expanding the Experience

The first step away from individual or group playback and critique of experiences developed with the introduction of the Empathy Studies of Arnold Buchheimer and the Interpersonal Process Recall technique of Norman Kagan, Michigan State University. Buchheimer and Kagan went beyond straight playback. For the first time, researchers tried to look deeply into the biases of the supervisor and the trainee in the examination of the counseling experience. This approach to supervision requires that the counseling session be taped and that the client group be recalled or interrogated by the supervisor as they view the playback of the just completed counseling session. The counselor, who is watching the recall, either over closed circuit television or isolated behind a one-way mirror, receives invaluable feedback from his clients, about their feelings during the counseling session.

The emphasis is on the feelings of the clients, and this is the major difference from earlier supervisory styles. In the earlier styles the "examination of the life of a counselor" focused almost entirely on the style and skill of counselor. This will always be a part of supervision, but it is supervision in a vacuum. The IPR feedback technique allows counselor and supervisor to "reality test" their assumptions.

Evolution of New Techniques

As our "counselor training experiences" were examined more and more, the awareness grew of just what a narrow experience it was! At the most our trainees could see only two groups for six or seven sessions in one semester. If the counselor happened to draw a bright, verbal, middle-class group of youngsters for his practicum, then his experience was self-evaluated as good; these kids usually show up for every meeting and have a lot to talk about, and the counselor needs only to help them gently to continue.

If the counselor draws a less bright, poor, silent group, he may try everything he knows to help them and still "fail."

Unfortunately, the relationship between the excellent but narrow practicum experience and the broad New York City Public Schools experience was not close.

It was obvious that we needed to offer a much wider band of experiences to our trainees so that when they entered the schools, they could be able to draw on a broad repertoire of skills and styles to meet the tremendous challenge of helping big-city youngsters.

We have made progress toward this goal. Recently in a one-week span, 20 employment counselors were able to experience 10-15 different approaches to beginning a group. In one semester, our trainees received intensive training in five specific group counseling techniques, such as Reality Counseling, Behavior Modification, Humanistic Education, and the Use of Play Techniques as well as microcounseling skills of leading, observation schema and planned intervention. Before the improvement of technological procedures, this was not possible.

New Thrusts

Sensitivity training and the newer affective education techniques led us to see how growth and change are possible in a relatively short time (week-end groups seldom run over 20 hours). These changes are induced by the activities and behaviors in the group experience. Much has been written about the nature of the experiences. Without defending or supporting the "group movement," it is obvious that these group activities, which are usually highly symbolic, must meet two criteria: relevance and transferability. If these criteria are met, the participant may suddenly see "real time" relationships as they truly are for the first time. This planned experience speeds the process of insight.

Technology can speed this same process in counselor training.

Just as sensitivity group members learn to match their patterns of behavior with their goals, counselor-trainees, through the use of televised stimuli, simulation experiences, encounters with clients who are coached and individualized modules can begin to match their own counselor behavior with their goals for the counseling session.

Televised Stimulus—Increasing the Spectrum

The TV monitor comes to life. A young man appears on the screen—black, Afro, militant, whiskers, angry. As he looks directly at you he spits the following words:

"You goddam honkey. You don't know me—I don't want to know you. Just stay out of my life. Just leave me alone! I'm sick of your meddling. Go back downtown and leave me alone!!"

(Stops the videotape recorder, turns to the trainee)

Supr: How do you feel about that?

Trainee: I don't know—it's scary. How can I ever talk to him?

Supr: You said it was scary—you mean you are frightened by him?

Trainee: Well . . . no. I don't think so—maybe more apprehen . . . oh—yes I'm frightened. Any time I see a group of black guys in my neighborhood, I wonder about them.

Supr: What do you mean—you wonder about them?

Trainee: You know what I mean. Why are they here? What are they up to? The other day I crossed the street to avoid passing a group of them. I know it's silly but I can't help it.

Supr: OK. You know you are frightened. Suppose this young man you just saw on the screen were sent to see his counselor, you. What would you want to happen?

Trainee: Well, I guess I would want him to listen to me and understand that I really want to help him.

Supr: And what would you say and do to bring this about? Keep in mind, that you'd be frightened.

Trainee: I'm not sure . . . I guess I would try to tell him that I hear him even though I probably can never fully understand.

Supr: Let's try something. A similar client is waiting to see you in Rm 1420. See if you can deal with him right now and we'll talk, after.

By videotaping "staged incidents" the supervisor can control and manage the experiences of the trainee. The range of experiences can be broadened to include practically any facet of human behavior.

The shy retiring man can be matched with overbearing girls who have been instructed to bully him. The Don Juan types can be matched with equally seductive types. Using this style, the supervisor is involved with helping trainees to deal with their "soft spots" with the hope that their repertoire of behaviors is expanded.

Other types of groups which lend themselves to this format are in-group/out-group encounters, non-participants, silent members, sexual overtones, gossipy-flight groups.

Using this form of simulated experience, in addition to ongoing "real time," the supervisor can broaden the experience of the trainee. Simulation packages via TV are steps to soften the entry of the counselor into his own school.

Simulation Experiences—Looking Into Biased "Sets"

You have been hired as a teacher to teach a small group of students. In 15 minutes you will teach the curriculum specified and evaluate your work. Your session will be videotaped for later critique.

Using this simulated teaching experience our trainees are helped to see the "set" each of us develops to what a teacher is and does. One trainee approaches this vague setting in a rigid I-will-transmit-information-to-you set. Another enters the situation in a more open we've-got-a-silly-task-to-complete/does-anybody-have-ideas-how-we-can-accomplish-it? Whatever the teaching set may be, it is crucial that our trainees examine their own "sets" and relate it to their counseling role. Usually, the beginning counselor does what feels right. After a simulation experience, he is more likely to plan his behavior to fit his goals for counseling, especially after viewing his "class" via videotape replay.

Coached Clients: Role Playing
with Face Validity

Counselor supervisors have always used role playing as a method to help the student explore and make ready his repertoire for counseling. To the role play model of asking some of our trainees to play certain roles to certain counseling styles, we have added face validity.

The High School of the Performing Arts is located near the Laboratory. From their student body, mostly students who have chosen acting as a career, we have formed a cadre of coached clients, youngsters who are paid to participate in our curriculum as clients. The role assignments vary as our needs do, but basically, the clients are in "role" from first to last contact with the trainees.

Although there are some "incurable hams" in their lot, the group is believable. Participants in the program are unable to tell them from their own "real time" clients.

Perhaps a word of caution should be mentioned here. When coached clients are involved in this process, time should be allotted for their own "real time" counseling. Often, when dealing with certain roles, their own response is one that needs further exploration of self.

Also, this technique demands funds to pay the clients unless some kind of course credit trade-off is arranged (i.e., drama students "act" as part of their own course requirement).

A typical coached-client group might be instructed to deal in intellectual flight from personal feelings so that the trainee can try out planned interventions to bring the discussion to the "here and now."

Or the group may be coached to portray in-group out-group themes so that the trainee can polish his intervention style to facilitate examination of this phenomenon.

The range of planned experiences can cover any group experience in the literature or the memory of the supervisor. But it must be well planned and requires supervisory time before and after the session.

Much of our training program is dependent on the trainee's

involvement in individualized self-contained instruction.

The counselor must have certain bits of knowledge, must have certain attitudes and must have certain skills in order to function in a particular counseling setting. The individualized module is an attempt to develop these three areas.

Individualized Modules: Knowledge, Attitudes, Skill

We have attempted to eliminate time and space as a constant in part of our program. The intent is to move toward an individualized specialty orientation for some specific areas. For example, on a given workshop night (once per week per semester) the trainee is asked to choose from among Affective Education Groups, Reality Counseling Groups or Career Counseling in Groups. If a trainee wants experience in all three, he then makes arrangements to study the materials, which are filed in the videotape library, on his own time. An example of this would be the videotape *Reality Counseling in the Bronx.*

In this tape, the viewer is led through a complete session with a class of third graders led by an experienced counselor and teacher. Crucial decision points are identified as discussion and study points for the viewer.

An example of the *attitude oriented* package is the "wrong decision sequence." In this experience, the viewer is faced with students making obviously wrong career choices. He is asked to evaluate his values and feelings regarding these decisions. The intent is that the trainee begin to "feel" that the client is the person best equipped to make decisions concerning his life.

Although most of our material is designed to encourage supervisor and trainee dialogue, some of it is designed to be used as self-contained individual study packages. One such module is *Questioning as a Facilitative Skill.* In this unit the trainee hears protocol materials of other trainees using questioning styles. The accompanying manual provides a directory for cognitive understanding of questioning styles and finally trying out new behaviors.

In a group experience, developed by Professor Leo Goldman, trainees who need awareness and practice in the use of different counseling styles are seated in a room, each with a cassette recorder ready to record his or her counseling response. After seeing a protocol from a group counseling session, they are asked to make a response which is non-directive or behaviorist or directive, etc. After each segment, each member then plays back his response for critique by the group. In addition to providing instant feedback for each trainee, it helps him to gather other ideas with which to expand his own.

Summary

I have tried to provide a feeling for one program in counselor education which is heavily dependent on technology. As can be seen, our values of what is important to the growth of a group counselor have heavily influenced our work. The reader will no doubt agree with some, disagree with others. One value, based on experience with many styles and techniques of presentation, permeates everything we do.

Trainees need a chance to argue, talk back, mull over, test out and finally to arrive at their own conclusions as to what counselor each will become. The use of audio-visual materials could easily neglect this. To overcome this possible error, we have built into all our presentations, sometimes painfully, but always thoughtfully, the human contact. We have programmed discussion pauses, key questions, distressing dilemmas and attitude probes. Only in this manner can we use our technology and avoid our technology using us.

23.
A Fully Equipped Computer-Assisted Group Counseling Research and Training Lab

John Vriend

Imagine having unlimited funds to construct a group counseling research and training facility. With today's technology, what could be built? Watching television—professional football games, with isolated camera feedback, with instant replay, stop-action, slow motion, split-screen techniques, or the roving reporter at the political convention with his communication tether to the principal commentator in the scanning-over-all Mount Olympus booth, or seeing the communications back-up personnel and equipment at "Houston Central" during an Apollo moontrip—any unsophisticated citizen can figure out some ways to adapt such razzle-dazzle technology to a few schemes of his own. Harnessing the computer is a little more difficult, but, with an elementary understanding of some of its delivery capability, it is not to be eschewed by the aggressive group counseling daydreamer.

Assumptions

For the sake of the model to be presented, however, it is important that we waylay the supposition that we are merely daydreaming, that the model represents just a futuristic conception, something which may or may not arbitrarily metamorphose into being in the year 2000. We therefore need to re-emphasize that we are dealing in *today's technology;* the model itself can be built as early as tomorrow. Also, we assume the following:

1) There is a need for such a facility, a super-endowed experimental laboratory for pushing at frontiers in both the advanced training of group counselors and in group counseling research. An analogous laboratory in the medical field is the fully equipped operating room used for surgical research and as a theater for the training of surgeons,

or, to name another analogy, the now famous laboratory which Masters and Johnson were able to construct for their human sexual response studies.

2) The proper place for such a laboratory to come into existence would be a training institution to which a steady flow of counseling psychologists and counselors would pilgrimage to receive intensified, in-depth, advanced knowledge, skill and competency building in group counseling, on both a short- and long-term basis. Such an institution could even be independent of a university, supported by an agency such as the Ford Foundation or the National Institute of Mental Health, having group counseling research, development and advanced training as its paramount reasons for being. Let us assume an as-yet fictitious National Foundation for Group Counseling Research, underwritten by both government and private funds, motivated by the spirit of philanthropy and the search for behavioral scientific truth, the national Mecca for study in the discipline.

3) Once some of the components of the model are understood, they can be instituted in existing research and training systems and laboratories. Indeed, places currently exist where some dimensions of the model already are being operationalized.

4) All of the aforegoing assumptions add up to the fact that the model, presented pictorially in Figure 1, is a wholly pragmatic portrayal of what is significantly possible in today's world, given sufficient commitment, money and manpower.

Figure 1 Explained
Group Counseling Room
At the National Foundation for Group Counseling Research headquarters there are many group counseling rooms, none of which is the same, all of which have been used for different purposes, but the "lab" room, as it is known to Trainers and Trainees alike, is something special.

First of all, it is round and its ceiling is dome-shaped, a half sphere, with powerfully bright recessed lighting in the superbly sound-proofed white covering. The acoustics are almost inconceivably sharp: even the softest breathing, when silence descends on the group, becomes audible. One can almost hear the sound of an eye blinking. While at times the furniture items and arrangements have included some bizarre combina-

Figure 1

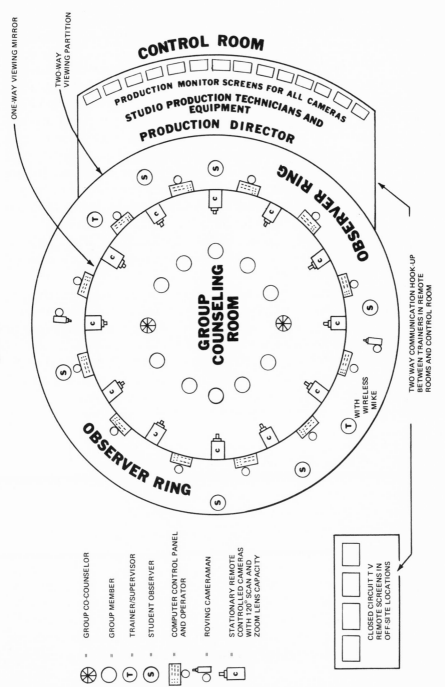

CONTROL ROOM

ONE-WAY VIEWING MIRROR

TWO-WAY VIEWING PARTITION

PRODUCTION MONITOR SCREENS FOR ALL CAMERAS

STUDIO PRODUCTION TECHNICIANS AND EQUIPMENT

PRODUCTION DIRECTOR

OBSERVER RING

GROUP COUNSELING ROOM

OBSERVER RING

WITH WIRELESS MIKE

TWO-WAY COMMUNICATION HOOK-UP BETWEEN TRAINERS IN REMOTE ROOMS AND CONTROL ROOM

CLOSED CIRCUIT T V REMOTE SCREENS IN OFF-SITE LOCATIONS

⊛ = GROUP CO-COUNSELOR

◯ = GROUP MEMBER

Ⓣ = TRAINER/SUPERVISOR

Ⓢ = STUDENT OBSERVER

▦◦ = COMPUTER CONTROL PANEL AND OPERATOR

= ROVING CAMERAMAN

c = STATIONARY REMOTE CONTROLLED CAMERAS WITH 120° SCAN AND ZOOM LENS CAPACITY

tions, sprung from the minds of the co-counselors to meet certain called-for prescriptions arising out of the interpersonal data of some members, such as is needed in role-working (see the Dyer-Vriend chapter in this book) or blackboard briefing sessions, generally speaking the room customarily contains 12 not-too-comfortable stainless steel and black leather chairs which are stationed in the traditional circle, each situated on the unbelievably soft, plushy white carpeting so that the mounted stationary cameras assigned to each member can do their appointed task of recording visually the member's behavior in the group session. The circular side wall of the room is made up of a continuous one-way viewing mirror, presenting a rather confusing distorted-image-surrounding experience for group members when they start out: it is over-simulating at first, an implosion of slightly elongated images of the fronts and backs of heads, an over-simulation one soon learns to ignore most of the time, but to relish and focus on when the action in the group flags or becomes tedious.

As sparsely depicted in Figure 1, the cameras are indicated in relationship to the 10 group member and co-counselor symbols, but one must imagine the chairs, the bright-white dome, the lights, the all-encasing mirror, the rug, and the fact that this cast of characters do not play out their appointed rounds removed from the rest of the world, privately ensconced in some secluded hideaway. They are observed, scrutinized, monitored, and their living in the group is televised to others, as well as made permanent in videotape and audiotape record. In the case of the co-counselors, at least, someone outside the group can even talk to them: they've been surreptitiously and appropriately "bugged" for the sake of their own skill and competency development.

Group Counselor Trainers
Since training group counselors to be optimally effective is such a heavy and valued part of scheduled on-going programs at Foundation headquarters, the Trainers comprise an elitist corps of experts among the total staff, their importance rivaling that of the Research Designers. (Indeed, in most cases the Trainers are Research Designers themselves.) In any event, they must coordinate their efforts with those of the Research Designers and, along with the co-counselors who might be leading a particular session, execute and orchestrate the kind of

behaviors needed for the ruddering of experimental variables.

While the chief involvement of the Trainers during a given group session is with the co-counselors leading the group, their function far exceeds that of being a "coach" who now and then sends in some "plays," as could be inferred from a cursory consideration of the meaning of the communication hook-up between Trainer and Trainee. But this dimension of the Trainer-Trainee relationship is a significant one and not to be undervalued: a part of the extensive research being conducted at the National Center is exploratory of it. The wireless microphone carried by each Trainer enables him to talk to the particular co-leader who is "bugged" to receive his messages. (See the Cohn chapter in this book.) This absentee-cueing, in turn, is picked up by a second microphone worn by the Trainer for the purpose of having his remarks to the co-counselor reproduced on selected taped records in "voice-over" fashion, according to the judgment of the Production Director and his technical assistants in the Control Room. An array of programmed absentee-cue schedules has been and is being tried out, but it has become regular practice to have this one-way communication connection between Trainer and Trainee even when it does not enter into a particular research design, for it has long ago proven its worth as a training adjunct.

Without going into all the explanatory details which would enable an interested party to fully understand the Trainer role and responsibilities, it can be revealed that each Trainer is a fully qualified expert group counselor himself, totally knowledgeable about known group counseling dynamics and techniques, a teacher of demonstrated excellence. It was learned long ago that one of the chief ingredients for imparting group counseling skills and competencies is the protege or apprenticeship system adopted at the Foundation. While there are occasional re-appointments for one adjustive reason or another, the usual arrangement is for each Trainee to become the training responsibility of a particular Trainer during his entire tenure in the learning program, and in post-training follow-up, as well.

As shown in Figure 1, the Trainers have free mobility and can walk about at will in the Observer Ring, thus enabling them to interact with sundry on-lookers, the Roving Cameramen, or Computer Control Panel Operators. While Trainers usually station themselves at opposite sides of the Ring the better to read the facial and other physical behavior of their assigned Trainees, there are not infrequent times when they get together to confer on operational strategies or options which were unaccounted for in the preplanning for a given session by the apprenticeship co-pairs.

Observer Ring

The Observer Ring is a concentric circle around the Group Counseling Room, a 12-foot wide passageway allowing a viewer to walk entirely around the counseling group and see the action from any angle. Like the Counseling Room, it is sound-proofed and air conditioned, and one could scream or beat a drum in the Observer Ring and members of the counseling group would be oblivious to the noise. It can accommodate more than two hundred observers with the custom-built floor tiering that is available for those occasions when a large audience is invited to witness a given event, such as some of the demonstrations of innovative dramatic techniques which have lately become of such great interest to so many professionals. The usual number, however, is under 30, and this includes, in addition to the ever-present student observers, the two Trainers, the 12 Computer Control Panel Operators, and the two Roving Cameramen with their portable equipment, who have learned to be expert at taking zoom and angle shots which focus in on any untoward or emotion-indicating physical behavior of group members or leaders. The "photogs," as they have come to be known around the Center, are bugged by the Production Director who, when he is aware of the need or the opportunity to do so, can direct their attention to the filming of special effects.

It is dark in the Observer Ring, but indirect floor lighting in key places is important for safety underfoot, the Computer Control Panels are unobtrusively lit (different colors for different buttons), and in the two dozen observer seats (hydraulically adjustable to heights of six feet) a tiny light illuminates sufficiently a writing surface for note-taking. Inasmuch as all sound from the Group Counseling Room is piped into the Observer Ring, earphones are unnecessary. The mirror which allows one-way viewing is between the counseling group and the observers, but not between the latter and the Control Room. Separating the Control Room from the Observer Ring is regular glass, which permits visual communication between the Production Director and the Trainers or Cameramen.

Audio-Visual Delivery Capability

Perhaps it should be emphasized again that the National Foundation for Group Counseling Research exists primarily for training, research and the development of useful techniques, practices and even products for the advancement of group counseling as an applied science, as behavioral truth, as an effective rehabilitative treatment, as a self-enhancing service to all. Thus, the Center does not exist for the sake of the "lab"; rather, the lab exists for the sake of the Foundation and all for which it stands. The distinction is important, for we must realize that not all of the research, and precious little of the training, takes place in the lab. But what *does* go on there can hardly take place better anywhere else: the lab is a nerve center, the heart of all that is possible when training and research in group counseling are thought of seriously.

While it is true that most training experiences at the Foundation headquarters are experiential, students participating in group counseling and other experiences as members, endlessly participating in structured social exercises, practicing as co-counselors in numerous groups, living through a rich variety of programmed activities which tax their powers and challenge their energy reserves, that is far from the totality of their learning. In the Center constant use is made of the closed-circuit TV system, and many of the scheduled programs emanate live from the lab. (An impressive number of these programs, through the television cable system, and the educational channel cooperation, are transmitted to other training institutions and commercial stations around the country.) The students observe hours and hours of group counseling in the lab. They must serve as Computer Control Panel Operators, developing enormously important zeroing-in and screening-out skills and mental sets. They themselves must study all the videotape records, including the personal one made for each performance, of every group session in which they participated, whether as member (yes, each Counselor in training is a committed member of an on-going counseling group scheduled for lab appearance at regular intervals) or as co-counselor. In addition, they go through all of the important audio and video records which the Foundation has developed which are pertinent to their particularized learning programs. It is these productions which have come to be so valuable to the profession, a storehouse of leader-modeling, do's and don't's, illustrations of practices, common human behaviors in groups, an ever-expanding library of group counseling lore, know-how, technology.

What the lab delivers, or can deliver, audio-visually, includes the following:

1) A videotape record can be made of each individual in the group, taken by the wall-positioned remote-controlled camera, which can move as the individual moves, and which has a telescopic lens. Thus, the technician in the Control Room operating the camera can make it move on a vertical axis from face to hands, or swing it horizontally to catch a side view, or telescope-in to show only the eyes, or mouth, or neck-muscles of a subject.

2) For each group session a master videotape is made. This tape is a work of art which can be improved upon through post-session editing and splicing, but seldom is, for the Production Directors have become extraordinarily proficient in their principal function of on-going image selection. While the group is in session, the Director decides which of the possible 14 camera images to bring into focus, including those of the Roving Cameramen. Additionally, he is able to direct the photogs and Control Room technicians to pick up special effect shots which he sees as possible. While instant replay techniques are available to him, he seldom uses them in the production of the master videotape. What he calls on for frequent duty, however, are the multiple split-screen combinations which enable a viewer to watch two or more closeups simultaneously of group members in heavy personal interaction.

3) The closed circuit TV system, in any given live programming, receives the imagery which the Director determines shall go into the making of the master videotape. Any other tape or film, of course, can be piped into the system.

4) Some experimentation in groups smaller than 10 is currently on-going with stop-action, slow-motion and instant replay techniques being employed within the group itself. TV monitor screens are set up in the Counseling Group Lab Room as companion equipment for each group member, and group members are given control over what will appear on their personal screen, including various kinds of playback options. The varieties of controllable structures for research purposes are endless. (Much of the inspiration for these studies has come from the pioneering work on interpersonal process recall done by Kagan and his associates at Michigan State University. See the Kagan chapter in

this book.) One possible structure, for example, would be where everyone in the group focuses on, and works with, the personal group interactive data of one member who operates his own companion equipment in what seems to be the most productive way, according to the goals to be reached in the given session.

5) Probably the most elaborate and significant function of the lab audio-visual delivery system is the "Production Company," as those staff members of the Foundation have come to be called who are engaged in the production of group counseling training tapes, both audio and video, films and other materials. While in the early days of the Foundation's existence all materials were developed for in-head-quarters use only and were considered totally experimental, today the thousands of training aids developed at the Center have been turned over to a distribution firm for marketing, and the revenue thus produced has been a great help in defraying some of the Foundation's understandably extensive operating costs.

6) Master audiotape records are made of each group session, but the lab has the capacity to make isolated voice transcripts of individual members as well. The latter, executed by technicians in the Control Room, are designated by the Production Director according to usually preplanned needs which arise out of consultation with the Trainers and co-counselors. They have proven to be extremely practical for research purposes, for leader skill building and for the achievement of desirable counseling outcomes for group counselees. In particular, separating out individual interaction from the group matrix of action and doing content analysis studies has become a rich resource for abetting the attainment of individual member goals, so members are routinely programmed to go over their own audio records, in the event that a personal video record was not made, between the scheduled group counseling session.

Computer-Assisted Research

As can be seen in Figure 1, a dozen Computer Control Panels and Operators are situated next to the one-way viewing partition at evenly spaced intervals around the perimeter of the Group Counseling Room. These panels are uncomplicated keyboards of lighted punch buttons which have a single go/stop capacity: the key is pressed to start, and pressed again to stop. What happens between "start" and "stop?" The computer records that that interval of time, in relationship to where it temporally occurred in the total group session, had whatever quality was coded and assigned to the key. The code assignment changes, but the keys do not.

Thus, at Computer Panel Station No. 1, Key A might be coded to represent "self-references," Key B "member-to-leader-directed responses," Key C "apparent daydreaming, tuned-out behavior," and so on. At Station 1, the Operator observes his group member designate and punches the proper key when the designate's behavior in the group warrants it, and the computer stores the information.

While much of this kind of data can be gathered from a content analysis of tape recordings, such a process is extremely time-consuming and laborious, and accuracy of diagnosing verbal behavior and assigning meaning to it is considerably more difficult than in the computer-assisted system developed at the National Center.

As the particular behavioral data of a particular group member is quantified and stored in the computer's memory system, all kinds of important answerable questions can be asked. For example, over the course of the counseling meetings in a given group, has Annie Larkin, who has been working on the personal goal of overcoming her fear and becoming more involved, actually shown in later meetings an increase of initiating and responding behavior compared to her earlier meetings? What was the percentage of this increase? How did it correlate with the amount of time George, Carl, or Melba were dominating group activity, the three members who were the most intimidating for Annie according to her own declarations? Annie, of course, is a sharer of the computer's answers to such questions, and the results of her efforts to be more dynamic in her interpersonal dealings with others in the group act as a spur to more concerted efforts, a positive reinforcer of great potency.

This computer-assisted dimension has become important to effective counseling treatment schedules, as can be seen from the above illustration, but the boost it has given to meaningful group counseling research has been inestimable. Not only has this computer power enabled researchers to learn about significant relationships between member growth and leader behaviors, for example, but also it has helped them to look at group variables (such as size, length of session, and so on) in a fresh way. The current research causing so much excitement around the Center, the "Humor in Group Counseling

Series," has already attracted attention around the country in reaction to early reports made at several professional association conventions. The staff assigned to this project has learned conclusively that there is a grossly high correlation between the amount of humor generated in a group and the amount of self-enhancing behavior growth for the greatest number of members, between humor and the amount of group cohesion, and between humor and the extent to which members want to be in the group and are willing to establish and work on individual goals. Dire, dour, gloomy, or sour-faced groups, those with no expectation promises for comedy relief or playtime fun, are etiolated structures for losers.

Future Promise

The imaginary fully-equipped group counseling training and research laboratory which has been pictured, it should again be brought to the reader's attention, does not yet exist. There *are* group counseling training labs which incorporate some of the features of the model shown (see the Tarrier chapter in this book), but nowhere does a lab exist that has them all. In particular, no such training facility has harnessed the computer in the fashion herein illustrated.

Short of programming a computer to convert language sounds of conversing humans into a printed script of the dialogue, a breakthrough which may one day happen, the use of the computer as herein described constitutes a revolutionary notion for counseling researchers.

What makes the future promise of the described model so important, however, is not the thrilling first-rate training and research it can liberate, but the fact that the process of group counseling itself contains such an enormous potential for improving the quality of human existence through supercharging personal effectiveness. Any development which increases the quality, power, validity and reliability of that process and helps it become an ordinary everyday service to more and more people across the land ought to be voted into existence.

I so move.

24.
Absentee-Cueing: A Technical
Innovation for Training Group Counselors

Benjamin Cohn

Counselor education programs generally have three levels of concentration—didactic material aimed at imparting facts about adolescence, occupations, testing and similar areas; theoretical material including techniques of counseling; and the practice and supervision of the counseling process.

The weakest part of the counselor education program tends to be that segment responsible for the training of counselors to do the counseling process. The counselor is a specialist in a school because he has had training in areas related to career choice, college placement, tests and measurements, and the like. The part of his training which truly makes him unique in the school system is his ability to counsel, to become involved with an individual or a group of individuals using his techniques to move the students toward self-determined decisions.

This unique counselor characteristic is most difficult to teach—and frankly it is not learned by most counselors. Because most counselors do not know how to counsel, they become "advisors," rationalizing their ineffectiveness. To learn to counsel effectively, the counselor must have a good background in the psychology of the people with whom he is dealing as well as an approach that offers direction in the relationship. He must also have a good command of his counseling techniques and access to supervision in the counseling process.

The supervision of counselors either in the one-to-one relationship or in a group presents problems. The relationship is supposed to be confidential. The relationship is with one person—the counselor. The initiation of material is supposed to be from the student.

In the group the problems are exaggerated by the number of group members. The counselor is supposed to be accepting and responsive to each individual and to the group as a whole. The non-verbal as well as verbal material may come from members other than the one who is speaking. The responsibility to the group requires the counselor to relate to and clarify a variety of statements from individuals to the goals of the group. Each member is responding not only to the counselor but also to other members, and their interactions can at times be geometrically increased. In controlling or manipulating individuals or the group, the counselor must be subtle and adhere to the "game plan" or theoretical approach to which he subscribes. Because groups require prodding at times, the counselor needs to have planned productive structures in "his hip pocket," so to speak, to move the group along. In other words, the counselor working with a group must be trained and experienced to a greater degree than a counselor working with an individual.

His effectiveness is greatly enhanced by his degree of experience as a counselor. To the new counselor the practicum or supervised experience is all he has had before he "faces the world."

The *old way* required the new and inexperienced counselor to work with the student or group, be recorded either on audiotape or videotape, and discuss his "mistakes" with his supervisor. The mistakes that were made were discussed, new approaches recommended and, hopefully, the mistakes were not made again. Also, hopefully, the same situation would arise again to substantiate the wisdom of the supervisor.

A *new way,* described here, still allows for the permanent record to be made with magnetic tape. However, to add to the relevant dimension, immediate feedback and evaluation, the supervisor can make on-the-spot suggestions and recommendations to the counselor. The counselor can, in turn, apply the suggestions and recommendations to an almost identical situation, which has a high probability of occurring in the same group session, in an effort to evaluate its effectiveness. For example, the counselor asks the student "How do you like social studies?" The student replies, "Fine." The supervisor then cues the counselor to ask the student to go into detail and state his personal *feelings* about his social studies class. The student now replies, "It's okay. I have difficulty with social studies. The teacher is okay, but she seems to expect too much from me . . . "

How It Works

In addition to the audiotape recorder and videotape, the supervisor uses a *wireless microphone* to contact the counselor as he works with his group. Visual contact with the counselor is still made by the training supervisor through a one-way screen or a TV monitor. The counselor receives cues from the supervisor through an FM radio and earplug. The FM radio fits into the counselor's pocket. If desired, the customary stiff antenna can be replaced with a flexible cable that can be placed in the shirt sleeve or pants leg or just left hanging.

The supervisor has his wireless microphone tuned to an off-station on the FM radio in the counselor's pocket. Because there are no wires connecting the sets, and both ends of the set are battery operated, both supervisor and counselor are mobile. They can move around. If the group session is observed by a group of other counselors in front of a monitor, as in Room B below, the supervisor can get questions or suggestions from the group and pass them on to the counselor for his use with the group. The communications with the counselor are heard by him alone and do not interrupt the group interaction. Suggestions and questions can be relayed to the counselor at times when the verbal action in the group is not directed to the counselor.

The Equipment Used

Any pocket-size FM radio can be used. The microphones are typical wireless microphones ranging from the do-it-yourself type costing about $6.00 to expensive microphones with individual transmitters selling for as high as $150 to $200.

Both microphones pictured are made in Japan. The smaller microphone is a wireless model selling for about $20.00. The larger microphone sells for roughly $50.00.

Points to Remember for Use of the Wireless Microphone

1. The counselor and supervisor should agree on the theoretical approach to be used in the counseling process.

2. The counselor should know the goals of each segment of the counseling process.

3. He should be well versed in the use of techniques.

4. There should be practice sessions to acquaint the counselor

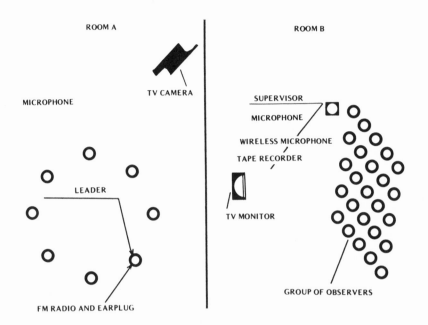

ROOM A

MICROPHONE

TV CAMERA

LEADER

FM RADIO AND EARPLUG

ROOM B

SUPERVISOR

MICROPHONE

WIRELESS MICROPHONE

TAPE RECORDER

TV MONITOR

GROUP OF OBSERVERS

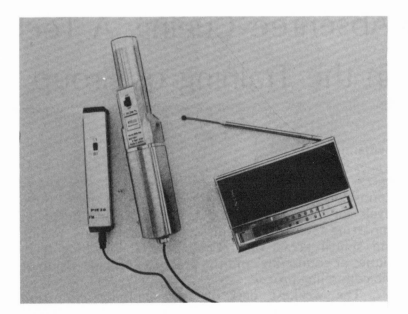

with the phraseology of terms used by the supervisor in describing techniques and pursuing goals.

5. The supervisor, in communicating with the counselor, should pay particular attention to making clear, concise and precise statements, with no qualifying adjectives or adverbs and without "rehashing."

6. In making his suggestions and recommendations the supervisor should wait for a time when the group members are talking to each other or when they have reached the point at which the counselor can share his attention between the group and the supervisor's statements.

7. The supervisor should restrict his comments, questions and suggestions to counseling process and techniques.

8. The supervisor should stifle those questions or comments directed at satisfying his curiosity.

Herold, Ramirez and Newkirk (1971) describe the value of this type of equipment for supervising classroom teachers, and make many references to the use of this equipment in supervising counselors, psychologists and therapists.*

Summary

Using the wireless microphone has one very important advantage over other systems presently used in most practicum courses. It allows the counselor to be supervised in a live setting where suggestions and recommendations can be tried and observed on-the-spot. A secondary value is that it allows the counselor to feel as though he is not alone. In those tense moments when he cannot think of anything to say or any direction to take, the supervisor, if he chooses, can help. One of the reasons group counseling is not being tried with more counselors is probably due to the fear of being in front of a group or being responsible for a group and not knowing how to get the group to move. During these early experiences it is comforting to know that someone is there to help.

*Herold, Philip L., Manuel Ramirez and Jesse Newkirk. A Portable Radio Communications System for Teacher Education. *Educational Technology,* November 1971, 30-31.

25.
A Study of Group Encounter in Higher Education

Jim Bebout

In the fall of 1969 I began a four-year research study of the value of intensive personal growth groups (encounter groups) for a predominately student population in Berkeley.[1/2] Three years of research have been completed. Data are now available on more than 1,000 participants in 100 groups. This chapter will report on some of the major findings. The task was to discover what personal changes, if any, could be attributed to participation in an encounter group, what were the natural processes occurring in such groups, and what qualities of leadership were necessary to conduct these groups successfully.

The project has the advantage of the West Coast popularity of the encounter group movement, the psychologically and socially adventuresome nature of Berkeley students, and an ongoing successful group program across the street from the Berkeley campus—the Personal Encounter Group Program (PEG).[3] The majority of the students are young, single, partially or not employed, majoring mainly in social sciences and humanities in their third to fifth year of higher education. They come from small, intact, working white families in the middle- to upper-middle socioeconomic ranges. More than one-half had no previous group experience; but many have had brief contact with professional therapy or counseling. More will be said of their entering characteristics later.

Increasing efforts are directed toward "educating the whole person." "Whole" persons, students too, have a world view, a social environment, a value system and emotional needs—needs for a sense of belonging, self-esteem and growth in personal relationships. It is commonplace these days to characterize higher education as "factory-like" and to consider the educational process as a "rite du passage"

281

allowing considerable "freedom from" but accompanied by marginal social status, alienation from meaningful community and "unrest."

Specifically, this vision evokes the psychosocial needs of students for discovering or affirming their identity and finding constructive modes of adult human relationship. These goals are embodied in recent efforts toward "affective" education.

In the past, emotional growth was left to fraternities, house-mothers and coaches. The ambition now is to discover means within the practical scope of the institutions of education with which to offer not only intellective, scholastic development but also, in the sense of Carl Rogers' "significant learning," to effect enrichment of students' emotional lives and promote their holistic personal growth. New channels of interaction are required and one of the most promising of these has been the intensive small group process (Egan, 1970; Rogers, 1970; Schutz, 1971; Solomon and Berzon, 1972).

The groups in our sample are called "encounter" groups and rely on a here-and-now focus on feelings arising within interpersonal interaction in the group. The groups are meant to be supportive, exploratory, and to generate more or less intensive experiences furthering people's personal/social growth. To the extent that personal growth *is* facilitated the groups are therapeutic. They are not "problem" or "attack" oriented by design, and an individual's right to a defense is respected. We try for a "fail-safe" approach. No programmed effort is made to interpret people's psychological histories or to formulate them within some particular theory. Responsibility for change rests primarily with group members rather than with leaders, and dramatic breakthroughs are valued less than lasting increments in emotional growth and sensitivity to others.

The groups try to achieve emotional openness, self-disclosure, risk taking, trust, intimacy, behavioral enactment and willingness to engage and confront others and perhaps to change. These ingredients are probably common to many approaches to encounter groups. Some distinct features of the sample are that group members are self-paying volunteers from the Berkeley university and community, and groups meet in the community rather than at resort areas, classrooms or professional development centers. All groups are led by non-professional leaders selected and trained over six months within the PEG Program. The average cost for each participant is 30 cents an hour.

Each group is composed of about 10 members, balanced in sex and age, generally within a 10-year age span. Groups meet once a week for 10 weeks totalling at least 60 hours of face-to-face interaction.

The areas most likely to be affected by an encounter group experience were defined as: self-concept, self-esteem, self-actualization, individual and interpersonal problems, socioemotional alienation, interpersonal values and outside relationships. To assess change in these areas participants were administered a battery of measures before, during and twice following their group experience—once immediately after the group and three to six months later for follow-up. The tests given and their related constructs will be discussed along with the findings for each.

Findings

Entering Characteristics of the Sample

Virtually nothing has been reported on the characteristics of the people who volunteer for an encounter group experience. We were particularly interested in the expectations, needs and self-view of the members in our sample for several reasons: to provide an evaluation of the group experience in terms of the stated desires of the participants, rather than in terms of preconceived theoretical goals; to make some determination as to whether the student population served should more appropriately enter professional counseling or psychotherapy or other traditionally-provided campus services—i.e., to find out if our sample needed therapy more than an encounter group, since they are not the same thing; and, finally, to be able to guess what elements of the student body find a personal growth experience most attractive (or unattractive).

Questionnaire responses indicate that a typical member enters a group with the important expectations of: "Increasing my capacity for deeper relationships," "Finding out how others really see me," "Being able to express my feelings," "Being sensitive to others' feelings," "Being able to share things with others and get closer," and "Changing some of the ways I relate to people."

Initial test scores on a Q-Sort test indicate that members include many positive personal and interpersonal traits in their self-concept, for example "I am concerned and interested in peoples' feelings," "I like to get close and make friends," "I take responsibility for myself" and "I do not feel helpless to deal with my problems." On the negative side, this sample subscribes to statements like "I think a lot about my problems," "I would like to change many things about myself," "I hold myself back" and "I am often disappointed with myself."

We've found that members generally see themselves furthest from their ideal-self in terms of "Self-Satisfaction," "Social-Inhibition" and "Sex." There are sex differences: males feel less adequate in the areas of "Intimacy" and "Expressiveness," whereas females feel less "Self-Reliant" than they would like to be. Comparing Self and Ideal Q-Sorts, the members of this sample show a wide range of self-esteem before taking part in their groups, but generally fall within low-normal limits. (See Figure 1.)

The most frequently expressed problems are "feelings of non-belonging or isolation," "inadequate relations with the opposite sex," "depression" and "uncertainty about future occupation." Clinically diagnostic symptoms are reported by less than 10 percent of this sample.

These and other test results suggest that the people in our groups are rather "normal" in the context of modern urban, young-adult living. They want to discover deeper relationships and to understand themselves better. They are people-oriented and positively motivated toward more supportive, intimate, expressive and comfortable interactions with others, but not through channels of conformity, dependence, or institutionalism.

The Impact of the Group
Self-Concept

Many specific and general changes occur in participants' self-concept. The Self Q-Sort test contains 63 items which participants arrange in sets along a continuum of "most like me" to "least like me" to provide a measure of self-perception. Of the 30 most characteristic Q-Sort items, 23 changed significantly in a positive direction after the group experience ($N = 331$). Items which appear more "intellective-cognitive" show the least (non-significant) changes (such as "I take time to figure people out," "I don't believe in pushing myself" and "I am reassured when I know someone is in charge.") The greatest changes were found in the following characteristics:

I am satisfied with myself (more)

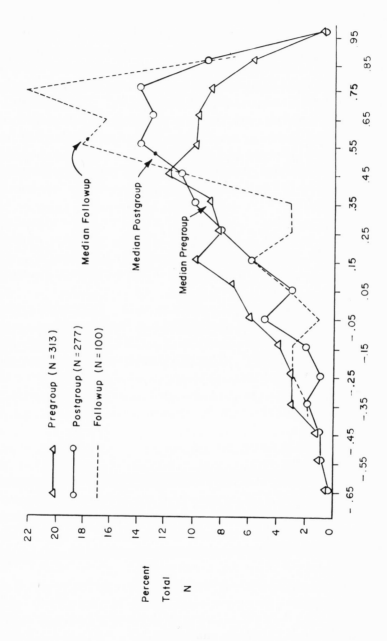

Figure 1

Distribution of Members' Self-Ideal Correlations

I like being touched (more)
I can dish it out as well as take it (more)
I feel helpless to deal with my problems (less)
I contribute something to others' lives (more)
I'd like to change many things about myself (more)
I like to get close, to make friends (more)
I have warm relationships with people (more)
I am shy and timid (less)
I think a lot about my problems (less)
I feel I can take care of myself (more)
I take responsibility for myself (more)
I am afraid . . . of getting too close with people (less)

Does this more positive perception of oneself last beyond the group? Our measure of Self-Ideal concordance—the correlation between Self Q-Sort and Ideal Q-Sort—provides a global estimate of "self-esteem." Figure 1 gives the distributions of self-ideal correlation at pregroup, postgroup and followup. All differences are statistically significant: Self-Ideal concordance increases from pregroup to postgroup and from postgroup to followup. Members gain in perceiving themselves more the way they would "ideally" like to be. The substantial increase from pregroup to followup suggests that these gains materialize over time or subsequent experience.

To check whether the reduced follow-up sample was selectively more positive with regard to the encounter group experience, 34 postgroup outcome variables were examined, testing the significance of the differences between the followup respondents and the rest of the sample. Only one difference was substantial enough to obtain statistical significance: non-respondents at followup (three to six months later) were less "close" to other members in the group than those responding ($p < .01$). Trends suggest that members who do not complete their testing may be more "counter-interpersonal" than other members. However, these findings could be accounted for by sampling fluctuation.

Multi-dimensional analysis of Self Q-Sorts indicates that items on this test measure various dimensions of self-perception. The Self Q-Sort differentiated 11 parameters of self-concept: "Self-Reliance," "Expressivity," "Productivity," "Sexual Adjustment," "Intimacy," "Self-Satisfaction," "Social Inhibition," "Criticality," "Toughness," "Indifference" and "Dependence." Positive change was predicted for the first seven cluster dimensions of self-concept, but no directional hypotheses were made for Criticality, Toughness, Indifference or Dependence. All predicted changes were significant except for Productivity ($p < .05$), signed ranks test. Several self-concept dimensions changed, although they were not predicted. Criticality decreased for females, not males, and Toughness increased for males but not females. Not only did the total available sample ($N = 336$) increase significantly in terms of their areas of deficit ("Self-Satisfaction," "Social Inhibition" and "Sex") but also in their special areas of Self-Ideal disparity by sex: males scoring higher in "Intimacy," "Expressiveness" and females higher in "Self-Reliance"; beyond this, men seemed to get "tougher" and the women "softer" by their own view.

If these findings continue to be significant relative to control group changes, and are maintained, it would suggest that such changes in attitude toward oneself are an added benefit from encounter group participation.

Self-Actualization

Using six sub-scales of Shostrom's Personal Orientation Inventory (POI) test, it was predicted that "self-actualizing" tendencies would increase as an outcome of encounter group participation. POI scores for a sub-sample of 65 females and 70 males were significantly higher at postgroup ($p < .025$) on measures of "Inner-Direction," "Feeling Reactivity," "Spontaneity," "Acceptance of Aggression" and Capacity for Intimate Contact." Females scored higher on "Existentiality" but males did not. Similar changes have been found by Foulds (1970). It should be noted that the significant gains are largely in terms of the affective life of the participants.

Alienation

Socioemotional alienation is a commonly reported problem. It is easy to suppose that alienation should lessen with encounter group experience as the aim and prospect of these groups is to generate a meaningful relatedness between people. The Social Feeling Index is made up of rather antiquated items (e.g., "Most people have so much trouble of their own that they aren't concerned about mine," "My life has been barren and meaningless") but does provide a crude index of this variable (McClosky and Schaar, 1965).

A modified version of the Social Feeling Index was completed before- and after-group by 272 participants. The average Alienation score at pregroup was 63.1, and at postgroup, 57.3. The difference between the two means is significant at the .01 level. Members identify with fewer statements of alienation after their group experience.

By an analysis of a sub-sample, it is known that there is a slight relationship between higher scores on socioemotional alienation and general dissatisfaction with the university as an institution (including its academic aspects). Further study of the relationships between students' valuation of educational components (faculty, student body, administration, the university as a whole) and their level of socioemotional alienation is now being carried out and will be reported elsewhere. At this point it can be suggested only that students who feel generally alienated in life and society are probably more dissatisfied with school, implying that gains in emotional satisfaction through encounter group participation may benefit students in terms of their roles in academia. However, there is also a suggestion in the data now under analysis that, following an encounter group experience, students are, if anything, more likely to drop out of school.

Individual Problems

The ten "most important" individual problems selected by each member before group participation were re-presented immediately after the group along with three rating scales. Members rated "Change in the way you feel," "Change in actual behavior" and "How much did the group contribute to helping with this problem" for each of the 10 problems. Mean ratings of improvement and group help correlated significantly (.84), such that those problems seen as most improved are those with which the group was most helpful. Many average ratings are substantially above the "zero" point: the largest gains reported reflect greater self-confidence, self-understanding, self-acceptance and mood change ("Difficulty understanding your own feelings," "Feelings of inferiority," "Difficulty asserting yourself," "Depression"); and greater ease and emotional satisfaction in relationships ("Difficulty in making friends," "Feeling of non-belonging," "Isolation," "Difficulty being comfortable with others"). The encounter group shows least effect on school and work problems.

Self-ratings on degree of change and peer-ratings by fellow group members also indicate significant gains (p < .001). Group members concur in reporting positive change for individuals, but generally report a smaller degree of change than do the individuals themselves.

Interpersonal Values and Relationships

On entering, the participants volunteering for an encounter group seem much less traditional than students in general in terms of stated interpersonal values (Gordon's Survey of Interpersonal Values Test). On this instrument, our Berkeley sample (N = 300) appears much more in tune with values of independence and non-conformity than college students in general. Differences between pregroup and postgroup scores show several significant changes: "Benevolence" as an interpersonal value decreases at postgroup for both sexes (p < .05); males endorse more independence items (p < .01) and females score higher on support (p < .02) but still lower on conformity (p < .05). The reduction in "Benevolence" scores is likely due to a number of "do-goody" items for this sub-scale that are disavowed after the group.

A second major instrument used to assess change in the interpersonal domain was the Relationship Inventory (Barrett-Lennard, 1970). This test was administered to "friends" of participants nominated at pregroup. By direct observation of over 100 groups, it was apparent that many "outside" relationships were undergoing considerable change. Many marriages were in jeopardy or dissolving, many friendships and love lives being discovered or broken. Thus, consistent changes in the measures of "Positive Regard," "Empathic Understanding," "Conditionality of Regard" and "Genuineness"—the variables tapped by the Relationship Inventory—were impossible to predict. Nevertheless, a sample of friends' RI scores (N = 83) indicated that "Empathic Understanding" increased significantly from pre- to postgroup (p < .05).

Meaningfulness of the Group

Besides thousands of written reports from participants regarding the value and role of the group experience in their life, a schedule was administered asking group members to rank their encounter group experience among the eight most significant or meaningful events in their lives to determine something of the total impact of the group. By this means it was found that about 46 percent of the participants report the group to be among the more meaningful experiences they have had (ranks 5-8), 39 percent rank the group lower than all other events chosen, and 17 percent report the group to be of extreme significance (ranks 1-4) (N = 283). The greatest impact was felt by the younger members and by those with the least prior group experience.

Discussion and Summary

For years encounter groups have been characterized by wildly differing polemics. In our program we have found significant and constructive changes in participants almost wherever we looked. There is not one known psychiatric "casualty" in the past 2000 members, in spite of casual screening and the admission of several post-institutionalized psychotic patients. This is probably because of the group model adopted, and the success of the leader selection and training program.[4] Although instances of "scapegoating" are observed periodically, there is group pressure to move someone toward the stated goals of encounter groups, and apparently many people experience personal changes. There is no way in which our data support the characterization of these groups as "emotional fascism" or "brainwashing." It is perhaps true that an encounter experience increases one's sense of and regard for personal independence and non-conformity in a self-actualizing manner. If this change is equated with "turning Pinko" or revolution, then encounter groups may become the new politics.

What we have observed is easy to summarize: the encounter groups in this sample do little for productivity, work or school problems. More experienced and older individuals receive diminishing returns from a group. Humanistically-oriented people do not change in this inclination much, unless to become more so. And these groups accomplish almost nothing for classically "symptomatic" problems such as phobias and somatizations.

On the other hand, there are many significant positive changes reported by members and others who know them. Members indicate greater self-satisfaction, increased self-reliance, more comfort with sexuality and less social inhibition. They feel more inner-direction, spontaneity and more acceptance of their own aggression. Self-actualizing tendencies are greater. They are less lonely and less alienated. They experience progress in a number of individual and interpersonal problems and fellow group members concur in this improvement. Members' friends report greater empathy in their relationships, and members seem less attached to shallow forms of "benevolence." Finally, in self-reports members attest to a great number of personal learnings, more self-awareness and personal growth. These outcomes are particularly dependent on the nature of the group and the leader.

At this point, these results can only be considered provisional, pending the analysis of experimental control subjects and additional followup data (now being analyzed). Careful and complex study of the data in terms of the effects of group-type, group-composition, leader style and indigenous process are necessary for the full understanding of the merits of this new approach—the encounter group—in increasing human potential and its value in the realm of affective education.

References

Barrett-Lennard, G. The Relationship Inventory: Revision Process. Mimeographed Paper, University of Waterloo, 1970.

Bebout, J. and B. Gordon. The Value of Encounter. In Lawrence N. Solomon and Betty Berzon (Eds.) *New Perspectives on Encounter Groups.* San Francisco: Jossey-Bass, 1972.

Egan, G. *Encounter: Group Processes for Interpersonal Growth.* Belmont, California: Wadsworth Publishing Company, 1970.

Foulds, M.L. Effects of a Personal Growth Group on a Measure of Self-Actualization. *Journal of Humanistic Psychology,* 1970, *10,* 33-38.

McClosky, H. and J.J. Schaar. Psychological Dimensions of Anomie. *American Sociological Review,* 1965, *30* (1), 14-40.

Rogers, C.R. *On Encounter Groups.* New York: Harper and Row, 1970.

Schutz, W.C. *Here Comes Everybody.* San Francisco: Viking Press, 1971.

Solomon, L.N. and B. Berzon (Eds.) *New Perspectives on Encounter Groups.* San Francisco: Jossey-Bass, 1972.

Notes

1. Funded by National Institutes for Mental Health, Center for Studies of Child and Family Mental Health, Grant Number MH17703-04; sponsoring institution—the University Y.M.C.A. (Stiles Hall) at Berkeley.
2. Sensitivity training, T-groups and human potential groups are more similar to than different from encounter groups.

3.   The Program Director is Dr. Mimi Silbert. For information, write to: Dr. Silbert, 2400 Bancroft Way, Berkeley, California 94704.
4.   For information, write to Dr. Mimi Silbert.

26.
Integrating Life's Possibilities by Comprehending Technology and Group Reciprocity

Anna Louise Miller and
David V. Tiedeman

Technology's Effects on Groups

Technology's Impact on Inner Systems and Mind. Technology implosively impacted people and their groups during the past quarter century. In relation to groups, the impact equalized the importance for man's psychological development of what used to be considered primary and secondary groups. As a result, we hold that man now needs to be shown 1) the importance of groups as he progresses through life and 2) how his effective use of such groups can aid his development in life. Good mental health depends on man's ability in the future to seek and find groups to replace the family, which no longer serves the singular purpose it once did. How did this condition come about and why is our remedy necessary?

Among the many and startling new and improved old inventions which occurred since World War II, two kinds implicitly changed people and our American society and thereby explicitly changed our relationships to the structures of that evolving society as well. Consider, as one example, the internal systems effects of tranquilizers and other new drugs. By balancing his chemistry, man now controls his health, his feeling of well being and even his perceptual relationship to the world.

Consider, as the other example, the external systems support of the extracorporeal, adjuvant assistance of the airplane, the telephone, the computer and other mechanical devices available to extend man's presence and mind. We now have visual participation in a world community. News is no longer impacted by lack of communication systems; for all practical purposes a communication lag no longer exists. TV brings the world into the front room, and willy nilly, implosively changes the world view of all exposed to it.

These major external structural changes have emerged in the form of "systems technology." Perhaps the single greatest accomplishment in this area was the placing of a man on the moon, a feat that staggered while intriguing the imaginations of men and proved one of the most outstanding examples of the adjuvant systems capability of man's mind. Another example of the creative capacity of man through systems technology is the computer-assisted instruction now available to children in a remote Indian pueblo community via satellite from Stanford University (*San Jose Mercury News,* 1972a). Further, employees from five Mid-Peninsula industries have been able to earn advanced degrees while attending class at their place of employment through Stanford University's Association for Continuing Education (*San Jose Mercury News,* 1972b). In other words, it is becoming possible to *communicate to* instead of *commute to* those structures and institutions needed for growth in life. This new type of access and the advanced speed associated with it place us in a different relationship to our world, which as we shall show necessarily implies an equalization in the importance of the former primary and secondary groups in which we interact.

We postulate a relationship between the structure/utility of groups and the rate of technological advance. With this relationship in mind, we *first* show how the primary and secondary groups have been modified as a result of technological advance, *second* indicate the potential of using groups in education to appraise students of their total environment, *third* show what new groups have emerged as a result of technology, *fourth* show how the concept of education and the potential of groups can be extended beyond the 12th grade, and *finally* consider counseling practice and organization necessary for the new situational or crisis counselor we thereby deduce.

Modification of Primary and Secondary Groups. The primary and secondary groups have been most affected by technological advances in the field of transportation. We live today at a pace unexperienced by any people since the beginning of time. We are now cognitively and technologically, but not emotionally, propelling ourselves through time at an amazing speed, and the "action and reaction occur almost at the same time" (McLuhan, 1964, p. 20). To understand our acceleration of self-transport in time, look at the following table showing the technological advances in the field of transportation and their rate of acceleration from the beginning to the present day:

Number of years to accomplish	Year	Means	Speed
	Prehistory	Walking	3 m.p.h.
	6000 B.C.	Camel	8 m.p.h.
Millions	1784 A.D.	Horse-drawn coach	10 m.p.h.
65	1825 A.D.	Steam locomotive	13 m.p.h.
	1880 A.D.	Advanced steam	
58		locomotive	100 m.p.h.
22	1938 A.D.	Airplane	400 m.p.h.
	1960s	Rocket plane	4,000 m.p.h.
	1960s	Space capsules	18,000 m.p.h.

(Adapted from Toffler, 1970, p. 26)

In short, it took us millions of years to increase the speed of travel from 3 to 13 miles per hour; about 60 years each, first to accelerate the rate to 100 miles per hour and then to quadruple that speed; but a mere 30 years to increase that speed over four hundredfold.

This kaleidoscopic existence has made its impact particularly on the primary group. Because of the accelerated speed at which we travel, we have more time, make more contacts, and thereby give ourselves a sense of "less time." Social relationships exist in shorter intervals as a result, but occur more frequently. We move in and out of groups so quickly that we fail to establish long-term commitment to any group. Therefore, if not secure in the self on which we must then primarily depend, we feel alone and alienated, even in our primary family group which has consisted of our most intimate associations. Part of this alienation also comes from the fact that both mother and father are working, are more mobile, and mostly experience their social life outside the family. As a consequence, the child now experiences his social life primarily with his peers, and continuity in the family group is beginning to disappear as families all go in different directions and are more outer-directed. What used to be a fusion of individual personalities into a common life and purpose of the family group has become a dispersion in the activities with people outside the family.

Now let's look at the secondary group—the less intimate group in which relationships are more impersonal, rational, formal and contractual. Examples of secondary groups are special interest groups—national, political, religious, professional—and business and bureaucratic organizations. Technology has increased interactions among groups of this type since secondary groups more appropriately match the pace of living that technology has made possible. Also, since they are contractual rather than lineal types they become natural bridges helping man over developmental and other crises.

So what happens as primary groups become less cohesive and secondary groups more numerous? Alienation becomes generic "And the ever-more-completely altered environment is, in turn, continually altering all the creatures" (Fuller, 1972, p. 83).

One of the most obvious antidotes to the alienation partially brought about by technology has been the emergence of encounter, sensitivity and T-Groups, sensory awareness groups, body awareness groups, body movement groups, creativity workshops, organizational development groups, team building groups, gestalt groups and Synanon type groups. These constitute only a partial list. These groups have much in common: they are usually small, relatively unstructured and set their own goals and directions. The leader and group members are oriented toward the process and dynamics of personal interactions.

For all practical purposes, both primary and secondary groups are therefore now equally important in bringing a person to psychological well being and integrated functioning. We feel that this equalization must now be acknowledged in educational practice. We must not be or become:

"Little humans
Preoccupied with the immediate needs
Of their physical regenerations
(Who) have locked
Their zoom-lens focusing mechanism
On the close-ups only
Leaving it exclusively to their intuition
To remind them
Once again in a surprised while
Of the vast long-distance focusing
Of evolutionary events" (Fuller, 1972, p. 72).

To avoid this "zoom-lens tendency" we need to assist the individual to look outward from his inner frame of reference, in order to get a total impression of himself and his possibilities—those aids and assists he can call on for growth in life. Man needs to learn that school is only one type of group he needs as he lives and that on completing his education there will be other groups which will assist him in his never-ending evolving search for meaning.

Education in Group Behavior

The Current Group Scene and Its Fault. In school groups we currently address such problems as career concerns, personal adjustment—but with emphasis on the past—and similar categorical topics. Such group sessions permit the student to see that others have similar problems and that he is not so different. He thereby gains in identification with others and is further enabled to talk unaided and more openly about those things that concern him as he grows and interacts. This is important to the adolescent and young adult. However, equally important is knowledge about the world he is going to be living in, some of its realities, and how his values and aspirations fit best into its schemes of career, life style and leisure time.

Existing group counseling has used zoom-lens mechanisms to focus on what is termed the student's problem. We have no quarrel with looking at the problem, but we do take issue with the fact that this problem is seen only in the psychological context, not as a part of the student's total gestalt. A student's gestalt includes his self in relation to his environment. The environment is at the moment dominated by speed, instantness and rapid obsolescence. The student experiences this time and motion with much more flexibility than the counselor as he has "cut his eye teeth on the ring of technology." But we do not in group counseling bring the ramifications of speed, instantness and rapid obsolescence into the student's total awareness. Group counseling up to now has not assessed the student's problems from the technological as well as the psychological frame of reference. Since it has thus dealt with a minute part of the student's sociological base, it is difficult for him to get a sense of the centering of himself in his technological environment and a look at his problems as first related to the environment and then to the people within that environment.

Since the brain apprehends and registers, stores and retrieves sensorial information and the mind alone can and does discover heretofore unknown integral pattern concepts and generalized principles (Fuller, 1972), we believe those in counseling are presently using their brains more than their minds. Unfortunately, their students are therefore being educated on quite minuscule perceptions. It is time to take our "blinders" off and perceive the world as a whole, so we can communicate that perception to students. At that moment, we will begin to look at the students' part in the world in relation to their total gestalt. In so doing, what kind of panoramic view will we give the student about his environment and groups in relationship to the needs that are aroused as a result of that environment?

Groups Formed and Forming as a Result of Technology. Technological changes rearrange relationships among people and things. Relationships once stationary and fixed in a person's life are therefore now experienced as changing at an accelerating speed—both coming into being and disappearing more rapidly within a person's life.

We feel that the kinds of groups formed in response to these technological changes are usefully arrayed as in Figure 1. Circles are depicted with a hub and three rings in the Figure.

Figure 1 has a two-fold purpose. It suggests something about groups which adolescents and young adults need to comprehend; it suggests some of the variability in counseling which looms on the horizon. But what will remain unexpressed in this figure and chapter are the implications for a technology of group process itself which must come about to provide the help needed to accomplish comprehension of technology and group which can no longer be avoided. We are momentarily incapable of writing all that, although there are well established procedures for helping another both to know group effects on consensually achieved decisions and to know one's self better while learning which should not be overlooked as we mutually conceive and construct the needed group technology. But enough of that; back to the Figure.

The center circle or hub represents the old primary group—the family with parents and children. This is a self-determined group, that is, a group which does not have the reasons of "others" as a basis for its existence.

Surrounding the self-determined hub group in Figure 1 are other determined groups, those which have no biological reason for their existence; they have only man's interdependency needs as reason for being.

The first ring of other-determined groups consists of institutional groups. School, church and work groups are examples. We note that

Figure 1

The Enlarging and Changing Group Scene

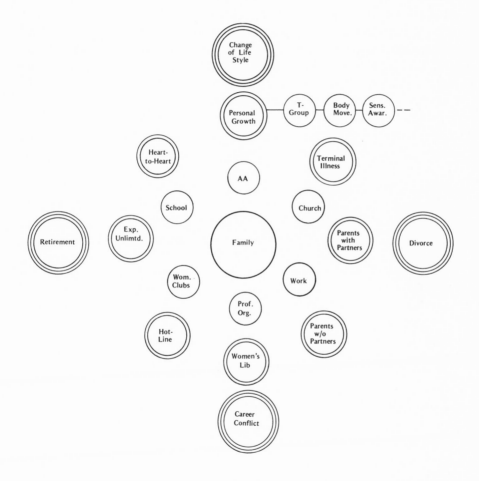

these groups are older and therefore well established or institutionalized in our culture. They perseverate because they still fulfill some needs but also because an organization exists in each and organizations tend to perpetuate themselves. We have also placed Alcoholics Anonymous in this first ring of circles because it is an older functional group which has become somewhat institutionalized just like school, church and work.

As we incur more and more change in society new needs are aroused, and groups formed in response to those needs dovetail into them. Thus more situational and functional type groups will appear as technology continues to present more alternatives, with better and faster ways of improving our quality of life. The reality of more group input into life because of rapid structural changes introduces the imperative that groups must now be comprehended as the nexus of mental health for people going through life. As indicated in a previous section, secondary groups have for all practical purposes become primary because they provide bridges and psychological support once provided almost entirely by the family, the only primary group of yore. Also, more kinds of groups are in existence that speak to the needs of young people as well as adults. For example, there are birth control centers where young women can get contraceptives and have abortions performed without parental consent, and the like. Technology is making a different life possible; this different life is causing short-term adjustment problems; and groups are formed and being formed to meet these problems. We note some of these newly forming groups as the second ring of circles in Figure 1. Since these are the emerging groups they deserve some further mention so they will be more in our awareness.

For instance, in terms of career we used to be able to say, "If you get a good education you will get a good job." That may still be true ultimately, but today's NOW actually being experienced forces conclusion that 1) the economy is not supporting "hiring"; rather it is tending to focus on a "tighten your belt" philosophy; 2) minorities are being given priorities in jobs; 3) there are geographical areas that cannot readily absorb those with a B.A. or even an M.A.; 4) some occupations are experiencing over-supply, e.g., engineering, teaching; 5) many students graduate from high school and college without any type of negotiable skill; and 6) people are moving to communities where they don't have contacts for jobs.

These problems cause groups to arise which assist people while experiencing one or more of the above conditions. For example, there are groups called "Experience Unlimited" which consist of people who band together to help each other get jobs, sharing knowledge about jobs, who they know, and what they know about job openings.

Another NOW is that due to the changes and distractions in our life, we don't give as much time to talking with each other as we did earlier, and such groups as Heart-to-Heart and CARE have formed as a result. Today a person telephones somewhere when he needs to talk with someone. There are numerous groups of this nature across the country all devoted to assisting the lonely of all ages.

If an individual is depressed to the point of despondency and suicide, there are hot-line groups formed to talk with him.

Other groups arising from NOW expectations are:

Parents-without-partners get together to talk about their special problems—children and their own personal development as a result of being alone. There are also parents-with-partners' groups.

Creative Initiative groups form to assist adults, both divorced and married, to formulate goals for their lives and to talk about ways to reach these goals.

Groups appear which are devoted to personal growth. However, various approaches are taken in respect to growth. For example, the body awareness, body movement, sensory awareness groups and the like.

People having trouble with weight have formed clubs to help each other in their pursuit of losing weight.

The women in the country join together in various Women's Liberation groups, aimed at equalizing women's position in the culture, now that women do have more time to be concerned with other than household problems.

A number of hospitals form terminal illness groups, where people can deal openly with the topic of death.

And then looking ahead beyond NOW expectations we speculate that some of the groups on the horizon and even coming into being are 1) divorce groups—for people involved in divorce; 2) change of life style groups—for those wanting a different way of life; 3) career conflict groups—formed for those adults who feel they have reached a stalemate in their life and want a change; and 4) retirement groups—for those who want to talk about the adjustment in retirement. These coming-into-being groups are shown in the third and outermost ring in Figure 1.

Most all the groups we have mentioned are important as they don't try to rehash the past, but deal and will deal with problems currently being experienced. However, these groups require a new type of counseling, the crisis type we identify further in closing.

Generalization with Implications
for Counseling

Generalization. We should begin to think of groups in learning—not groups in school—groups that assist us in moving smoothly and effectively *as we learn and grow through life.* We must become able to move in and out of groups as needed until we reach that final group—our terminal illness group. To effect this change we need first to recognize and enunciate it. We will then need to train crisis counselors "who will be experts not in such conventional disciplines as psychology or health, but in specified transitions such as relocation, job promotion, job loss, divorce, or sub-cult hopping" (Toffler, 1970, p. 387).

Implications for Counseling. We have herein recognized and enunciated the need for crisis counseling. At the center of that need is comprehension of the interdependence of individual and group. This is the goal toward which mature understanding tends. The person and the group are dependent on each other. But the interaction must be experienced as—and become—a reciprocating one, that of interacting independently but still being dependent on the interaction with each other.

We have highlighted the impact of technology on this comprehension. We have noted that technology has made need for comprehension both more immanent and more imminent. Technology has created more need for various types of groups. We have depicted some of the increased group density and variability in Figure 1. But we believe the primary group no longer suffices to let people understand the place of various groups in their individuality. Safety no longer exists in the family; it exists in comprehending technology and group interaction.

We therefore need to establish programs to train our crisis counselors as we now have programs to train our therapeutic counselors. (We define crisis not as a life-or-death situation but as a period in an individual's life where he needs assistance for a short interval.) It may seem at first that there is no difference between the crisis and therapeutic counselors, but we believe there is a vast difference because the crisis counselor will not be concerned primarily with a person's past but with how he can help the individual adjust to his present situation or short-term crisis. In addition, he considers the future and possibilities more—making self more than just being self.

In establishing needed new programs for crisis counselors, we must also place these new counselors in the school system. Crisis counselors for school practice have to be trained to help the young see their world totally, noting the various types of groups they may enter for short-term assistance after completing use of their instruction group (school). Since school crisis counselors will be trained from the holistic point of view, they are more likely to pass this view along to their students than the presently therapeutically trained and oriented counselors. The therapeutic counselor and the crisis counselor can exist side by side and serve equally important purposes. But therapeutic counselors are *not* crisis counselors.

Crisis counselors will be able to visit a person's group consciousness with him and thereby further mature his individual comprehension of the dependence of his independence on the concept of the extended self or group. We have started ourselves forward along that line of thought—a start, a mere step. Take it from there. Man's sanity depends on such comprehension and action by a new breed of counselors.

References

Fuller, R. Buckminster. *Intuition.* New York: Doubleday and Company, 1972.

McLuhan, Marshall. *Understanding Media: The Extensions of Man.* New York: Signet Books, 1964.

San Jose Mercury News, January 27, 1972a.

San Jose Mercury News, May 4, 1972b.

Toffler, Alvin. *Future Shock.* New York: Random House, 1970.

27.
Effectively Leading a Group
in the Present Moment:
A Highly Artistic, Probabilistic and
Professional Task if One Would By-Pass
Traditional Myths About Group Work*

H. Jon Geis

In reviewing an otherwise excellent book on research in psychotherapy, Victor Raimy recently concluded that for some time to come practitioners still will have to continue to do their work "mostly with their wits" (Raimy, 1972). Having spent over six years as a professor in graduate schools training psychological counselors and psychotherapists, the same amount of time as a chief clinical supervisor at a major therapist training institute in New York City, and also as a more than full-time psychotherapist in private practice for many years—on the frontiers of personality disturbance and reality problem-solving situations of all kinds, night and day, attempting, in the crucible of moment-to-moment requirements for effective action, to continually improve theory and practice for helping people—I still find striking the innocence of university-based writers, researchers and trainers with regard to the range and depth and complexity of the personality and reality situations with which these professionals must deal if they would actually, efficiently and maximally help people.

On the other hand, among the practitioners who do write about their work or about whom we otherwise hear, in many cases I am also struck by their emotionalized attachments to one generalized "right" way to the truth of helping people or to what are in many cases their unthinking evasions from making their operating theory and practice

---

*This chapter is written for the developing group leader—one who wishes to know how to work more effectively with groups in the Present Moment and who, if only because of this desire, is very likely to do so. It is for the developing group leader who has zero hours of experience leading a group and for the developing group leader who, like the author, has many thousands of hours of experience.

explicit in their non-specific claims of "eclecticism."

Beginning my own work with counselees and patients in hospitals, agencies and schools more than fifteen years ago, I soon found these leading practitioners and university authorities unusually wanting in the specifics of moment-to-moment interactions in which I was engaging with the people I was trying to help. Neither in individual supervision nor in extensive readings was I able to find very much of the help I sought, even though the intensity and breadth of my efforts to seek supervisory help did yield some few profitable hooks, from time to time, upon which to build my own general and precise understandings of theory and practice. So it has been, with great difficulty and persistence over many years, that I have had to forge what has largely been my own conception of psychological theory and practice. This conception has guided me in that vast complex of meanings and possibilities which exist in any Present Moment experience for the group leader or individual psychological counselor or psychotherapist.

My concern in this chapter, however, is not to make a claim for the correctness of my own views and practices. My aim is to focus the reader's attention upon the endless possibilities and meanings to be found within what I call the Present Moment that is constantly the experience of anyone engaging in the process of psychologically helping people—no matter what label is used to identify the worker's role or what school of theory and practice is followed—on an individual or group basis.

In discussing with the editors of this book what I might contribute, we decided that I might identify and challenge some of the long-standing myths which they and I believe have been such useless baggage and uncritically thought-through aspects of group work. However, when I sat down to challenge these myths—in part out of my own professional experience, which has included approximately 5,900 hours of group work and 31,800 hours of individual psychotherapy or psychological counseling sessions just within the last decade—I came to the realization that it was of primary importance to help the developing group leader understand and find more meaningful the creative possibilities in the Present Moment. Under some circumstances these myths might or might not be true or useful. It was of secondary importance to clarify the nature of the myths themselves. This led to the clearer formulation of my goals for this chapter. They are:

1) To help the reader attend to a frame of reference for experiencing himself, his group and its members with ever-expanding possibilities for his creative and constructive feeling, thinking and acting in the Present Moment;

2) To help the reader appreciate more deeply the meanings of the group leader's experiencing in the Present Moment and the fact of the rich, almost infinite number of variables and events possible;

3) To help the reader understand that there are no certainties or absolutes in group work and that even the myths may hold or not hold in particular cases; in actuality at the very best there are guidelines and specifics which may be drawn upon as "best" courses of action in certain typical situations, but each event must be experienced, thought about and acted upon creatively as a new event in the Present Moment;

4) To help the reader appreciate the dynamic rather than fixed and absolute nature of some particular myth areas and "certainties" well known in the field of group work;

5) To help the reader generalize his appreciation of the goals set in this chapter to other "certainties" and myth areas, and to his own creative experiencing in the Present Moment;

6) To help the reader appreciate the importance of operating, as a group leader, from theory, experience and thoughtfulness, and in an aggressive, fearless and open-minded attempt to learn and develop himself professionally and personally in a continually evolving manner.

In short, I would like to help the reader sense more deeply the infinite array of dynamic possibilities, the choices, the opportunities for effectiveness and for difficulty, the hint of things to be avoided, the possibilities not to panic but to face oneself, to work on oneself to rid oneself of great and subtle fears, and to improve one's group leadership abilities.

I would like the reader to come away from this chapter with a greater personal sense of what it means to engage the task of leading a group in any Present Moment.

An Orienting Frame of Reference
The Present Moment and the Future Moment
Basically, the Present Moment is a simple concept. Suffice it to say here that it is that moment in time, unlike any other, which for the individual—as for example, for the reader—is occurring now. It comes

and is gone, to be replaced by another Present Moment. It is in this Present Moment that all of the group leader's thinking, deciding, feeling and acting—to help or not help, or to hinder, his group members—takes place. It is for the benefit of Future Moments, rather than for the Present Moment alone, that the group leader almost always acts the way he does (i.e., to achieve some long-range goal from short-range or "now" stimulus conditions).

Intrinsic Experiences and Outcome Experiences

In terms of goal orientation, the group leader's experiencing may be thought of in two ways: he may engage either in Intrinsic Experiences, those undertaken solely for the effect of the moment, for himself or for his group members (e.g., making a joke for his own ego satisfaction or evading a member's remark because of his own personal fear), or he may engage in Outcome Experiences, those designed to achieve some Future Moment goal (e.g., making a joke to break group tension or not responding to a member's remark in favor of focusing on something more important).

Atomism Within a Long-Range Perspective

Within the Present Moment the conceptual frame of reference which the group leader most ideally should experience is what I call an atomistic point of view within a long-range perspective. This means that the group leader pays the most precise attention to the details of his inner and outer experiences yet considers these—at the same time—within a long-range awareness of other possibilities regarding the group, himself and the group's individual members.

A Three-Part Orienting Theory

As I have noted elsewhere (Geis, 1969, and Chapter Two of this volume), any individual who operates within any kind of professional helping role must work—within the Present Moment—from a three-part, interrelated theoretical framework: (1) a theory of what people-in-the-world are like, (2) a theory of what is good for people-in-the-world and (3) a theory of the stimulus conditions which may constructively influence people-in-the-world as a function of their characteristics and what is believed to be good for them. In the examples which follow we shall see how the group leader operates within the Present Moment—

ideally as consciously and cognitively as possible rather than mostly intuitively—in terms of these theoretical categories and the atomistic/long-range perspective.

Acting Artistically and Probabilistically
in the Present Moment

Whether or not one is open to and aware of it, the process of living is complex, difficult and often painful. To experience it as not being so is, most likely, to be ignorant or psychologically in trouble. To experience it as *only* these things also is, almost certainly, to be ignorant or psychologically in trouble. The use of reason, evidence, fearlessness and expertise in the roles we undertake in life—all to be acquired with great effort over much time—and based upon the primary value of truth-seeking, may help us more fully, but never completely, to actualize ourselves, with increasing satisfaction in our personal and professional lives. Effective and successful professional group work, like every act of successful personal living in the Present Moment, is an artistic and complex endeavor.

As may be held about living itself, more fundamentally even about the nature of Reality, there is no single assertion about group work that may hold for *all* circumstances but virtually anything may be appropriate at some particular time—in some particular place, with some particular group member, in some particular group, using some particular theory, with some particular goal(s), with some particular ... etc. For every "right" thing that exists in the Present Moment, that same thing may be wrong at some other time (or wrong in the Present Moment because of the view or unawareness of the observer). For every particular thing that exists, its opposite may exist, in the Present Moment or in Future Moments, or its absence may in fact be the case (or these may exist in the Present Moment, similarly, because of the particular frame of reference or the ignorance of the perceiver).

Before the fact, *before* the Future Moment, *any*thing is possible, *any*thing is potentially useful to influence an existent. On the other hand, although nothing is certain, all things are not equally probable. Depending upon a dynamic interplay of many things, looking ahead from the Present Moment to a Future Moment, things have a greater or lesser *probability* of coming to pass, and so we look ahead and act *probabilistically,* and without fixed certainty. At the same time, and most crucially, we must distinguish between *poss*ibility and *prob*ability. (This is one of the most common distortions, to be sure, of *both* my therapy patients and the many hundreds of counselors and psychotherapists I have supervised. In short, it is a distortion fundamentally true of *people*.)

A group of people is like a stone. Or a flea. Or a pineapple. Or a star. Or an orgasm. Or a cough. Or an idea. Or a group of any of these things. Or all of them together. Or anything else in the universe, existing or in the experience of the individual conceiving of it.

To influence these reality existents to react in particular ways for any Future Moment one must have certain goals in mind, stimulate the existents appropriately and—at any Present Moment over the long-run process of working to change them (seconds, hours, days, months, years beyond the Present Moment now existing)—ideally, bring into play appropriate intelligence, professional expertise, experiential background, theory and action skills.

In view of all the foregoing orienting remarks, perhaps the reader and developing group leader may more clearly appreciate that the effective action of the group leader in the Present Moment, like effective living itself, must be—whatever else it may be—both artistic and probabilistic.

Some Prevailing Myth Areas
The Structure of My Own Groups
To examine Present Moment experiencing as it relates to some of the major myth areas in group work, I will briefly present the structure of my own current helping groups and draw from these groups for discussion incidents taking place at the time of this writing. I do not believe that the kind of clientele, setting, or professional concerns basic in my own professional helping activities—no matter how different they may *seem* to be compared to those of the reader, both in overt content and in underlying dynamics and process—need prevent *any* helping professional from relating to the major concerns of this chapter: (1) The meaning of Present Moments and Future Moments in group leadership and (2) clarity about some particular myth areas.

Currently I am leading seven psychotherapy groups. These groups meet for one-and-a-half hours weekly with the same continuing members. Three of the groups are fifteen-person groups, the other four

Situation No. 2. Judith, a member of one of my small groups, is being accused by other group members of controlling the group situation for her own interests. She begins to complain about the way the group is being run, with obvious implications for criticism of the professional behavior of the group leader—myself. I say nothing. After four or five minutes of this interaction between her and other group members, she turns on me angrily and says, "And *you—you* just sit there. Aren't you going to *do* anything or *say* anything?" I sit there calmly, paying attention to her but not responding with any word or movement. Is my behavior correct in the Present Moment? What would an effective group leader, in the Present Moment—do?

Situation No. 3. The fifteen-member group has been in session about twenty minutes and the last of six members has presented a brief progress report, stemming from the psychological homework he undertook to work on at the previous week's session. I am about to ask who in the group would like to present a problem, for group help, this session—allowing the group to structure its session—when I decide to act in the following way: I say, "Let's get Sally to talk. I have a feeling it's important for her to talk tonight. Tell us, Sally, what have you decided to do about school, and moving out of your parents' home and in with your boyfriend, Jim?" Sally is a pretty nineteen-year old from a lower middle-class socioeconomic background. She is an only child who lives with her rather "old-fashioned" parents. Basically quite bright, but with little awareness of her ability, and with deep inferiority feelings, she works as a salesgirl in a job she hates, flirting with the possibility of trying some hard drugs and living with her boyfriend Jim, who has recently been paroled on drug and theft charges. Did I, as group leader in the Present Moment, act correctly? What would an effective group leader, in the Present Moment, in the same situation—do?

Situation No. 4 In one of my small groups, a young man, Noel, twenty-one, pressures the group to help him know what to do to prepare for his upcoming final examinations at one of the national service academies. For the past year-and-a-half he has improved his grades only gradually and now stands in danger of flunking out from the military program altogether if he does not pass these end-of-course examinations with relatively high grades. The group members jump on him for demandingly "wanting easy gimmick answers to solve all of your problems." The examinations are three weeks away. What should I, as group leader, do? And what do you think the effective group leader, in the Present Moment, would do?

Situation No. 5. An experience similar to this one happened to me some years ago, in one of the more difficult of the New York City public schools. I was responsible for a twenty-member group of "problem" disadvantaged adolescents in twice-weekly counseling sessions. The children were all about fourteen to sixteen years old, mixed with regard to sex, race and disciplinary problems, etc. Some were quiet and retiring; many were impulsive, acting-out and overtly hostile. Six sessions had passed when the following incident occurred: Milton P. had not spoken very much during this particular session. The group was focused on whether it was to their self-interest to do any of their school homework or to put out effort to get better marks. The discussion was, from my clinical point of view, quite promising, particularly in view of the slowly but steadily improving nature of the previous sessions. At this point in this particular session we were half-way through the 40-minute period. The group was rather noisy, fairly irrelevant to the topic, but, with my efforts, able, on the whole, to stay with the topic and develop it. Several group members were at the side of the classroom looking out the window, making small noises and otherwise evading the topic. Suddenly Milton rose in the middle of the group and silently began to blow up a huge balloon. The all-too-obvious question came to me: What should I as group leader, in the Present Moment, do? And what do *you* think an effective group leader, in the Present Moment, should do?

Some Prevailing Myth Areas*

Five Present Moment group situations have been presented which suggest the nature of the experience within which the group leader is

---

*As this chapter was nearing completion, the editors persuaded me that its readers might give its contents less attention because of a lack of identification of their own work and professional goals with my own work and goals. They suggested that my frequent use of the term "psychotherapy" and references to my "patients" may lead the reader astray in the time-worn confusion between "counseling" and "psychotherapy." To help avoid such difficulty, and to increase the potential relevance of my own considerations for those of the reader, may I say that I consider *all* forms of psychological helping activity—from psychoanalysis to involved—a bombardment of external stimuli as well as the group leader's own internal experiences and the interaction between these experiences and the external stimuli. In the consideration of myth areas which follows in this chapter these situations will be drawn upon in a variety of ways. Since a number of aspects in an orienting frame of reference have been presented and examples of five different kinds of group situations have been provided, it is now time to move to the principal focus of this chapter, namely, the identification and productive analysis of some of the major myths about group work. It should be understood that there are perhaps more than a hundred other important group areas—or what I also call "myth area issues"—which could be dealt with as mythical. Certainly less than ten percent of all the possible categories are dealt with here, and not more than several issues under each group work myth area. What is most relevant for the reader's consideration is the *meaning* of any particular myth area issue

psychiatry to school counseling—as "psychological counseling." I am taking the liberty of quoting from my previous chapter in this book:

"Psychological counseling is an activity in which a person who is trained and experienced in the psychological theory and practice of understanding and changing human behavior seeks to influence, mainly but not exclusively by the technique of talking, the perceptions, thinking, feelings, emotions and actions of one or more counselees [*hence the relevance of group work*], with the intention of producing short- and/or long-range changes in the counselee and/or in his reality situation which are more self-benefiting and self-actualizing and less self-defeating and self-inhibiting, with regard to what the counselee and/or counselor define as the counselee's self-interest as it relates to his personality and/or his reality problems."

For all persons who lead a group the following further quotation is relevant:

"Even though many counselors do not [believe that they] operate primarily within a psychological framework . . . it is impossible to divorce the subject matter of an interview (e.g., which course of study to choose or how and whether to lose weight) from the psychology of the counselee and the psychological skills helpful in getting the material thoroughly considered by him."

"Psychological counseling" then, is an umbrella term which applies to many forms of "counseling," "psychotherapy" and related activities where a psychological emphasis is involved or of concern to the professional worker.

Finally, a quotation from C.H. Patterson (1966), a leading critical authority in the field, is relevant: "There are no essential differences between counseling and psychotherapy in the nature of the relationship, in the process, in the methods or techniques, in goals or outcomes (broadly conceived), or even in the kinds of clients involved."

as it applies to the Present Moment experiencing of the group leader.

Myth Area No. 1: The role of theory: having a theory is not important.

This is one of the most absurd statements in all psychological helping work, yet it is an orientation very frequently encountered. It is absurd because, in the first place, every human being *already* has a theory. That is, every human being has a set of ideas which guide him in his interactions with the world as he goes about in the service of his own values. The great difficulty with the theories held by most people is that they are rarely fully conscious, and, to the extent that the individual is unaware of them, he is more likely than not self-defeating, since he operates blindly on the basis of vague intuitions and momentary impulses.

Pursuing this thinking within the role of a professional psychological worker, one can see readily that the worker, similarly, *already* has an operating theory as he interacts with his group members. The real questions to be answered, of course, are (1) *what kind* of theory for helping group members does the worker hold and (2) to what extent is it the best theory he might have for understanding reality and influencing change in his group members?

Having a coherent theory—ideally one that is fully in consciousness—is *crucial* in group work. It is difficult to understand how a group leader might expect to act helpfully if within his professional role he did not have, at some level of awareness, such a cognized theory, made explicit to himself. From these assertions it may be seen that even group leaders who claim to operate intuitively do in fact have a theory. The difficulty—the *huge* difficulty—is that this theory is only or mainly intuitive, and therefore, as in everyday living, it is accordingly less beneficial and more self-defeating with regard to the group leader's professional goals.

My focus on the importance of theory in this chapter may seem to contradict its entire title and specifically the focus on the vitally important *artistic* nature of Present Moment experiencing on the part of the group leader, but it does not. Artistry cannot be divorced from intelligence or from theory. In any artistic undertaking intelligence, within a frame of reference based upon reasoning, is a required though not a sufficient condition for carrying out one's goals satisfactorily. It is the thrust of this chapter to communicate not only the meaningfulness of an artistic experience in the Present Moment group leadership undertaking but to explain that it is one which, necessarily but also desirably, must include the group leader's maximally activated use of his intelligence. Such intelligence, of course, finds its finest support in being expressed within the matrix of a scientific attitude, a scientific method, scientific findings and the artistic integration of these and other aspects, as connected to the group leader's Present Moment action skills within his own best theory to date for the work he is here-and-now undertaking.

Several crucial aspects of a cognizable theory may here be noted. The first is almost too obvious, but it is often overlooked: the theory should include Future Moment connections; that is, connections between Present Moment events and the group leader's conceptualized Future Moment goals.

A second aspect important in a theory is the connection between elements of the theory and empirical referents. Specifically, the group leader ought to—ideally in consciousness, cognizably—connect the conceptual elements of his theory with memories of events within his own experience, which apply to these elements, together with his appraisal of external events in the Present Moment and potential Future Moment situations.

It should be clear that I acted as I did in the five situations given as examples—or in fact chose not to act at all—as a function of the theory inhering within my experience in the Present Moment. My own theory was not a personal theory but one framed in professional terms, for the appropriateness of the situation in which I was to play a professional role. What I did with Doris was to intervene physically between her and Barbara at the Moment just short of a likely physical assault on Barbara. I moved because my professionally developed and cognized theory in the Present Moment was explicit in my thinking that Doris was building up to a pitch of emotionality which she would not be able to control—she very likely could attack Barbara physically; not only could she hurt Barbara, but also she could set back everyone's progress a great deal. I was confident in Present Moments before the Present Moment of action that I could allow the Present Moment to develop (and desirably, according to my theory of what is useful for the group and the individuals involved, it should develop so) to the point at which

I acted—and I knew that the antidote for Doris' violent feelings would be: love. That is, according to my own technical theory I believe that love and internal security are extraordinarily related and Doris' impulses toward her roommate were based not only on the particular provocative incident, but upon her own fear of inadequacy, worthlessness and self-rejection, which precipitated the explosion in the group. (That is, Doris' covert acceptance of herself depended upon others' acceptance of her and resulted in her overt violent reactions and covert emotional disturbance.) Knowing then that these fears lay underneath Doris' increasingly violent reaction, I knew from theory that the antidote for fear is love, and I moved in to intervene physically, then soothingly, reassuringly and lovingly with words and physical love and security. I held Doris in my arms, told her that the group and I actually loved her, and counseled that she might do better to "wait a while," to sit down and, after the group session, in private consultation, to take the issue up with me and her roommate.

When Judith turned on me in an angry attack, I did nothing, based upon the theory that it would be useful for her to vent her feelings upon me as a group leader, someone she felt very emotionally attached to, yet in conflict with, as is understandable with counselees and patients in relationships with their therapists. I believed that it would be useful for the group and for her that I *not* respond at that time.

I did indeed have a plan and one of Judith's major problems was her need to manipulate the group, based on her fear of not being "in control," adequate, not being what she "should be." Knowing that the group would have many Future Moments, as would Judith, I chose to frustrate her impulse and action for the greater long-range benefit. While I operated from a conscious theory, based on past experience, and knowledge of Judith and the Present Moment situation, I nonetheless made a judgment which was both artistic in its execution and probabilistic in its orientation toward Future Moments.

In both the first and second situations just noted, I employed my theory-based technical principle to the effect that, "Everything may be worked out satisfactorily, even in a situation which is seemingly extremely dangerous, if I play a conservative role, do not panic, and play out my options over the long run." Another way of putting this principle is that, "Anything that is done wrongly may be undone." These principles are cardinal aspects of my theory and I employ them in any Present Moment group situation for maximum effect in influencing reality existents in long-range Future Moments.

Although there were really a great many principles interacting dynamically within my consciousness in the Present Moment of the previous situations, several other principles of interest, which I was then thinking, were: (1) I wanted the group to work the problem out and felt that it would be an important learning experience for them to do so—for the group's purposes as well as for the major participants—until the very limit of usefulness, when I would have to take overt control; (2) I "knew" that things would be all right in the group and that things could be worked out well, based upon past experience, knowledge of Judith and the present situation, the previously noted principle, and the notion that when anything is going wrong, I, myself, would move in to cover the situation as closely as necessary, in time, energy and involvement; (3) then knowing that the group situation would work out to be reasonably well resolved, I wanted that satisfactory solution to be learned by the group members as an example of a principle which could be generalized to external world situations in their everyday lives—that *other* situations could work out satisfactorily, could be handled without one's panicking, feeling tense or anxious, or acting self-defeatingly. All of these aspects, and more, relate to a cognized theory which I held in those Present Moments.

Briefly, in the other situations: I could not have moved to suggest that Sally talk without a technical theoretical frame of reference, knowing what happens to people psychologically at particular Moments in time. This seemed a particularly crucial Present Moment for Sally, within which we might shift her to a more constructive orientation or let the Moment go by to her possible detriment. Probabilistically the likelihood was in favor of using the Moment for her future benefit, though this was not certain. As a matter of fact, it proved that I was correct and the group and I did in fact use the Moment to help Sally more constructively.

With regard to Situation No. 4, I allowed the group members to interact with Noel so that—all flowing from theory—he might get *both* a specific "gimmick" answer, which indeed is useful at times (such as a special way of talking to oneself to quell anxiety before an examination or the mechanics of examination-taking) and a greater awareness of the factors lying *beneath* his surface request for an external way of working with his problem. His group was particularly oriented toward "depth" psychology and psychodynamics, and—based on theoretical reasons, believing that he could profit from both aspects—I allowed the group to attack his position so that what evolved was the best over-all product for him. Too, what I predicted from theory for the group also happened: the other group members learned that "gimmicks" some-times are very useful, and that all is not "depth" psychology.

As for Situation No. 5, I allowed Milton to blow up his balloon, waiting to see the reaction of the other group members. Based upon some of the foregoing principles, I then developed the situation as one which would not be productive for the *other* group members, and group pressure was brought to bear upon Milton to help him see that his behavior was self-defeating. This point of view was a theoretical one, as was my understanding that Milton was feeling a pull for attention, which in turn was based on fear or anxiety and feelings of inadequacy, and that these personality characteristics should not be attacked directly—so I supported Milton while encouraging the other group members to draw him out to clarify the situation so that he might save his self-esteem yet give up his group-deviant and self-defeating behavior.

The consideration of the role of theory in group leadership should not be left without noting, at least, what is a somewhat different and important deficit mode of functioning in this area of group leadership: *rigid adherence to theory*, whether conscious or unconscious, may be as outstandingly self-defeating in group leadership as may be the relative or total absence of theory. Rigid adherence to one's theory is a rather pervasive phenomenon found among psychological helping profes-sionals who are in the early years of their careers and also among workers who have been in the field for a great many years. Yet there is some evidence, of a formal as well as an informal sort, that years of experience do tend to increase the practitioner's openness and flexibility toward those whom he seeks to help.

Because of limitations of space and the lack of its centrality to the major meaning of the present Myth Area, a more than brief identification of this aspect is not appropriate here. However, the reader may note in this deficit mode of the group leader's functioning what has been and will continue to be the implication of a major concern of this chapter: the group leader's imperfect perception of, and the resulting self-defeating action with regard to, the nature of Reality.

The artistic and effective manipulation of Reality can take place only insofar as the group leader has a clear perception of Reality. The imposition upon the actual Reality of a construct that is at variance with it is a distortion which results in less effective behavior. The group leader should seek to hold as hypotheses rather than as conclusions, imposed for personal or other rigidity-based reasons, his clinical speculations about the nature of his group members' Reality. Holding clear hypotheses, yet being free to perceive differently, not being bound by those hypotheses, and thereby to act differently within the Present Moment, is the essence of truly artistic and probabilistic yet professional group leadership.

> *Myth Area No. 2: The group leader's role: the group leader should not be (too) active. He should reveal his personal feelings to make the experience "real."*

A useful analogue to the role of the group leader is that of leader of an orchestra. I see the group leader as, and experience myself as, an orchestra leader who at the same precise Present Moment has the responsibility for a great number of external Others, so as to help them contribute maximally to the over-all experience of the group, yet at the same time also to contribute maximally to their own and every other member's own possibilities for excellence—within the member's, group's and leader's own goals for excellence. At the same time, the group leader must consider—within this Present Moment—the inter-action of himself with the group members and their goals. To complicate the matter further—again, within the same Present Moment—it has been my personal experience that it is not only necessary but desirable, and certainly possible, for the group leader, to view and experience the Future Moment possibilities for individual group members, and the group as a whole, simultaneously in terms of an extraordinary number of different levels of analysis of the Present Moment problem and in terms of an extraordinary number of directions in which any particular action may be influenced.

As one looks out from the perspective of one's personal experiencing of the Present Moment, as group leader, one may see the group in terms of a variety of depth psychological levels of fact and possibility and, at the same time, interacting dynamically as a unit within this experience, one may view the Future Moment possibilities prospectively in a hugely logarithmically expanding dynamic lattice of possibilities. For example, looking upon Doris' interaction with her roommate and the group in the Present Moment, I was cognitively (and to a lesser extent intuitively) aware of a great many things happening at the same time—external, internal, within individuals, at a variety of levels within the same individual, with interaction aspects between levels and between individuals, etc., and at the same time I was aware of a huge variety of possibilities which might probabilistically, at different levels of probability, have occurred in Future Moments ranging from a few seconds to years ahead. In the other four situations I felt the same way, with the same depth-time personal-professional frame of reference, as I feel in other interactions with patients in the Present Moment.

It goes without saying that the group leader desirably should be *able* to be as active as possible, as his professional goals and the situation dictate, both technically and emotionally. It has been my experience, after supervising hundreds of counselors and psychotherapists and teaching a number of courses on group work, that most group leaders take a professed public position of "non-directiveness" with relation to the possibilities for active intervention, due to some notion, of which they themselves often are unaware, that to hold back and not take responsibility for action in this situation is emotionally "safe." For example, the group leader's responses of clarifying and reflecting feeling are quite obviously "safe" techniques, since they deal only with what the group has presented and take no new initiatives which would place personal responsibility on the leader; hence they would be unlikely to make him anxious.

From this point of view, giving responsibility to the group is emotionally "safe" and in my experience is far more often the basis of practice and even institutionalized theory—a myth area which might well have been included in this chapter relates to the oft-heard professional dictum "Let the *group* do it!"—rather than a technique pursued knowledgeably and advisedly within a particular group session. Related to all of this, of course, is the notion that many developing group leaders—in fact, to my knowledge many professional group leaders who work with groups a great deal—actually are quite fearful of participating actively in their own groups, whether they admit to this or not.

On the other hand, though much less frequent a happening, it is of course a fact that many group leaders are *too* active and *too* interventionist, both for poorly thought-through technical and theoretical reasons, in the minority of cases, and more importantly for personality reasons peculiar to the group leader. Many group leaders rush in rather than holding back and dealing more conservatively and artistically, when the situation might dictate the latter approach as being more appropriate. The basic problem, whatever the elaborated psychodynamics may be, is of course the anxiety the group leader would feel at *not* intervening, *not* dealing with the situation, *not* pursuing something or, on the other hand, allowing something to continue which might be personally threatening to his concept of himself as a group leader who is adequate or likable. It is not the overt behavior of acting or not acting which may indicate whether the group leader is acting out of his personality needs rather than an objective professional judgment of what is good for the Present Moment group situation; it is the underlying feeling and psychodynamics of the leader—underlying anxiety may motivate either defensive acting or not acting, either kind of overt behavior being disguised as within the leader's professional role.

To deal with that threatening thing "out there" actually reflects an insecurity within the group leader where he himself feels personally vulnerable, attackable or damageable. This is a function of his own personal psychodynamics. The fact that nearly all Americans, more in point, probably all human beings, tend to feel such threat means only that the threat is normative (usual with most human animals) rather than something the group leader must settle for—rather than something which cannot be eradicated. It is my decided opinion that the group leader should strive for and attempt to attain—most desirably in personal psychotherapy—feelings of security within himself so that he may operate entirely securely within any and all potential group situations to help his group members.

It might seem obvious but it is nonetheless a fact that in case situations such as those of Doris and Judith (the first where violence might erupt in the group situation and the second where I was personally attacked—psychologically), the group leader, as would be true of most people, would normally feel personally threatened. I have worked on myself for many years to the point where I, as a function of my own understandings and theory of anxiety and danger (not elaborated within this chapter), have developed to a point where, almost without exception, I do not feel *personally* threatened *no matter what* kind of external violence occurs or *what kind* of internal concerns are cued off within me by the external existents occurring dynamically within the Present Moment (e.g., Judith rejecting me; my feeling that I might make a mistake with Doris; Sally rejecting me for putting her on the spot; Milton P. "making a fool out of me," or in a situation occurring at the time of this writing, a psychotic person whose identity I do not know persistently making threats to "kill" me).

People tend to take two major overt styles of adapting to their internal insecurities: to withdraw behaviorally, in one form or another, or to rush in to attempt to overwhelm the situation, thereby forestalling (as fantasied) the anxiety or threat to themselves. They tend to develop adaptive personality styles which prevent anxiety and tension from appearing, because such styles are useful for preventing the situation from developing into an experience which might *appear* potentially to be threatening to their internal security. This latter form of overt adaptation to internal anxieties may be more subtle within our developing psychological encounter and sensitivity group culture, but it is nonetheless true that many group leaders find natural outlets for their personality neuroses—again, normative or usual within American society—within the popular ethos and even the popularized theoretical underpinnings of the group work they undertake. Defensive or anxiety-based intervention on the part of a group leader should not be confused with constructive, wise, member-helping intervention which includes the leader's internal sense of security and freedom *not* to intervene or, on the other hand, not to avoid intervening when it is otherwise appropriate to do so.

Another aspect of Myth Area No. 2 is the notion that the group leader "should reveal his personal feelings to make the experience 'real.'" Perhaps the notion of the importance of the therapist or counselor presenting himself as being "real" or "authentic" or "himself"—revealing his "real" or more basic or underlying feelings about the counselee or patient—began with Carl Rogers' highly stressed emphasis on having a "genuine" or "congruent" therapeutic relationship. It goes without saying that many psychoanalysts, many years before the advent of Carl Rogers, believed it important to introduce their own particular feelings about themselves and the patient—technically called "countertransference"—into the analytic session as a constructive part of the patient's ongoing therapy. More recently, and with some significant usefulness, I think, William Glasser (Glasser, 1965) has presented the importance of the therapist involving himself with personal examples from his own life, which I have identified elsewhere as using oneself as a role model (Geis, 1969).

More importantly, I think, the group leader may reveal *himself as a person* to the counselee or group member. For example, I might have chosen to reflect my genuine—that is, underlying, covert and authentic—negative feelings to Judith when she turned upon me angrily but it did not seem useful for helping *her and the group* at that particular time. I was nonetheless fearless about doing so. At the same time, I might have felt fearful of revealing "love feelings" for Doris, holding her in my arms soothingly when she was about to attack Barbara, but I did not feel these feelings. Not feeling fear allowed me to reveal what was authentic. (However, had I felt fear—which I still do occasionally, in fleeting experiences, from time to time, it *may* have been appropriate for me to have done so.) The most important point with regard to this area of concern, though, is not the usefulness of such a technique *per se*, but the *appropriateness* of using such a technique at any particular time, in any particular situation. In my observation, group leaders with whom I have been in contact seem to prize the fact of revealing that they, themselves, are "real" in any particular instance as a virtue in itself, almost entirely without regard to what ought to be their major goal, namely using themselves in that Present Moment to influence group members for the members' own self-benefit. In short, displaying oneself as "real" with regard to a group member desirably ought to be used as a technique to achieve an Outcome Experience for the group member(s) within the professional role of the group leader rather than as an Intrinsic Experience for the benefit of the group leader himself.

Myth Area No. 3. Goals should develop from the group process itself. (Related to Myth Area No. 4.)

In the real world—which is the only one we have and which has only one identity in the Present Moment, whether or not we are individually aware of it—human beings continue to confuse what would be "nice" with what *in fact* is the case. It would be nice, preferable, highly desirable if every group process really did have within it the ability, intelligence, efficiency, drive—in short, all the requisite constituents—with which to establish group and individual member goals which would be most group- and self-benefiting. Alas, this is not the case.

One need think only a minute to realize that mankind has improved itself beyond its cave-level existence primarily and almost exclusively because of its intelligence—namely, its ability to figure out what would be good for it and, as a consequence, what therefore it ought to do in particular situations. Moreover, what distinguishes human beings from lower animals is precisely that aspect of intelligence which allows the human animal to imagine potential Future Moment events and to plan, from the perspective of the Present Moment (and including, of course, remembered Past Moments), so that it may maximize its adaptation to this ongoing life process. Furthermore, the use of imagination applied artistically in the human animal's prospective and retrospective mental machinations maximizes the organism's potential living benefits for itself over the potential maximum of its life span. Most specifically, the *effortful* and *intentional* development of long-range goals is self-benefiting to the human animal.

It follows then, that to leave rather exclusively to the psychotherapy or counseling group and to some kind of mystical "group process" which will function as an end in itself the responsibility to structure itself and "heal" itself or otherwise set forth and attain *long-range* adaptive and actualizing goals would be foolish in the extreme.

Underlying the basic notion that goals "should" develop from the nature of the group process itself—even in the best of circumstances—is an implied assertion about the nature of Reality. Namely, that this in fact not only is possible but, more basically, that it is likely or almost certainly probable. It is my own assertion, as a highly experienced professional group leader and one who believes he is quite knowledgeable about the nature of Reality, that such is not the case, and if the group were to be left to its own vagaries, there is very little likelihood that at best more than a little productive group work would be accomplished in a long period of time. Moreover, there is a *high* probability that self-defeating and even self-destructive things would happen in the group, to the group as a whole and to individual members.

(As an experiment in a group course I taught at New York University in 1965, I conducted a quite leaderless, "client-centered" type of group, allowing the group to determine for itself, with only a supportive role played by myself, which goals it would set for itself in individual sessions and during the semester. After seven to eight weeks of two-hour group sessions, fraught with high frustration and no accomplishment of any constructive kind, I was forced to admit that this type of group experience was a failure, and I moved in with structure.)

In short, left to its own devices, the same as would be true with an individual human being in the world, and barely provided with, at best, a kind of security within which to experience itself, a group may, in my judgment, have some small chance of achieving some good things; it may have the greatest possible chance of achieving nothing constructive, and it may have some small chance of achieving negative outcomes. Moreover, virtually the *only* chance the group would have to achieve *highly actualized goals* would be to have the appropriate and wise influence of group and/or other leaders for the many Future Moments ahead in time.

In the situation with Judith, I was choosing to allow her and the group to develop their goals. But this was because *my own* goals were for them to have some personal experience with autonomy—so that they could learn this more readily over a long-range basis—and to work out some of their own problems in the Present Moment situation, rather than to continue to find dependency in the "safety" of my own leadership. Basically, my long-range perspective within the atomistic view of the Present Moment dictated my intending to allow the group ambiguity even if it were to be experienced over a succeeding series of sessions, over months if need be. Sessions in which I am seemingly giving up the leadership role, however, only indicate that I may be giving up part of my overt, not covert, leadership, and these experiences are quite unlike the situation at New York University just described. At such times I usually intersperse the hour-and-a-half session with many influential statements and actions—"reflecting feelings," being provocative, evocative, even shocking—even though at some periods and even in an over-all sense I may seem to be mainly, though not exclusively, "non-directive." One principal aspect of my role as a professional is to *influence direction,* which sometimes may seem to be obvious and overt, at other times non-existent, although my covert choice at these times is quite decidedly not to give overt direction. In my own professional world I discard as irrelevant what "should" be and instead concentrate on the realities of the Present Moment and the probabilities of the Future Moments.

It is my belief that in nearly all instances a group should not start its session with a highly fixed, rigid, particular structure, just as any individual psychological helping session should not begin with such a structure. The main reason for this is that if the leader of a psychological helping group completely structures the beginning of the session with a response which allows only a limited range of therapeutic responses on the part of the members—sometimes fixedly structured responses are subtle, such as "the group was rather angry at the end of the last session"—this may rigidly influence direction and close off the members' feeling that they have an option to respond in ways *other* than those indicated as therapeutic by the leader. On the other hand, to have no structure at all could lead to chaos, inefficiency, possibly even great and insurmountable difficulties or dangers for the group and its individual members, or an interminable amount of sessions required for even the most minimal change (in my view, decidedly true of Rogers' "non-directive" approach and also most psychoanalytic methods). Therefore, what I have found to be most desirable, from my experience, is some kind of *semi*-structure. The particular kind of semi-structure depends upon the presuppositions of the group leader and his professional goals for the group in the potential Future Moments of the ensuing session.

With my groups the situation is somewhat different, although my basic goals are the same. With the large, fifteen-person groups I begin by asking for two-to-three minute psychological homework or status reports, usually receiving four or five of these. Then I ask, "Who wants to talk about a problem tonight?" If there is no outstanding reason not to do otherwise—such as someone, like Sally, in an emergency situation—I will then name the three, four or five people who, by raising their hands or speaking up, indicate that they wish to get help from the group. After the more formal group session with me, most of the group members will adjourn for another hour or two at a nearby coffee shop to continue therapeutic discussions—as they are specifically encouraged to do—and they may also call or otherwise contact each other during the week for help on their problems. (Insofar as group members have non-formal group or individual interactions with each other, they are encouraged to emphasize the therapeutic aspects of their encounters and involvements. Where therapeutic emphases are not apparent members are encouraged to keep the therapist and group informed of interactions with each other so as to maximize potential benefits.)

My approach to the beginning of small group sessions is somewhat different from that used with the larger groups, more like my individual sessions, since my techniques and the effects I wish to create in the session—again, the leadership of the professional with *his* (my own) Present Moment and Future Moment experiences and goals—are more along the lines of ambiguity, member experiences with anxiety, member autonomy experience in asserting or not asserting themselves to "want to speak today" or other member responses which may engage the group, individual members or the leader in contacts which the leader may deal with artfully as he so decides. As with the individual sessions, generally I begin with a decided semi-structure, which throws the burden upon the group. If things do not begin or continue satisfactorily—in my professional judgment—in any Present Moment I alter the direction and content of the session, and I—and this is crucial for this myth area—overtly or covertly influence the session goals as *I*, Jon Geis, therapist, psychologist, group leader, helper and person, wish them to go.

Normally I begin most of my individual sessions either with a few seconds of silence, to see whether the patient or counselee has something important he wishes to raise (if he does this and it is not in my professional judgment important enough for us to continue, I will alter the direction and content of the exchange). If he does not raise anything, or if he says or does something irrelevant in my opinion to his therapy or counseling, I will offer him some kind of semi-structured stimulus condition, such as, "What should we be talking about this week that's important to you?"—or—"What did you do to change yourself this week?" (also having the advantage of implying and reinforcing the importance of and need for *his* efforts actively to do things to change himself)—or—I might growl a bit, pull at my trousers, swing around in my chair, and look expectantly as if the burden is upon *him* to say or do something important—or—I might speak or act with some sarcasm, depending upon the sophistication of the person with me. All of the foregoing are examples of attempts to structure the session in a way which is relevant for the psychological and reality development of the individual with whom I am involved, yet taking care not to bias his response and to assure its being therapeutically relevant. (For example, many patients, particularly those who have worked with other psychotherapists, expect to be able to talk about anything at all, no matter how therapeutically irrelevant—flowers, Yankee Stadium, some trivial incident in the week, their impression of my office, or dramatic but irrelevant incidents from their history. Rapport and effectiveness are to be found sooner and more strongly in going quickly to the heart of therapeutic, psychological and reality problems, rather than allowing the individual—again, on balance, depending upon professional judgment, the individual's defense system, readiness and other factors—to evade what is important for him to deal with.)

Myth Area No. 4: Group process should not be structured, gimmicked, or theme-centered. (Related to Myth Area No. 3.)

It almost seems unnecessary to comment upon this myth area in view of the discussion under Myth Area No. 3, yet this particular fallacy seems to carry an autonomy of its own among the many school counselors, psychotherapists, psychoanalysts and psychiatrists with whom I have personally spoken, have heard about, or whose works I have read. At issue here—although it may seem trivial and unimportant to the reader—is the fundamental understanding of *causality*. Specifically, as I have mentioned earlier and will mention later in this chapter, with regard to particular existents which lead influentially to particular effects or outcomes, I am concerned that the reader make the connections between Present Moment experiences of which he is aware and later Future Moment outcomes or effects. If we would fundamentally examine the nature of Reality we would find that the fundamental issue of our professional therapeutic, helping concern is which stimulus conditions might probabilistically lead to which group member outcomes or effects.

From this point of view we must ask whether the introduction of what heretofore has seemed an "artificial" aspect of the group experience should not in fact be introduced. If the goal, after all, is to achieve certain specified outcomes, then is it appropriate—even, moreover, is it ethical—that we, as professional group leaders, unthinkingly do not include seemingly "artificial" or "gimmicky" adjuncts to stimulate the group experience and process toward Future Moment goals with which we are, in the first place, mainly concerned?

In the behavior of every organism, of every human being, is a potential goal orientation or motivational state—this orientation or state being already present, as a fact in itself—and the problem, then, for professional group leaders is to influence the Present Moment goal orientation of the individual group members, whatever these orientations may be, in such a way as to make their individual development maximally positive in view of the leader's understanding of desired goals with relation to group process. That is, since goals, at least non-specific ones, are *already* involved in all behavior, the task for the group leader is to redirect the goal orientation of the group members in the Present Moment toward long-range goals—Outcome Experiences rather than Intrinsic Experiences—which are therapeutic and actualizing, in view of their present circumstances and the leader's theory of what is "good" for people-in-the-world (Geis, 1969).

In the five example situations presented in this chapter, I have made the choice in some cases to take over overtly and structure the session so as to be more likely to achieve certain possible Future Moment goals for the group and individual members. In the case of Sally, it worked. The erupting violence of the Doris and Barbara incident, in combination with the later individual counseling session, was defused because of my structured intervention. Noel was helped to understand certain "gimmick" but altogether practical suggestions which would help him to tackle the study procedures necessary to pass the final examinations, as well as the more subtle material relevant to his situation, mainly from a long-range, Future Moment point of view, which would help him understand on a "depth-psychological" basis the *meaning* of his block and of his evasive efforts in tackling the study material.

The field, as I have observed it in personal experience and in writings, tends to be oriented toward one of two extremes: either with (1) a highly structured "group guidance" approach with specific, mainly practical and immediate reality content goals or (2) a highly unstructured and loose "experimental" situation within which the group members will somehow "find" themselves, with at best the semblance of psychological security of a duly stipulated group "leader" who will save them from harm should they behave or feel in unwarranted ways. (This latter fantasy tends to be dislodged the first time the group "leader" does something to indicate his own insecurity or inexpertise.) As I have suggested earlier, the artistic, highly delicate, probabilistic and professional task is to introduce into the group experience in the Present Moment at the precise time that exact kind of structure, or lack of structure, which will induce and influence certain likely Future Moment outcomes for the group members as a whole and individually.

To begin a group session with a fixed structure is, again, not necessarily an inappropriate act. To belabor the obvious: it depends upon what particular goals the group leader seeks for his particular group members, under what particular conditions ... etc. There are many different kinds of groups—including some kinds of psychological helping groups which may be labeled "counseling" or "therapeutic," and some particular sessions within these kinds of groups—where a fixed structure is highly desirable and most likely to lead to certain Future Moment Outcomes.

Part of the myth area relating to the prohibition against structuring the group process more specifically relates to the frequently heard dictum that "the group leader should not 'lecture.' " (A second frequent meaning of "lecturing," not discussed here, relates to the psychological worker's moralizing—asserting directly or indirectly that the counselee or patient "should" or "should not" do something or be a certain way—or implying that the group member's personal worth and adequacy are contingent upon his behavior or other characteristics related to him.) This is akin, almost, to saying that the group leader should not provide information. As a psychotherapist and as a psychological counselor, I consider myself in the main a teacher who is highly skilled psychologically, and I regard my patients actually as students. There are many times in group and individual sessions when I will give short "lectures" informing the patients about certain aspects of psychodynamics, reality, philosophy or other topics relevant to their concerns at the time. At times these lectures may go on as long as ten or fifteen minutes, often with the patients interacting with me. Beyond my own practice, however, all of us can think of many examples of lecturing to groups which lead to highly useful goal attainments of various kinds—acquisition of information, reality clarification, even personality change. Such a "mythic" consideration as that regarding "lecturing" again focuses the issue squarely upon the group leader's goals for his particular group members and the particular conditions of their group process.

Normal academic education in the United States society, whether elementary, high school, college level or industrial, for all its faults, must have some virtues: the introduction of certain kinds of structures inevitably has had some telling impact upon the increments of learning acquired by the students involved in course material. That is, some structures and some "gimmicks" already used within the vast educational enterprise in American society have been highly profitable, whatever may be the deficit areas of this enterprise.

Gimmicks may include almost anything which is not thought by group workers to fall within the "natural" experience of the group process but on the other hand is introduced as something "artificial." Slide films, role playing techniques, physical touching and massage of group members, the use of music, blackboard lecturing and note-taking materials provided (which I use in my Minithon and Marathon group sessions), adjunctive textbook materials, and the like—all of these are what might be called "gimmicks." Nonetheless such adjuncts to interpersonal experiencing clearly may be seen as useful *under the appropriate conditions.* Again, such "appropriateness" depends upon the particular group leader's particular goals for his particular group members . . . etc. in Future Moments.

One interesting aspect of "gimmickry" is that some group leaders, and those who write about groups, seem to rely all too heavily upon the use of such gimmicks as *major* aspects of influencing group and individual change, rather than as adjuncts. It clearly seems to me that the theory and skills of the group leader must necessarily be primary in achieving group goals, without which all adjunct materials and experiences must play secondary roles. It is true, however, that one may program a group of individuals through certain prearranged experiences, in line with the hardware techniques used in programmed learning, but even here the underlying theory and goals must be clear, whether or not the group leader takes a major role in influencing the group. My own feeling is that many university-based writers and practitioners in the field of counseling resort to gimmickry and hardware as major aspects of their group work. They do this either out of ignorance about the deeper psychological aspects of theory and practice in group work or because they are secretly afraid of putting themselves actively on the line with group members without using such adjuncts or having them available, so that they may be "sure that something is happening." To feel, at least, that "something is happening"—better yet, that "something" is "good"—provides the concreteness and certainty which forestalls all manner of underlying anxieties in the insecure group leader. Other writers on group processes may have little actual knowledge of group or individual dynamics and may overemphasize gimmicks and hardware simply because this is the area in which, for whatever personality or professional reasons, they have developed a special focus.

The notion that the "group process should not be theme-centered" is the unthought-through belief that to purposefully structure a group session with a particular theme—such as the meaning of anxiety, depression, self-discipline, self-awareness, the mechanics of doing effective school work, sex-love problems, techniques for changing one's personality or orientation to finding a job—is somehow unhelpful or destructive with regard to the "real" purposes of the group. Curiously, many professionals seem to believe—with regard to groups which, they admit, desirably should deal with themes such as these—that it is quite all right for such themes, for example, to emerge spontaneously in the group session, as a function of the group's own in-session concerns. When these themes are introduced either at the beginning of or during the session by the group leader, however, it is somehow believed to be antagonistic to group goals.

For years I, myself, have very frequently been confronting my individual and group patients (persistent confrontation is one of my most frequently used techniques) at times vigorously structuring themes I believed to be most relevant for their progress, and in retrospect I see this still to be a highly useful aspect of the professional helping role, when artistically woven into the session. Other examples with which the reader might be familiar are those of the drug-oriented therapy groups, popular "personality change" courses such as those of Dale Carnegie, and the like.

Again, all of this has to do with the nature of the goals the group leader has in mind for his group, which, of course, are considered in conjunction with the ongoing goals of the group members themselves. I believe that if the group members do not structure their own goals early in the session, then, at this time, the group leader should structure the group's goals. Goal setting is an important part of individual and group psychological work.

I recall a demonstration interview some years ago which another professor and I undertook with a student in a graduate class in counseling. The other professor demonstrated his non-directive or client-centered technique on a young woman with guilt feelings, leading her to feel she had gotten nowhere in the fifteen minutes they had spent together. I then actively helped her understand the meaning of her feelings and what to do to change them within the first five or six minutes of my own interview, actively structuring goals and solutions alike in conjunction with the counselee's own problem presentation. My friend and colleague then told the class, still proud of his "non-directive" work, that "sometimes I have worked with clients as long as nine months before we have any idea of what goals we are seeking."

Myth Area No. 5. There should be no individual counseling or advice-giving in a group session.

The assertions involved in this myth area flow, as they do in the other areas, from lack of full awareness and technical understanding of the many dynamically interacting particulars of the Present Moment situation. More specifically, the assertion that there should be no individual counseling, advice-giving, or the like on the part of the group leader or others seems to be a variation of the idealized yet most often unrealistic notion that the group leader "should let the group work it out." As I have mentioned earlier, it would be all well and good if the group could, in fact, and would, in fact, most efficiently, "work it out": the indubitable question, then, as always, gets back to the issue of whether it is better to have "it" "worked out" in the best and most efficient way possible, all things considered, or whether the group leader should take his chances and let the group proceed, willy-nilly, itself to help the individual group member, if it will and can. Again, the notion that anything "should" be carried out is based on the underlying assumption that in fact it *can* in reality be carried out.

The major questions in particular Present Moment circumstances in group experiences must deal, in all respects, with the *nature of the goals* for individual group members as well as for the group process as a whole. (Although in my judgment the group process experience desirably should be focused primarily and even exclusively on the furthering of self-benefiting Future Moments for *individual* group members—considered one at a time or viewed collectively, yet simultaneously, as individuals—rather than for "experiences," no matter how beneficial, for the group as a whole.)

The group leader is ascribed the role of a professional helping person, because he is to a greater or lesser extent an expert in Reality, the psychology of persons, a responsible and trained helper, more or less, and also because he chooses or accepts the responsibilities of group leadership. At certain times, then, the question may arise as to whether it is better for the individual group member to go without receiving counseling or information which would be, in the Present Moment and in rather immediate Future Moments, to his self-benefit—sometimes even of an urgent or emergency nature—or whether it is better (1) to take a chance that in the given limited period of time available the group may help the individual sufficiently or (2) that the group leader himself take up the responsibility to counsel and advise the group member on an individual one-to-one basis so as to maximize the likelihood that the group member would profit.

As a rule of thumb in my own groups I assess the urgency nature of the situation and try always to make sure that the group member will receive some significant benefit from the ensuing Future Moments of group experience. In doing this, however, I first determine which if any group members may on an individual or collective basis probabilistically be of minimum to maximum help to the group member in question. If I think such may be the case, I let the group member(s) try to help the individual, interrupting when I think things are not proceeding usefully. ("Proceeding usefully" is a phrase used to stand for my judgment of the constructive dynamic combination of group and individual members' goals, particular events in Present Moment and Future Moment situations, theory and experience projections, my own feelings and analysis of the Present Moment interrelationships among all present, and other factors—in short, this too is a complex Present Moment gestalt experience combining analyzing and intuiting with action skills.) The functioning leader's role is to work on a one-to-one basis with the individual group member to *ensure* that he comes away from his Present Moment experiences with some significant contributions to his self-benefit, whether or not these contributions relate overtly to the major or minor problems presented or are more subtle increments in his personality development, covert in him and visible only to the leader because of his professional expertise.

As I work with my groups, the question in my mind is not really whether I can successfully help the individual group member—since I know that 99 percent of the time I can, if I work with him alone—but whether it is better to intervene to help him or her *myself* rather than to "let the group work it out," because, after all, the nature of a group's session is primarily designed to help *all* group members, not just a single individual presenting a particular problem of interest mainly or exclusively to himself. When possible, then, I let the group "do it." When this seems not possible or unlikely, then *I* "do it." In a Present Moment world where nothing is certain this approach necessarily is highly probabilistic.

What actually happened in Situation No. 3 is that I in fact took over the group leadership activity exclusively after Sally had been encouraged by three group members to talk for several minutes. Because there was such a wealth of material needing to be covered, both in terms of Sally's reality problems and the personality underpinnings interacting with them, I interacted with Sally on a one-to-one basis for about thirty-five minutes, laying out a full map of the problems—both visible and underlying, with the benefits and dangers available should certain courses of action be followed—a period throughout which Sally was encouraged to reflect on her reality and personality problems and to make Moment-to-Moment judgments and decisions within this individual counseling process.

At the end of the time period Sally was asked whether there was anything further she wished to say with regard to the problem, and group members similarly were invited to comment. Then she was asked to summarize the significant things she had learned from the interaction. After she had pulled six or seven points together, I added three or four more. Then I asked her whether she would make some decision about a course of action with regard to all of the material, getting her to agree to report on her psychological homework—undertaken to implement her decisions—at the group meeting the following week. During all of this interaction Sally had tape-recorded her session on a tape cassette (I provide the tape-recorder and ask my group members to bring individual tape cassettes in case they present a problem) and I asked her to "analyze it carefully a few times during the week and take notes on the important points," to which she agreed. This was an excellent example of individual counseling which, it turned out, forestalled some likely dangers and was undertaken primarily because of the emergency nature of the situation. Normally, however, I rarely let an individual's problem presentation to the group end without bringing in important material and tying it up in an over-all "map" or "package" so that the group member can see it usefully and act upon it. Also, as appropriate, from time to time I interject my own notions quite actively to the group member during the individual's interaction with the entire group.

If the leader keeps in mind his over-all group goals, as well as his specific goals within any Present Moment, he must conclude that individual work between himself as leader and one group member sometimes is most desirable, even for prolonged periods, as well as is individual counseling between that member and another member. Group *interaction* is not always so crucial nor is it always desirable. Many professionals in the field tend to elevate almost to sanctity the notion of *group* process as a thing in itself rather than seeing the group as one kind of instrument or vehicle—and only one kind—within which particular goals may be attained, most importantly for particular individual group members.

It might be recalled that even among Gestalt therapy enthusiasts it is highly regarded for the group leader to work on a one-to-one basis with individual group members. The lead in this regard was set by the founder of the Gestalt therapy orientation, Fritz Perls, and came to be known as "working with Fritz." The technique has generalized to many different types of encounter and sensitivity training groups, where the individual group member is seated alongside the group leader specifically for the purpose of working with him.

Myth Area No. 6. The group as experience: the group has a life of its own unique to it, is a microcosm of the world outside, has a basic "wisdom" of its own, and should be treated as an "experience" rather than also, mainly or exclusively as an information-getting tool.

There tends to be a truism in the tradition of psychotherapy and psychology, going back many, many years, and one with which I disagree, that an aggregate of people somehow constitutes a "new" experience, a "new" phenomenon, in essence a new existent. Although the issue is more complex than may be considered in detail in this limited space, it might be pointed out here what is a simple, observable set of facts: (1) Any collection of reality existents no matter how grouped or formed, and no matter how dynamically interacting with one another, is still a set of the same reality existents. (2) However, the perception of the particular observer *may itself be experienced* as indicating that there is some kind of "different" reality constituted by the group as a whole—"out there" or "in the air," as it were. What group authorities and workers frequently refer to as the group "climate" or "atmosphere" actually is a perceived set of traits and responses in *individual* group members which create the impression—in the mind of the observer—that there is some kind of existent separate and apart from the individual group members, each of whom exists as a distinct entity, while all together constitute nothing more than an aggregate of such existents. This "aggregate of separate existents" actually is a set of individual behavior tendencies, existing in discrete individuals, to react *vis-a-vis* one another in certain modal ways which enable the observer easily to perceive them as a gestalt phenomenon rather than as individually yet at the same time synchronistically reacting entities. In short, in my judgment there has been a confusion, from the time of the early crowd psychology to present-day authorities on groups, between the reality existent that is the experience of the group leader and the reality existents outside of the leader, namely the aggregate of group members. What I *do* believe to be true is that while there is no special "new" "thing-in-itself" or existent constituted by a group, *a collection of human beings has more potential power to influence a single human being than does almost any other fact of reality.* In actuality, it is the susceptibility of the individual group member to group influence, rather than, vice versa, the group's influence upon the individual, which is most fundamental to understand. Nonetheless, the group—as an aggregate of persons perceived in a gestalt experience by the individual—is virtually unparalleled in powerful influence.

In some of the situations I have cited as examples, it would have done me no good whatsoever to think of the group as some kind of "special" reality set apart from the factual realities and the interactions among individuals, which I knew to exist. Knowing, for example, how *individual* adolescents are likely to behave in a particular kind of group situation, I was then able to influence the aggregate of group members to help Milton not disrupt the developing constructive group process but in fact to turn his balloon-blowing act into a learning experience for him and for the other individual members.

Another highly interesting myth which is related to the consideration of the group as an experience is the notion that a group has "a basic 'wisdom' of its own." This view is held typically by many leading writers on counseling and psychotherapy. The reader will note that this attributes to the group as a collectivity some special capacity which is beyond that of the individual members themselves. Not only must I disagree that such a capacity exists and as such may be relied upon dependably to solve the group's individual and collective problems, when an aggregate of people convenes, but I must also assert—as I believe is true for individual human beings—that there is no innate, basic long-range healing power of the organism or group of organisms, collectively, in itself or in themselves. This is a confusion of the basic adaptive capacity of the organism in the Present Moment with a *long-range* Present Moment orientation. For human beings, adaptations and actualizations for Future Moments must be, necessarily—due to the unique symbolizing capacity of the human animal—of an extraordinarily complex sort. It is in this sense that it would seem impossible for the human organism, not to mention an aggregate of human organisms, to have a Present Moment innate, basic and long-range healing power which would serve it in self-benefiting rather than self-defeating ways.

It would be "nice" if individuals and groups had this reliable "wisdom," but it does not square with the facts of reality. In my own professional work, I use an enormous variety of stratagems, both overt and covert, to *influence* the people I am trying to help—whether I am working with an individual or on a group basis—to help themselves. I do *not* rely upon them to help themselves, but I maneuver the stimulus conditions of the individual or group experience so as to bring about the changes which, according to theory, experience and the individual's own goals and other relevant dimensions are most desired.

To elaborate on the notion of a "healing power" or "innate wisdom" within a group of persons or an individual: such a capacity would be true mainly in the Present Moment situations where the individual and/or group attempts to adapt on an equilibrium, homeostatic or compensatory basis. That is, it takes but a moment's thought to reflect upon the fact that an individual or group cannot "heal" itself beyond merely adapting to Moment-to-Moment stresses. Certainly it cannot in a Present Moment framework do things which will actualize itself for long-range purposes, not without using its intellect and/or instinctoid programmed capacities. In short, without fusing its intellect and/or instinctoid programmed capacities, all that a group or individual can do on a Present Moment basis is adapt to Present Moment stresses—nothing more. Healthy biological healing has an organic, future oriented thrust which moves beyond the Present Moment in its orientation. That is, the biological adaptive orientation is futuristic or prospective in that it is oriented toward more than the Present Moment orientation in its organic thrust. Psychologically, emotionally the human organism is more complex. In short, the psychological-emotional make-up of the human being is so fraught with potential negatives, due to the unique intellectual and consciousness component of the human organism, that—before the fact, in the Present Moment— it cannot be asserted with assurance that the human being is, more likely than not, bound to "heal" itself in self-benefiting ways.

Thus, the reader may ask, will not the group or individual tend to seek out—over many Present Moments (say, over an hour-and-a-half group session) aspects which it will use to develop itself for greater self-benefit? The answer, largely, even for such a relatively lengthy time, must depend upon the capacities, skills and intelligence of the group and/or its individual members. In other words, what kinds of people are going into the experience, what are their values, what are they seeking to do? In most cases, since wisdom is hard-won in life for any human being, and very few human beings possess it—hence the development of a profession of psychological helping persons, who include wisdom as one major aspect of their professional role—it is highly *unlikely*, particularly *before the fact*, that we could expect any group to develop for its own maximum, actualized self-benefit the best possible goals and means of achieving them. On a *probabilistic* basis, then, considering all things within any Present Moment, it is highly unlikely that the group and individuals can do for themselves what the professional helping person is by his very role definition there to do!

Getting back now to the reality problems all psychological helping professionals face, allow me to ask the reader the following questions: Does a mentally retarded child "have a capacity" to "heal itself?" Does a mentally retarded adult have this "capacity?" Does a psychotic group member "have the capacity?" Does a neurotic person "have the capacity?" Does an average American group member "have the capacity" to "heal himself?" Then, does a *group* of any of these individuals, however you would mix them, "have the capacity" to "heal itself?" What then does it mean: to "have the capacity?"

And even if we could argue that individuals and groups could learn to *function adequately* left to their own devices, what shall we say about the fullest possible—moreover the maximum—self-actualization for the individual human being? I have seen groups and individuals not only be "unwise" when left to their own devices, not only fail to learn to function adequately, not only miss out on the very hard-won long-range process of self-actualization, but do things which in fact not only are cruel but actually highly dangerous, in the fullest meaning of these two terms. In a situation like that of Sally, I have seen group members attempt to do—most often unwittingly, almost always with the sense of helping, but sometimes with destructive motivations—a great many anti-helping and anti-therapeutic things. As I tell my group members frequently, "On the whole, your friends are the worst possible people to get advice from." Unless I know the particular friend who is advising one of my patients, I take pains to urge that the patient *not* consult his friends for advice in important areas and I monitor his private and group advice-seeking from other group members with some care.

One last interesting aspect which might be mentioned in this myth area is the belief of many writers and practitioners that the group counseling or therapy experience "is a microcosm of the world outside." In my judgment the group leader will make a serious mistake if he views the processes of his groups as *necessarily* identical to the experiences which the group members have in their lives when they are not in the group. Obviously, at times there may be certain similarities, even apparent identities, between what happens with individual and group behaviors when persons are in a professional psychologically

As I have suggested earlier, viewed from within the Present Moment, a major dimension of my own professional experiencing in a group situation involves the concern about Present Moment-Future Moment connections. As a group leader I look toward the Future Moments from within a personal experience of a dynamic lattice of hugely, logarithmically ever-expanding possibilities for group members, while at the same time experiencing at many depth levels their Present Moment status. Insofar as he is able to use this frame of reference, the group leader then can plan his options ahead toward achieving various goals, and he may plan to use his thinking, experiencing and action skills accordingly in the Future Moments ahead. Time, then, is secondary; Future Moment goals are primary. What is most crucial for the group leader is how he chooses to use a given period of time, what he does—based upon theory, experience, Present Moment appraisals and the like—within a given period of time.

A frequent problem involving time is that of scheduling group sessions. Should they be forty minutes long, as is appropriate in many school settings? Is this too much or too little? One-and-a-half hours? Open-ended, which may run to six, seven or more hours? Firmly fixed for twelve hours—a Minithon—or many more hours, for example, thirty—a Marathon? Should they be "weekend encounters," as is becoming popular in the current "encounter" culture?

Hand in hand with the consideration of the length of particular sessions is the issue of the frequency of the sessions. Should sessions be once weekly? If so, how long should they be? Should they be twice weekly? Once monthly? (One of my colleagues has an interesting idea which he is undertaking to follow. He proposes to have four or five weekend group meetings yearly, hoping for as much or more group member change from such a series of sessions as he would get from an ongoing series of weekly hour-and-a-half group sessions, fifty-two sessions to the year.) It goes without saying that interacting with the problem of session length and frequency, as well as a number of other variables, is the all-important factor of the nature of the group leader himself—experience, intelligence, maturity level, basic talent for effective group work and use of theory, as noted earlier in this chapter.

It would seem important to remember at this point that the fundamental and ideal goal of any counseling, therapy, educational or related group session, series of group sessions, or encapsulated time period within a particular group session is: *more self-benefiting change in each individual group member.*

In summary, the "answer" to the questions involving length and frequency of group sessions must be based upon consideration of the wide variety of particular variables involved, as discussed throughout this chapter. On the other hand, I would hope the point has been made clearly that I believe that greater lengths of time are not *necessarily* better than shorter time periods.

Related to the problem of the length of time involved in changing group members—whether with regard to length of particular sessions, the over-all time period of a series of sessions, or the frequency of sessions within a delimited time period—is what I consider a most fundamental point: it is fundamentally my belief, and one borne out over many years of experience, that highly significant goals may be achieved within any *single* Present Moment if the right combination of group leader stimulus conditions and group member responses takes place. One of the major themes running through this chapter has been that it is the ideal goal of the group leader to maximize the expert use of the Present Moment.

For years I have sought to increase my own ability to use any single Present Moment with maximum effectiveness and artistry. Anyone who has been engaged in professional psychological work, whether individual counseling or group leadership, well knows the meaning of some particular Present Moments within which were brought together all of the ingredients necessary for the best possible outcome; moments often, for example, when a single word or gesture conveyed exactly the meaning necessary for a particular desired outcome. Because of space limitations I cannot here cite many of a countless number of such Present Moments from the countless such experiences I have had during the many years of my professional work. Daily, however, my own work is filled with just such Present Moments during which the artistic and technical execution of my own skills in combination with the patient(s) with whom I am working result in some therapeutic change or related outcome.

The most dramatic of such highly significant Present Moments, of course, pertain to the often highly delicate encounters I have with my many suicidal patients, where the wrong or right thing said or done may result in the person's move toward or away from suicide. For the most part less dramatic is my own daily practice of having very brief telephone contacts with many of my patients, who call because of a wide variety of real or felt emergency situations, during which time (on the average only several minutes) I generally have a highly succinct yet influential series of Present Moments with the person in distress. During such Present Moment telephone contacts I bring to bear a wide variety of techniques, understandings and the use of theory and experience to diagnose the situation and act influentially toward outcomes most of which are developing as potentials during the several minutes within which the patient and I are talking. This kind of highly economic use of time is an art to be cultivated by every psychological counselor and particularly by group leaders.

One interesting myth which should be neutralized is an idea which is found at least unconsciously, if not consciously, in the personalities of many counselors and therapists: that is, that "long silences should be avoided." In my supervisory experience, I have found that psychological workers in training—many of whom already have a number of years of experience as individual and group counselors or therapists—tend to react in two major ways to periods of silence on the part of the counselee, patient or group member(s): they speak a great deal or otherwise try to provoke the other person into speaking or into some kind of action, or they "sit it out" and have a kind of competitive "waiting contest." Both overt reactions are responses to underlying personalizations of the issues which generate underlying anxieties, the same kinds of reactions as explained under Myth Area No. 2.

Many psychological workers find it so difficult to tolerate long periods of silence—due to their own anxieties about what may or may not happen within an extended time period—that an unconscious myth has grown up that time should be used "productively," filled with action, where things "happen." Overt action, as I hope I have indicated elsewhere in this chapter, is not necessarily the major ingredient at all times to effect Future Moment change. Early in my own experience as a psychotherapist in training, in 1957, I recall finding it very difficult to tolerate long periods of silence between a patient and myself. I felt a press for activity. Only later, as I came to understand myself, through personal psychotherapy and extended self-confrontation and self-analysis, did I realize that it was *my own* underlying anxieties which dictated my reactions to my patient's and group's stimuli presented to me, not alone my professional concern for their well-being.

With regard to the five example situations cited, it may be seen that I acted overtly, as group leader, at the precise moment which I believed to be of importance for the individual's and the group's goals. Years ago I might have trembled with fear at Doris' mounting anger and potential violence, yet at this time I did not do so and was able to move most effectively in the series of Present Moments in this particular episode. I was able to be non-anxious at Judith's angry attack upon me so as to help her and the group move beyond that attack for their own developments. I saw what I believed was an important Present Moment for Sally and moved in immediately to invite her to discuss her problems, thereafter undertaking most of the problem discussion with her myself. With Noel and with Milton P. I tolerated the ambiguity of the situation—sometimes subjectively-seeming long periods of silence— to achieve an outcome which I sought. Basic to what I felt were effective uses of theory and action skills in these situations was the fact that I had no anxiety myself which wrongly could have motivated my group leadership at these times, having eliminated my own anxieties through years of work upon myself in subjective, actual and even physical risk situations.

In conclusion, the use of time in psychological counseling work is a pre-eminent dimension within which may be experienced the counselor's or therapist's highly artistic, probabilistic and professional Present Moment focus on Future Moment goals.

Myth Area No. 8. Group composition: groups should be small in size and the nature of each group member—with regard to sex, age, race, personal goals, emotional health, etc.—is of the greatest importance.

This is one of my favorite myth areas, probably because it is so patently absurd, as is the earlier discussed notion about the lack of "necessity" for using any theory! As with this latter aspect, and many of the other myth areas, it only takes a little intelligence and inspection to see that the basic questions are: (1) What are the realities involved? (2) What are the ideal goals of the group leader with regard to the group members? (3) Which particular stimulus conditions, undertaken by which particular group leader, are likely to lead to which particular outcomes, for which particular group members . . . etc.?

The question of group size is an obvious and fundamental one: the answer, too, is patently obvious, it has always seemed to me: advertising, television, Presidential elections, satellites in space, the individual's favorite sports team struggling to win and a huge variety of related situations have all shown us that under the right conditions actually *millions*, even *billions* of people may be influenced according to one individual's or organization's goals. And this may take place in a few Moments, at that! Instantaneously! Often I have thought that if we had a dirigible hangar which would house at least ten thousand people, with what we know about human psychology at this time we could influence these people in a short period of time with an impact which would have, predictably, a significant influence upon them for the rest of their lives!

From this point of view it therefore seems absurd that counselors and therapists quibble about whether there should be seven or eight (considered to be a rather "ideal" group therapy size), ten, fifteen, twenty or many more persons in the group which they are trying to influence. What *does* seem of crucial importance to me is that those persons who are concerned with influencing any particular number of persons viewed as a group should have a heightened awareness of their particular goals regarding these particular people, who may be arranged in a particular group number, in a particular setting, in a partic-ular . . . etc. That is, an understanding of all that is involved with regard to constructively influencing any number of people, for whatever goals, is what is required of a group leader.

Continuing within the myth area relating to composition of the group, a matter of very frequent concern (unfortunately more unconsciously than consciously) of psychological group leaders other than those who are formally trained and professionally labeled "psychiatrists," or "clinical psychologists," is the matter of having people in the group who apparently are in poor emotional health. The much misunderstood and maligned term, which does disservice to many persons, always a "scare" word, is: "sick" people (a companion word is "psychotic," and one can think of many others, as used by psycho-logical counselors of every professional label who choose, rightly or wrongly, for their own reality reasons or personality reasons, not to work with certain children or adults).

While it is true that some few individuals are too seriously disturbed to profit from a group counseling or psychotherapy experience, and others might even be disruptive or, moreover, in some extremely few cases dangerous, the fact of the matter is (based upon my own extensive wide-ranging psychotherapy practice, often with deeply disturbed individuals, and upon my psychiatric hospital experience, as well as my intensive supervision and training of many school counselors and other professionals who deal with the great bulk of the American population) that a very small percentage of individuals, perhaps less than one percent, need be excluded from *any* group membership experience because they would be set back emotionally or otherwise and/or because they would be highly defeating to the group purposes over perhaps ten group sessions or more. (What I am pointing out is that what may seem like a negative experience for some particular group members—the "emotionally disturbed"—may even out into a much more profitable experience if the group leader gives the group process time and treats the situation wisely.)

What is somewhat more likely, although it would still comprise a very small percentage of persons, would be those individuals who would be unlikely to profit, but not be disadvantaged themselves or be defeating to the group, from the group process. What is most crucial in this entire area of concern is what is most basically the "scare" or "threat" psychology found in many professional helping workers with regard to seemingly hyperactive or violent individuals, persons with underlying aggressive, depressive or seemingly non-understandable or bizarre mentation and emotionality, individuals with psychiatric "labels," ex-prison inmates or formerly drug-involved persons, and in particular the rather unconscious, out-of-awareness feelings of threat that many group leaders experience with regard to having any such individuals in their own group.

For example, both Doris and Milton P. in the example situations were what normally would be identified diagnostically as "emotionally disturbed" or "psychotic" individuals. Because I, as group leader did not experience fear in dealing with them, even though I was not *always* certain what to do in any Present Moment, my staying with them as group leader helped them have a highly profitable learning experience.

With regard to the *appropriate mixture* of what may generally be called "emotionally disturbed or disruptive" individuals with other group members, this too depends upon the expertise, fearlessness, patience, openness to new possibilities and the like which may or may not be true of the group leader. *One* very significantly different group member may not be a disadvantage to group progress; in fact it may be—and in nearly all cases, in my belief, may be *turned into being*— an advantage. Obviously, however, the more members in a group who are disruptive or otherwise so antagonistic to group progress—whether because they are hostile, acting-out, violent, withdrawn, retarded or short (yes, I said "short"—physically short!—since any single factor if taken to an extreme *may* be disruptive to the group!)—the more difficult it is to guide the group and its individual members into material that will be psychologically helpful to them.

Many psychological workers (in my judgment probably the vast majority, including school counselors and a great many psychotherapists) are quite reluctant to work with individuals who have been labeled or otherwise appear as "emotionally disturbed," "drug-involved," former criminals, the minority group members, the disadvantaged and poor, *et al.* This is what we can call the "problem of referral." In many instances it is, of course, highly appropriate for a psychological worker to refer an individual to another worker or agency who is more qualified to work with this person. However, most psychological workers know that more often than not agency and hospital waiting lists are so long that this discourages useful referrals (and often have a high percentage of workers who are in the early phases of training and a much smaller percentage of experienced professionals). Private practitioners have fees often out of reach of much of the population. In my experience most psychological workers use referral all too readily because of (1) ignorance of the exact nature of the seemingly "difficult" or "dangerous" case with which they may be working and (2) fears and anxieties, largely unconscious, which threaten their internal sense of security (through fears of physical injury, anger and disapproval from the counselee, disruption of their professional performance leading to mistakes, revelation of personal-professional inadequacies, the strange socioeconomic class, racial and other "differentness" of the counselee and a host of other factors).

It is my decided opinion that in the majority of cases most psychological workers who have any reasonable training and acuity at all, particularly if they seek more experienced and wise supervision, can take on and work with, often with surprising success, the majority of kinds of cases just identified. The well-known "wish to refer," particularly among psychological helping professionals other than psychiatrists, clinical psychologists and other kinds of trained psychotherapists, almost always has in it some large ingredient of unconscious fear. The psychological worker had better consult his own psyche, his personal and professional conscience and his desires for helping his clientele, as well as make an attempt to seek supervision, when such a time arises.

Also, insofar as group work is concerned, one or several seemingly "difficult" or "dangerous" individuals mixed in with a group of otherwise "normal" people will most frequently find the group leader receiving help from the other group members in working constructively with these individuals. A further point: the psychological professional ought to ask himself what kind of professional career he has undertaken if he is not willing to face the difficulties and occasional risks, mainly or almost always subjective, with people who need his help.

But on a related issue: Should group members be more heterogeneous in their characteristics? Should they be more alike or unalike? Again, unfortunately, and alas and alack!, this depends upon the group leader's conception of what goals he wishes to attain with regard to his group members—which particular goals, for which particular group members, at which particular times . . . etc.

I remember an instance some 15 years ago when a colleague of mine, in training, as was I, as a psychotherapist in our own four-person supervision group, worriedly noted to our supervisor that the patient he expected to meet soon for the first time was, as was he, a Negro, and that this almost certainly boded trouble. The concern was resolved rather immediately when the supervisor asked him two questions: (1) Was it more likely to be a problem for the prospective patient or for the therapist himself? and (2) Was it possible that there were any *other* significant features about the patient? What was happening here, of course, was that the neophyte therapist was elevating to all-importance a single feature of his patient which in fact is what happens in many cases when psychological workers become preoccupied with particular and single features of their group members or prospective group members, a preoccupation often based upon the worker's own anxiety, rather than the whole, almost infinitely wide range of characteristics-in-events-in-situations, which is actually the Reality.

It is important to keep in mind, of course, that the point I am making here is that almost *any* existent—or, as in this case, a group-member-in-a-particular-situation—probabilistically may be turned, at least, to some good outcome. One obvious and fundamental reason for this is that the group leader—even though he might be the most poorly trained and experienced group leader in the world—*intends* to influence a good outcome, and therefore—*probabilistically*—he is on balance more likely to do so. This is not to say, however, either that all existents or group members are *equally likely* to be turned to such outcomes nor that the group leader should make a choice to include anybody and everybody in his group. Again we have the distinction between the *poss*ibility and *prob*ability.

> *Upcoming Myth Area No. 9. Leader's and members' attitude to be cultivated: "You do your thing, I do mine. I cannot take responsibility for your life, nor you for mine."*

This in essence is what is called "the prayer in Gestalt Therapy," as written in a popular recent book by the founder of Gestalt Therapy, the late Frederick S. ("Fritz") Perls (1969, p. 4). The reason it is cited here is because Gestalt Therapy has rapidly and increasingly become popular with a great many would-be professional psychological counselors, particularly as it relates to a rather different and "encounter" set of therapy techniques and also a personality or philosophical orientation which is explicit mainly in some catchy maxims, through the encounter and sensitivity group movements, and filtering down through a variety of forms of psychological counseling and psychotherapy. One finds this "early 1970s ethic" on a large youth culture poster, for example, and I myself have heard it mentioned many times among young people and psychological counselors alike. The difficulty with this assertion and ethic, as I am afraid many of Fritz Perls' followers, and often perhaps he himself, do not and did not point out, is that it *may* be true or untrue, wise or unwise, ethical or unethical—depending again upon the particular individual experiencing the Present Moment.

There are times, within my judgment as a group leader, when it is quite appropriate not to take responsibility for the group member's development, anxiety, confrontation with reality, problem-solving need or other concern—even to the point where, as actually is happening at the moment of this writing, when I am actively considering terminating the psychotherapy of a young woman who has been in therapy with me for three years and actually has not finished her therapy, although she is no longer suicidal—the professional worker may forcefully and upon his own initiative act in such a way as to cause the counselee or patient to founder or have distress, in short to have to take "do or die" responsibility for himself. Ideally, of course, this latter situation is undertaken with the fullest possible awareness and expertise on the part of the professional worker in each Present Moment.

It has been my unfortunate experience, however, in recent years often to witness the altogether capricious and, in my view, frequently thoughtless assumption of this attitude—in short, "you are your own responsibility, not mine"—in the guise of helping the group member take responsibility for himself. Most professional workers, and many lay people, by now know of instances where this ethic was asserted to the decided detriment, never recovered, of the recipient. While it may be assertedly true that one is not *always* one's "brother's keeper," it is my own personal and professional value that within the professional helping role the worker ought to act thoroughly, wisely and cautiously (depending upon his level of professional expertise) when giving certain significant responsibilities to the counselee or patient within his charge, lest that person be irreparably and needlessly disadvantaged *because* of the professional worker. (It is another question, an important one which unfortunately cannot be pursued here, whether this increasingly popular "ethic" is in fact in itself *un*ethical.)

People requiring psychological help, which would include nearly all people, find it very difficult to take full and wise responsibility for themselves and their lives. Handling this kind of personal responsibility for oneself is indeed difficult, and it is a most delicate undertaking to help a group member, counselee or patient learn such responsibility for himself. What I object to most strongly in this upcoming myth area is the careless popularization of what is obviously an important psychological idea, value and ethic into an assertion set without due regard for the intricacies of the learning situation of the individuals involved. It is highly desirable for everyone to be able to take full responsibility for his own life but the way to help people achieve this status is not simply by blatantly asserting this notion and, for the group leader in particular, then leaving the management of relevant problems in responsibility entirely up to the individual involved.

Some Closing Remarks

The main purposes of this chapter have been (1) to communicate to *you*, the reader, the meaning of Present Moments and Future Moments in group leadership and (2) to clarify some particular myth areas which prevail in the field of group work. I have tried to cast doubt upon some of the standard categories, assumptions, modes of thinking and practices—with particular regard for only a few of the many issues falling within the purview of the myth areas I have selected for presentation—with regard to group work. And I have attempted to throw into larger and wider perspective the possibilities, operational as well as theoretical, with regard to these issues, especially as they relate to constructive group leadership on the part of the psychological helping professional. Actually, I feel that I have really only barely touched the surface, from my own experience and theory, with regard to the depth and breadth of what it is important to communicate about effective psychological group leadership.

For many years I have had the conviction, as I recall trying to persuade my supervisees first at New York University in 1964, that highly effective psychological counseling or psychotherapy can be carried on, as I said then, "in a clown's outfit in a coalbin . . . provided the psychological worker knows what he is doing." This rather extreme assertion makes one of the major points, I think, that I have attempted to communicate in this chapter: that, before the fact, from within the perspective of the Present Moment, depending upon a wide variety of variables, any particular psychological worker *may* influence any particular individual or group to behave in any particular way in any particular Future Moment for any particular long-range goal, for any particular . . . etc.

I have tried to communicate to the reader the nature of Reality in the Present Moment. I have introduced a number of new constructs, presented with terminology which perhaps seems neither truly scientific (although I believe I am attempting to be extraordinarily precise with regard to reality and theoretical referents) nor fully experiential in meaning. My writing, to communicate some of the issues and meanings in "group experience," probably seems rather "unlife"-like and not discursive or perhaps informal enough. Often it may have seemed tedious, repetitive and perhaps needlessly complex. As a partial excuse, however, I would argue that thus is the nature of Reality when grasped closely and in full awareness from within the personal Present Moment experience of the "hugely logarithmically expanding dynamic lattice" of Future Moment possibilities.

Most writers do not tell the reader "how to" do group work, and they neglect to do this for a variety of reasons, some of which I have already commented on, the most important reason, perhaps, being a major point of this chapter—that it is possible at best only to have guidelines rather than absolute specifics in this Present Moment for any particular Future Moment situation. Over-all, it is the *artistry,* including planning for Future Moments, and the Present Moment to Present Moment experience and skill of the leader, that makes the difference in effective psychological group work. At best, research, theory and even the shrewd and experienced professional's collective experience background may account only for generalities and guidelines, not for one hundred percent precise prescriptions for particular Present Moment situations. These aspects can never—I repeat *never*—account for the group leader's dynamically and artistically synchronized Present Moment mobilization of theory, expertise, personal awareness and fearlessness, and precise judgment and execution of the best action at any particular Present Moment so as to affect Future Moments of his Present Moment concern. In brief, textbook research, supervisors, outstanding theorizing—whatever one may name—will not totally help you in the Present Moment when the "chips are down." One must learn, in actual group leadership action, to help oneself.

Many things have been left unsaid in this chapter. To allude to only a few: I have not really touched upon what I consider to be the most desirable qualities and skills of the group leader, at his beginning best potential as well as at his expert experienced best. I have not, for example, in depth set forth an important fact which I believe to be true, namely, that "beginning" counselors or paraprofessionals or other persons aspiring to lead groups should in fact *attempt* to lead groups and that they should *try* to learn professional psychological skills and to improve personally and professionally from their group, group-related and individual helping experiences. Almost everyone desirably should *try* to lead a group—one need not have thousands of hours of experience already behind one to *try* to help people. It is at the point where we have little or no actual group experience that we must all, necessarily, begin serious learning. What is in fact desirable is to keep one's wits about oneself, to try to be adventurous, yet conservative, to think problems through, to plan, to seek the best supervision available (not the "face value" or institutionally prescribed available supervision necessarily—one can always pay, on an hourly basis or otherwise, for the supervision of someone more knowledgeable professionally than oneself), and one should value truth and self-confrontation above all.

I have not mentioned the notions of confidentiality; responsibilities to the institution or agency with which one may be involved; the physical nature of the group setting; personal-social involvements with counselees or patients; or whether in fact all groups actually *must* have a leader. And I have not discussed the desirability of alternate, more frequent non-formal or "pre"-group meetings; or whether the leader should in fact *promote* anxiety, conflict, disruption and the like rather than just attempt to eliminate these emotions; and whether in fact a group should be designed for more than helping people become happy and feeling better, but also to help them meet their "belongingness" needs and deal with the alienation anxieties erupting in modern society; and whether a group should help people learn how to minimize and tolerate ever-present negative experiences. These are simply a *few* of the things which might have been touched upon, but which space did not permit in this present work. There are many, many more.

Becoming an *expert* group leader is no easy undertaking; certainly it is one involving many years of time and sustained, intelligent effortful thinking in acquiring increasingly effective theory, experience and practice in action skills. It is an undertaking requiring self-confrontation, self-analysis, self-development and a maturity and wisdom, ideally, far beyond that of the average person in American society. It is not achieved merely by reading others' articles on groups, writing one's own articles and then reading others' writings based partly on one's own previous writings, etc.—and occasionally "looking in on a group" or "having a try" at leading it, leading a weekly group of students in "counseling supervision," carrying a few student advisees in personal-helping ways, or being a part-time "vocational-type counselor" in a student personnel office in a university. Nor is wide-ranging and depth experience in group leadership, as an expert, achieved through being a settlement house worker, former drug addict or criminal-now-turned-group leader, or "encounter culture" or sensitivity training enthusiast—although these role experiences certainly lead to *some*, though limited, kind of expertise.

Becoming an expert group leader is not achieved by becoming an expert authority on the literature of group process and dynamics. Action skills, particularly those which are designed to be *most* effective in dealing with problems of self-defeat and with actualization possibilities in the Present Moment, are not attained by reading the professional literature—or by writing it—particularly without extensive experience on the frontiers and within the extraordinary range of difficulties involved with group problems. In short, although almost everyone may lead a group without great danger, and most likely with at least some profit, if they work "mostly with their wits" (Raimy, 1972), to learn to do expert group psychological work demands an enormous amount of time (daily and over years), effort, critical thinking, self-confrontation, self-awareness and truth-seeking.

One cannot become a skilled courtroom attorney overnight, no matter how much one has read the legal textbooks in law school, nor a concert pianist in a day, no matter how much one has beforehand "read about" playing the piano, nor by reading books and articles about these undertakings and experiences written by people who almost exclusively have had little or no action experience themselves in them—but "know about" them secondhand. Nor can one learn these professional skills, in all their enormous range of depth and complexity, from persons who have spent a great many hours merely "being present" in these enterprises, in a passive way. Further, research designed to uncover the major dimensions of successful courtroom legal work and piano concertizing, no matter how excellent, will not lend more than a little help to those aspiring to experience and learn theory-as-included-in-action skills in these special kinds of Present Moment situations. The reason is, simply, that direct Present Moment experience is not in itself the same thing as is writing or speaking *about* that experience. Nor, it must be said, is thinking about an experience—to make sense of it—the same thing as that experience itself.

For the developing group leader, psychological counselor, or psychotherapist, the following notions, briefly, are important to keep in mind: consciously, intentionally and effortfully attempt on a continuing basis to build and increasingly refine and add to the theory which guides your Present Moment-Future Moment professional work in psychologically helping people; seek intelligent, wise and experienced supervision, wherever possible, but settle for the best you can get if that is *all* you can get; cover the situation with the counselee conservatively when in doubt; remember that anything done by *you* (almost) always can be undone; introspect, confront and get into your own feelings, thoughts, images and anxieties and try to be willing to face both subjective and objective risks with the people with whom you work; be aware of the continuing personal and professional development that you need, if you would achieve your personal-professional career goals—if you think that you do not need this development, then in fact you *do* need it; take an experimental yet conservative point of view toward your professional and personal development; take an active orientation toward learning your craft—be an activist engaging the material, issues, professors and supervisors, colleagues, your clientele, yourself; do not confuse actual helping actions or experiences in the Present Moment with sets of words—written words about "how to" involve yourself in experiences within your action skills, within yourself and also with group members and—on the other hand—do not confuse an exclusive focus on "experiences" and actions with a feeling about the uselessness of learning words from books and from supervisors, and with the words that you hear in the Present Moment group situations in which you are engaged.

Learn how to read critically through the wide variety of textbooks which will purport to inform you about how to "work with groups." In a great many ways—and I say this taking full responsibility for my statement—much of this material is quite irrelevant (although some of it may be somewhat interesting) for learning the action, theory and artistry involved in expert group work. Learn, and try actively, to extract from these readings what seems veridical and true to your own experience, and sensible to your intelligence, as contrasted with what is some author's attempt to present a variety of other people's notions, vague and abstract theories, discussions of peculiar and idiosyncratic cases without any depth analysis relating to theoretical and factual understanding as well as practical action skills and consequences. Again, it is still my "bias" that university-based writers and trainers generally have little experience with what in fact are the range and depth and complexity of the personality and reality situations which they must confront if they would *actually*, efficiently and maximally help people (rather than research what others and others and others and others have to say, largely without great personal experience, about helping people).

With regard to textbooks, journal articles and "authorities" in general, the only thing I might have to say other than that they are mainly "wrong"—in terms of helping you learn what is important in becoming an expert group leader—is that they are also "correct." It is *your* problem—for *you*, the reader—to make the distinctions as you will be attempting to do in your Present Moment group work. And it is *your* task and yours alone to learn how to distinguish good supervision from poor supervision, effective group behavior from poor group behavior, poor written technical material and poor university advisement from that which is excellent, mediocre, valueless or, worse—self-defeating.

If I would have only one more bit of advice to give you in this Present Moment, reader, it is this: *doubt* everything that I have had to say in this chapter. Professionally and personally, you will be the better for it.

References

Geis, H. Jon. Toward a Comprehensive Framework Unifying All Systems of Counseling. *Educational Technology, 9,* 3, March 1969, 19-28.

Glasser, William. *Reality Therapy.* New York: Harper and Row, 1965.

Perls, Frederick S. *Gestalt Therapy Verbatim.* Lafayette, California: Real People Press, 1969.

Patterson, C.H. Theories of Counseling and Psychotherapy. New York: Harper and Row, 1966.

Raimy, V. Review of A.E. Bergin and S.L. Garfield (Eds.) *Handbook of Psychotherapy and Behavioral Change: An Empirical Analysis. Contemporary Psychology,* April 1972, 207-208.

The Contributors

John Vriend

An established Contributing Editor of *Educational Technology*, **John Vriend** has long been an advocate of helping the counseling profession to mobilize its technological resources, editing as he did the Special Issue of *Ed. Tech.* on "Counseling Technology" (March, 1969) and writing an important chapter on "Computer Power for Guidance and Counseling" (in *Guidance for Education in Revolution,* edited by David R. Cook, Allyn and Bacon, 1971). His co-authorship (with John J. Pietrofesa) of *The School Counselor as a Professional* reflects his intense concern about professional upgrading. As Senior Editor of this book, he shares with his Co-Editor, Wayne W. Dyer, a dedication to helping the profession become aware of the importance of a technology of group counseling and a dedication to his own professional development as an effective group counselor and trainer of group counselors. He is currently on the counselor education faculty at Wayne State University, Detroit, Michigan, and edits the *Michigan Personnel and Guidance Journal* as well as the *National Vocational Guidance Association Newsletter.*

Wayne W. Dyer

Wayne W. Dyer is a member of the Counselor Education Staff at St. John's University in Jamaica, New York. His concern for the development of a technology of group counseling stems from his role as a trainer of group counselors, and the observation that effective group counseling is seldom practiced in the school setting, where he sees it as most urgently needed. He set as his own personal goal to be a contributor to a compilation of effective group counseling practices for all counselors and educational decision-makers, i.e., a Technology of Group Counseling. A co-contributor with John Vriend to *APGA's Counseling Today and Tomorrow Series*, he has conducted research and published several articles in the area of group counseling, while having led numerous counseling groups, with all age levels.

H. Jon Geis

H. Jon Geis, a Ph.D. in Psychology from Teachers College, Columbia University, is a psychotherapist in private practice in New York City. Forty-two, currently divorced and a bachelor, he has a 26-year-old informally adopted daughter, lives alone with four cats, and describes himself as "a man who tries to practice what I preach. Professionally, I am mainly a theorist at heart, although I am at the same time action oriented and experimentally so. In fact, I test out on myself, ahead of my patients, most of my theories and technical practices."

More fully describing himself professionally in the body of his chapter, Dr. Geis has taught on the graduate faculties of New York University, Yeshiva University and Columbia University and, until January, 1972, was the Director of Training and a chief clinical supervisor, emphasizing clinical strategies and psychodynamics, at a major New York City therapist training center. Dr. Geis currently is working on four technical books related to psychotherapy and is planning to undertake advanced biological or medical studies as related to his developing theoretical concerns.

Living his own life experimentally with relation to his professional concerns, he has parachuted out of a plane with a patient, nearly drowned in an underground jungle cave, shown male patients how to "pick up" girls in bars, and otherwise used himself and examples from his personal life, as appropriate, as tools for helping his patients and for constructing and refining his developing theories of personality and patient treatment.

He has a special interest in crisis intervention problems and in particular with emergencies related to chronic and acute suicides or what he describes as challenging experiences of "gambles with death."

T. Antoinette Ryan

T. Antoinette Ryan (Ph.D., Stanford University) directs the Adult Basic Education in Corrections Program in the Education Research and Development Center, University of Hawaii. She also is principal investigator for the Career Development Continuum Project, and conducts training activities in systems research. Her interests are primarily in learning theory, motivation, values and systems research. She has authored over 100 publications, including books, monographs and articles on counseling, guidance and systems.

John D. Krumboltz

John D. Krumboltz is Professor of Education and Psychology, Stanford University. He is the author of five books on behavioral counseling, and over 60 articles, monographs and published research reports. He is generally considered as the most outstanding proponent of behavioral counseling, having written, researched and practiced this goal-oriented approach to helping for the past 20 years. Under his editorship, *Revolution in Counseling* was published in 1966, and it has since become one of the most widely quoted texts in the counseling profession.

Beverly Potter

Beverly Potter has a master's degree from San Francisco State College in Rehabilitation Counseling (1968). She has had varied experience, counseling run-aways, jail inmates and parolees. She developed and implemented a special remedial program for Army men reading below 6th grade level. She has participated in Synanon, gestalt, encounter and women's groups. Presently she is an advanced doctoral student and Clinical Training Coordinator in Stanford's Counseling Psychology program.

Robert R. Carkhuff

Robert R. Carkhuff is Director, Center for Human Relations and Community Affairs, American International College, Springfield, Massachusetts, where he has concerned himself with programs in the development of human and community resources. He is also President of Carkhuff Associates, Amherst, Massachusetts, a consulting and training firm concerned with the development of a technology for human, educational and career achievement. Dr. Carkhuff is the author of more than one dozen books and over 100 articles on human and educational resource development.

Milton Schwebel

Milton Schwebel is Dean of the Graduate School of Education at Rutgers University. As a professor, he teaches a course for counselors and supervisors of counselors, and part of a course on the group process in community educational planning. His last book was *Who Can Be Educated?* (Grove). His forthcoming book (with Jane Raph) is *Piaget in the Classroom* (Basic Books). He recently completed a study on logical thinking in college freshmen.

Doris Jefferies

Doris Jefferies earned both her B.A. and M.Ed. at Wayne State University. Additional graduate work was done at UCLA and the University of Hawaii. She taught first grade and was an elementary school counselor in Detroit in the Developmental Career Guidance Project, directed by George Leonard in the Detroit Public School system. The Ph.D. was completed at the University of Illinois in 1970 with M.M. Ohlsen and C.H. Patterson as advisors. She has been on the faculty at Boston University and is currently an Assistant Professor in Counseling and Guidance at Indiana University.

George M. Gazda

George M. Gazda, a graduate of the University of Illinois, has been active for 15 years in the field of group work. He has authored or co-authored 50 journal articles and six books in group guidance, group counseling and group therapy. He is currently President of the Association of Counselor Educators and Supervisors and a member of the international consulting board for the *Comparative Group Studies* journal. Dr. Gazda is a member of the American Group Psychotherapy Association and the American Society for Group Psychotherapy and Psychodrama, APA and APGA. Currently he is Professor of Education,

College of Education, University of Georgia and Consulting Professor, Department of Psychiatry, Medical College of Georgia.

Roger W. Peters

Roger W. Peters holds a B.A. degree received from North Park College. He attended DePaul University and then the University of Georgia, where the Ph.D. was granted in June, 1972. Currently he is Assistant Professor of Psychology and Intern Supervisor at Central Missouri State University, Warrensburg, Missouri.

Wayne Rowe

Wayne Rowe received his Ph.D. from Michigan State University, where he did research on the use of groups in counselor education programs. While there he was director of the Behavioral Counseling Laboratory, a student-managed clinic for doctoral practicum experience. He was later the director of social rehabilitation at the Alternative Education Center in Grand Rapids, Michigan, and is currently Associate Professor of Education in the counseling program at the University of Oklahoma.

Bob B. Winborn

Bob B. Winborn is Professor of Counseling, Personnel Services and Educational Psychology at Michigan State University. He received his Ed.D. from Indiana University and has been assistant director of counseling centers at North Texas State University and Indiana University, where he investigated the effects of group work on the behavior of college students. Currently he is vice-president of the Division for Counseling and Human Development of the American Educational Research Association.

Walter M. Lifton

Walter M. Lifton is Professor of Education and Director of the School Guidance and Counseling Program, State University of New York at Albany. From 1939, when he worked with teen groups (Madison House Settlement, New York) through his baptism in group therapy while a psychiatric social worker (Army), followed by research interest reflected in his master's and Ph.D. theses, to a professional interest in group classroom techniques, and ultimately through the crossfire of riots and confrontation groups (Rochester), groups have dominated and influenced his personal and professional life.

Merle M. Ohlsen

Merle M. Ohlsen did his undergraduate work at Winona State (Minnesota). He received his A.M. at the University of Illinois and his Ph.D. at the University of Iowa. He is perhaps best known for *Guidance Services in the Modern School* and *Group Counseling,* and as APGA president. He is now Holmstedt Distinguished Professor, Guidance and Psychological Services, at Indiana State University.

Clarence A. Mahler

Clarence A. Mahler is Professor of Psychology at Chico State University. He received his Ph.D. at the University of Minnesota. He has specialized in group work over the last 18 years. His 1970 book, *Group Counseling in the Schools* is the culmination of these years of experience as a leader and trainer. He has taught at Oregon State University, University of Minnesota and New York University, and summer sessions at the University of Illinois, South Carolina State College and the University of California at Berkeley.

James E. Doverspike

James E. Doverspike is Professor of Education and Head of the Department of Counseling and Special Education at the University of Akron. Dr. Doverspike is a graduate of Pennsylvania State University and a member of the American Personnel and Guidance Association, American School Counselor Association, Association of Counselor Education and Supervision, Phi Delta Kappa and American Association of University Professors. Publications appear in *The School Counselor, The Guidance Journal, Counselor Education and Supervision, Elementary School Guidance and Counseling, National Catholic Guidance Conference Journal, The Personnel and Guidance Journal* and *Guide to Human Development and Learning,* William Brown and Company, 1963.

Allen E. Ivey

Allen E. Ivey was once a devoted encounter cultist, having been "turned on" at Esalen and Bethel. Increasingly, he has become concerned about the failure of behavior learned in groups to transfer to daily life situations. Much of his work in microcounseling has been concerned with transfer of behavior from the learning situation, be it video training or group work, to one's own life experience. He is currently applying microcounseling methods to training of psychiatric patients in communication skills.

James M. Sacks

In the mid-fifties **Dr. James M. Sacks** was an improvisational actor in the evenings while a University of Chicago psychology doctoral intern by day. He has since combined these interests, using psychodrama in his practice and at open weekly sessions at the Moreno Institute in New York. He is president of the American Society of Group Psychotherapy and Psychodrama, author of numerous articles and is now completing a text on psychodrama.

Barbara B. Varenhorst

Barbara B. Varenhorst is a consulting psychologist in the Palo Alto, California School District. She has adapted the "Life Career Game" for use with junior and senior high school students. She has written chapters on the subjects of simulations and group counseling in *Simulation Games in Learning, Behavioral Counseling: Cases and Techniques* and *Theories and Methods of Group Counseling in the*

Schools. Most recently she was a co-author of *Deciding,* a curriculum for decision-making published by the College Entrance Examination Board.

Norman Kagan

Norman Kagan has been employed as a teacher of emotionally disturbed and delinquent children. He has served as a lecturer on the faculty of New York University, and for the past ten years at Michigan State University where he is Professor of Education and Medical Education. At Michigan State University he has taught in the general areas of group counseling, appraisal of research, counseling practicum, doctor-patient relationship and paraprofessional mental health workers. Dr. Kagan has been a guest lecturer at some 30 universities.

Randolph B. Tarrier

Randolph B. Tarrier has worked in the counseling profession in all areas of education, from elementary school through the state department. He received his Ph.D. at Case Western Reserve University in 1968. Following brief teaching experiences at John Carroll University and Case Western Reserve University, and consulting experience with the State of Ohio Department of Education, he is currently Assistant Professor with the City University of New York. He is currently pursuing two major areas of specialization: the use of simulation in counselor training and exploration approaches to career counseling. His immediate task is to finish and package 30 videotaped instructional units for use in the training of counselors and teachers.

Benjamin Cohn

Benjamin Cohn is presently Director of Professional and Pupil Personnel Services with the Board of Cooperative Educational Services in Yorktown Heights, New York. He is also adjunct professor both at Manhattan College and Western Connecticut State College. He has lectured extensively at various colleges and universities around the country and has authored numerous articles in the area of group counseling. Dr. Cohn directed a USOE-funded project on group counseling in 1960 and directed the Arden House Conference to establish guidelines for research and group counseling in 1962.

Jim Bebout

Since his graduation from the University of Chicago and work at Carl Rogers' Clinic (briefly with Dr. Rogers), **Jim Bebout** has practiced in and researched the fields of group psychotherapy and encounter groups. His study of these groups at California State University at San

Francisco and in Berkeley has led to his current position as chairman of the Association for Humanistic Psychology Research Committee and interest in developing theories of co-experiential behavior.

Anna Louise Miller

Anna Louise Miller is a counseling specialist, Behaviordyne, Inc., Palo Alto, California. Her major interests are in individual development and the facilitation of hierarchical restructuring through self-understanding. She brings her strong background in group processes in career development and education to bear on this interest. She has written reports, articles and book chapters on vocational psychology and guidance.

David V. Tiedeman

David V. Tiedeman is Director, Project TALENT and the Institute for Research in Education, American Institutes for Research, Palo Alto, California. Dr. Tiedeman's major interests are in individual development and the facilitation of hierarchical restructuring through self-understanding. He is particularly interested in how the computer can be made adjuvant to the mind in the process of hierarchical self-restructuring.